JUL -- 2014

W9-BZO-571

WITHDRAWN

Getting LIFE

AN INNOCENT MAN'S 25-YEAR JOURNEY FROM PRISON TO PEACE

A Memoir

Michael Morton

Mount Laurel Library
100 Walt Whitman Avenue
Mount Laurel, NJ 08054-9539
856-234-7319
www.mtlaurel.lib.nj.us

Simon & Schuster
New York   London   Toronto   Sydney   New Delhi

Simon & Schuster
1230 Avenue of the Americas
New York, NY 10020

Copyright © 2014 by Michael Morton

All rights reserved, including the right to reproduce this book or portions thereof in any form whatsoever. For information address Simon & Schuster Subsidiary Rights Department, 1230 Avenue of the Americas, New York, NY 10020.

First Simon & Schuster hardcover edition July 2014

SIMON & SCHUSTER and colophon are registered trademarks of Simon & Schuster, Inc.

The Innocence Project logo is a registered trademark of The Innocence Project, Inc.

For information about special discounts for bulk purchases, please contact Simon & Schuster Special Sales at 1-866-506-1949 or business@simonandschuster.com.

The Simon & Schuster Speakers Bureau can bring authors to your live event. For more information or to book an event contact the Simon & Schuster Speakers Bureau at 1-866-248-3049 or visit our website at www.simonspeakers.com.

Interior design by Akasha Archer
Jacket design by Tom McKeveny
Jacket photograph © Rashevskyi Viacheslav/Shutterstock

Manufactured in the United States of America

10 9 8 7 6 5 4 3 2 1

Library of Congress Control Number: 2014000148

ISBN 978-1-4767-5682-0
ISBN 978-1-4767-5684-4 (ebook)

For Cynthia—
You have turned my mourning into dancing.

Foreword

IN THE MOVIE *CRIMES AND MISDEMEANORS*, A BRILLIANT AND DARK cautionary tale about a prominent, admired doctor who commits a murder and gets away with it, there is a character named Dr. Louis Levy, a professor of philosophy plainly based on Primo Levi, an Italian chemist, writer, and Auschwitz survivor who committed suicide in 1987. Dr. Levy was played by Dr. Martin Bergmann, a psychoanalyst who coauthored the lines he delivers as the Levy character in a series of interviews throughout the film. Levy/Bergmann gives a memorable and wise peroration just before the final credits, a statement that came to my mind the day Michael Morton was released from prison in Williamson County after enduring twenty-five years of hard time in the Texas Department of Criminal Justice:

We are all faced throughout our lives with agonizing decisions, moral choices. Some are on a grand scale. Most of these choices are on lesser points. But we define ourselves by the choices we have made. We are in fact the sum total of our choices. Events unfold so unpredictably, so unfairly, human happiness does not seem to have been included in the design of creation. It is only we, with our capacity to love, that give meaning to the indifferent universe. And yet most human beings seem to have the ability to keep trying. And even to find joy from simple things, like their family, their work, and from the hope that future generations might understand more.

Michael Morton was wrongly convicted of murdering his wife, a woman he dearly loved, and eventually lost all connection to his three-and-a-half-year-old son, Eric, the center of his world. He was shunned by most of his community, who came to believe he had committed a horrible crime. His in-laws turned against him. Despite the work of great lawyers who did everything possible, he was convicted in a trial that was both maddening and humiliating. It's an ultimate nightmare, beyond human imagination. How does one survive, much less prevail, after such an experience? How can one find the capacity to love and find joy again in simple things? Read this wonderful book, take this journey with Michael Morton, a gifted writer with a marvelous power of observation and clarity of thinking, and you will learn some surprising answers.

Starting in 1989, as the first post-conviction DNA exonerations triggered an "innocence movement" and the liberation—no other word adequately describes it—of literally hundreds of wrongly convicted men and women, a treasure trove of remarkable books by and about "exonerees" have been written. Michael Morton has produced a memoir of his twenty-five-year ordeal that, by any fair calculation, may well be the best to date—no disrespect to John Grisham intended! Michael Morton is the innocence movement's best approximation of Everyman—a self-described average, middle-class guy, living in a Texas suburb with a wife he adored and a three-and-a-half-year-old son, who gets up early to go to work. When he arrives home later that day, he learns his wife has been bludgeoned to death. He has no record, no experience at all with the criminal justice system. No reason to believe he could be suspected or, even worse, convicted of this terrible crime. It's like being struck by lightning without even knowing there was a storm on the horizon. Unthinkable. Yet from Michael's story alone, especially the way he tells it, any sane American will have to conclude that if it could happen to Michael Morton, Everyman, it could happen to me, it could happen to anyone.

I am certain this book will have far-reaching impact. Why? I can think of at least six reasons.

First Reason: The story itself is just so astonishing, especially the way Michael came to be exonerated, that it should induce a skeptical existentialist to literally get religion, a point Michael gently makes to me (the existentialist) on occasion. You will pinch yourself at some of the stranger-than-fiction dramatic turns in this story.

Second Reason: Michael is a courageous man, a person with true integrity and an unerring conscience. These qualities palpably drip off the page from his clean, fair, and generous narrative voice, which is never mawkish or sentimental. Permit me a personal note: On the eve of his exoneration, I presented Michael with an agonizing moral choice—you can get out of prison tomorrow, but if you are willing to fight some more, if you are willing to risk staying in prison for another six months or longer (I could not make guarantees), we have a chance to get the truth about how you were framed for a murder you did not commit, a chance to strike a significant blow against prosecutorial misconduct in a way that will generate some deterrence, a chance to get some legislative reforms. Michael said, "Let's play hardball." And our team did, with much greater success than we ever anticipated and without his having to remain a minute more in prison. Utilizing a unique Texas procedure, the Court of Inquiry, we were able to get Ken Anderson, the prosecutor in Michael's case who hid exculpatory evidence, convicted of criminal contempt. We hope that this lesson—the value of having direct court orders that prosecutors look through files and disclose exculpatory evidence—like other lessons learned in the Morton case, can effectively and fairly deter those prosecutors who deliberately and knowingly engage in misconduct. In this book Michael is far too modest about the courage he displayed when faced with this agonizing choice, so I feel compelled to give him up in this foreword!

Third Reason: Michael is a wonderful writer, with a dry wit that never deserts him, even at his darkest moments.

Fourth Reason: This story has already proved to be compelling in other media: Pam Colloff wrote a terrific, award-winning account of certain aspects of the case in *Texas Monthly*. *60 Minutes* did a striking segment they wound up airing three times. An excellent documentary, *An Unreal Dream*, produced by Al Reinert, Marcy Garriott, and John Dean, has been well received at film festivals and was aired in its entirety by CNN in prime time. But if you have read or seen any or all of these accounts, don't worry, you will find this book even more interesting.

Fifth Reason: Michael is a remarkably effective advocate. He has demonstrated an appeal to Republicans and Democrats, conservatives and liberals, prosecutors and police. In a state with Republican supermajorities in both the House and Senate, and with the conservative Rick Perry as governor, Michael's advocacy and example led to the passage of "Michael Morton" bills in 2013. One bill greatly expanded discovery in criminal cases. The other extends to four years the statute of limitations in attorney discipline grievances cases where prosecutors engaged in misconduct and innocent defendants were wrongly convicted, and that four years starts from the time of the defendant's exoneration. Based on this new statute of limitations, Anthony Graves, an African American who was wrongly convicted of murder and sentenced to death in Tyler, Texas, has filed a grievance against a prosecutor who hid exculpatory evidence when Graves was tried.

Sixth Reason: Michael is white. It would be hypocritical not to acknowledge this intractable reality of American life, even in the age of Obama: the media and the general public have always been somewhat more responsive and attentive to the narratives of white exonerees. This takes nothing away from Michael's unique achievements. His story illustrates the painful reality that a wrongful conviction can happen to anyone, regardless of race or economic background. Yet it's important to acknowledge that race effects pervade our criminal justice system, with people of color making up more than two-thirds of the 312 wrongful convictions later overturned by DNA evidence.

Finally, no prefatory words about *Getting Life* would be complete without contemplating how close Michael came to losing his own. No one knows this better than Michael. The first sentence he uttered the day he was released from prison was "Thank God this wasn't a capital case." Attitudes about the risk of executing the innocent are quickly and appropriately changing. Pew Research reports that support for the death penalty among Americans has dropped from 78 percent in 1996 to 55 percent today. Without question, much of this movement is attributable to cases like Michael's. Reasonable people can differ about whether capital punishment is a morally appropriate sanction for the most heinous of crimes, but reasonable people cannot differ about whether it is morally appropriate to execute someone who is innocent. Professor Franklin Zimring, in his masterful book *The Contradictions of American Capital Punishment*, has shown that attitudes in European countries, where capital punishment was repealed decades ago, are not dissimilar to those in the United States except that in Europe people do not trust the state to get it right. Remember, Michael had very good lawyers who performed well, but when a prosecutor, or any law enforcement official, chooses to hide exculpatory evidence, when winning becomes more important than playing by the rules, no system of regulation can effectively eliminate the risk of executing an innocent. This is not a hypothetical problem.

Michael speaks truth to power with moral authority that cannot be questioned, with Christian forgiveness that comes from his core. He has, indeed, defined himself by the sum total of moral choices he has made, choices that inspire and that command respect. This is a book you should read.

Barry C. Scheck
Co-Founder and Co-Director, The Innocence Project
February 14, 2014

Getting
LIFE

Prologue

THE DOOR CLOSED.

Not with a click or the sound of tumblers finally hitting their marks or the sturdy clunk of wood and metal meshing as if they were made for each other.

This was different.

It began with the long, hard sound of steel sliding against steel.

Like a train, the heavy door built speed as it barreled along its worn track, the portal to the real world growing smaller as the barrier of thick and battered bars roared into place.

It locked with a cold, bone-shaking boom that rattled me—literally—me, the guard outside my door, and any other inmates unlucky enough to be nearby.

I was alone in my cell, alone in the world, as alone as I had ever been in my life.

And I would stay there—alone—listening to that door close, over and over and over again, for the next twenty-five years.

Twenty-five years.

My wife, Chris, had been savagely beaten to death several months earlier. Before I had time to begin mourning, I was fighting for my own life against a legal system that seemed hell-bent on making me pay for the murder of the woman I would gladly have died for.

I was innocent.

Naïvely, I believed the error would soon be set right.

I could not have been more wrong.

As the years went by, I saw the three-year-old son my wife and I had doted on grow up and grow away. He believed his father was the murderer who'd killed the person he loved most.

And why wouldn't he? That's what everyone told him. On each of the rare occasions Eric saw me, my imprisonment—my inmate uniform, the guards and the guns, the bars and the buzzers—was a stark reminder that the world had decided I wasn't fit to walk free.

Ironically, Eric was one of the two people who knew what had really happened. He was in the house when something evil entered and destroyed our lives. At the time, our son tried to tell others what he had seen, but no one believed him.

And through all my time in prison, through all of my son's heart-ache, through our whole family's grief, the man who killed my wife was free—free to travel, free to commit crimes, free to kill again.

And again.

As the years passed, I watched the world go on without me through the keyhole of a door I could not unlock.

For a quarter century—a generation—my life was lived in peni-tentiary television rooms where you could get killed for changing the channel and on hard labor farms where violent men would feign fainting just to get a brief break from the unrelenting Texas sun.

I ate every meal in chaotic and cavernous prison chow halls where, as the old joke goes, the food was terrible, but at least you got a lot of it.

Needless to say, my dining companions were much the same—they were terrible and there were a lot of them.

If I was very lucky, weekends were spent in packed visiting rooms that were either too hot or too cold, and were always overrun by shattered families—virtually all of them walking wounded, scarred by addiction, abuse, and ignorance.

While I was desperate for company from the outside, whenever

I entered the visiting room, I knew there was a terrible downside for me, as well as for the people who had made the long trek to see me.

Everyone who visited had to try to act "normal" in an almost unimaginably strained setting. Because they loved me, they would ask that we pose for pictures together in front of the dirty, cracked walls washed in harsh fluorescent light. I would stand next to my family in their colorful street clothes, while I grinned grimly for the camera—year after year—getting ever grayer, looking more worn out, always in my poorly fitting prison whites.

Smile!

Click.

And on those visits, I would see my mom and dad—my biggest boosters, my eternal believers—spend year after year in shabby rooms surrounded by failure and sadness, aging before my eyes, struggling to smile through their pain, their shame, and their profound anger.

I was doing the same.

We spent all those visits and all those years talking about old times and planning for a future we could only pray would come to pass.

What none of us knew was that in the small town where I had stood trial, in a nondescript concrete warehouse where police stored old evidence—a dingy place packed with damaged cardboard boxes and haphazardly marked plastic pouches—was hidden the tiny piece of truth that would one day set me free.

Decades after I entered prison, a DNA test would change everything—not just for me and for my son but for the man who so unfairly prosecuted me. The DNA test would make huge changes, as well, in the broken legal system that tried to keep me behind bars.

For the cruel monster of a man who killed my wife, the truth came roaring out of the past with a vengeance.

This is the story of how I got a life sentence and survived what felt like a lifetime behind bars—only to have everything change again. I got my life back, and this time, I understood it.

Twenty-five years after I was swept away, the tide turned.

The wind changed.

The door opened.

PART I

PAIN

What has happened to the truth?
—JOURNAL OF MICHAEL MORTON, NOVEMBER 5, 1986

CHAPTER ONE

BY THE TIME MY FAMILY MOVED TO TEXAS FROM SOUTHERN CALIFOR-
nia, I was a fifteen-year-old wiseacre crushed to be leaving the big
city for the sticks. I felt like we were moving from the center of the
universe to Pluto. I mourned for miles in the backseat of our old car,
as my family left behind the Pacific Ocean for a sea of East Texas
pines, the California mountains for rolling hills and hotter-than-hell
summers.

But I had to admit that even California had nothing quite like the
Texas sky.

It can still take my breath away—big and blue, wide open and
welcoming. Then, in what seems like an instant, it can turn into a
wind-whipped canvas for bruised and brooding clouds, the horizon
streaked with lightning, a ground-shaking Old Testament storm on
the way. Then it will change yet again—bathing those of us below in
sunshine and forgiveness and peace—until the next time.

Since my coming to Texas as a teenager, that beautiful, terrible
sky has been the backdrop for each burden and every blessing that
has come my way.

THE HIGH SCHOOL IN TINY KILGORE, TEXAS, WAS A FRACTION OF THE
size of the school I had attended in California. I entered as a junior,

accustomed to thousands of students, packed hallways, and the ever-present possibility of gangs. Instead, what I found at Kilgore High School looked and felt like an episode of the old TV show *Happy Days*. The classes were small, the teachers were old school, the kids clean cut and smiling. They seemed younger than the worldly West Coast teenagers I had left behind.

And because I had just come from "exotic" California, I was lucky enough to hold a tiny dollop of mysterious cool for some of them. I wasn't exactly the Fonz, probably more like Richie Cunningham, but I had a background that boasted palm trees—something as rare as movie stars in Kilgore, Texas.

I got an after-school job as soon as I could, because I was desperate to have a car. The distances were tremendous compared to what I'd lived with in suburban California, and I wanted the freedom and self-determination that would come from sitting behind a steering wheel. So I started slinging patties at the town's spanking new Whataburger, saving money, making friends, and looking high and low for a car I could afford.

I ended up paying five hundred dollars for a powder-blue Cadillac Coupe de Ville that belonged to Mom's hairdresser, a flamboyant gay man named Ricky, who had inexplicably, but rather successfully, chosen conservative Kilgore as home base for his beauty shop. All I wanted to know was whether he had taken care of his car, and he certainly had.

It was a magnificent beast—with power windows, a plush interior, and an mpg of about three. The car was so massive that the first time I got it spruced up for a date, I used an entire can of Turtle Wax.

I loved it.

It's hard to be dapper when you are a small-town kid in a too-big car, but God knows I tried. My mother had raised me to be a good date, and I prided myself on taking girls out for dinner or to a movie rather than just racing through our barren downtown on the way to split a Cherry Coke at Dairy Queen.

I left Kilgore behind when I moved on to Stephen F. Austin State

University, eager to study psychology and make new friends in a fresh social setting. And that's where I met the person who would change the course of my life.

The first time I saw Chris Kirkpatrick was in a huge classroom amphitheater. She was standing several rows up from me, holding her books to her chest, talking with and taking the measure of my roommate. Luckily for me, he wasn't her type.

On this day, even from a distance, I could see that Chris was having none of his attempts at flirting. I couldn't hear the conversation, but I could see her listening to him with a bemused look on her face, the kind of look you'd give a carnival barker trying to fast-talk you into a crooked midway game.

I was giddy when she coolly walked away and I knew he had lost that round. That meant I might have a chance—maybe not much of one, but it was a chance I was willing to take. Within days, I had asked her to attend a party at our apartment, and to my surprise and never-ending gratitude, she said yes.

Chris was different from any woman I had ever met. She was *so* smart, not just school-smart or street-smart but world-class, real-world smart. Her BS detector was as accurate as a neurosurgeon's laser and could be lethal when aimed at someone or something that displeased her. She could take apart a lie, spot a bad choice, or point out what really mattered better than anyone I had ever met. After that first date, Chris and I were pretty much inseparable. Both of us believed our lives, and the way we felt about each other, would go on forever.

I would have moved in with her immediately, but Chris was a good Catholic girl. She wanted a wedding in her family church, with her family priest, with the prayers and priorities that she grew up with.

Raised a Protestant, in California no less, I lurched through the Catholic ceremony. But if it was important to Chris—and it was—it was important to me. I got through it without embarrassing her, and that meant everything to me.

She wanted a honeymoon in the place she had dreamed of visiting since childhood—Disney World. Even though I had been to Disneyland dozens of times when I lived on the West Coast, I wanted to please. We packed up and headed for the East Coast version of "the happiest place on earth."

And it suited us. We were not sophisticates, we were small town and simply giddy—to be together, to be in love, to be beginning our lives.

Even today, so long after I lost her, Chris is still very much the same, very much alive in my memory.

She met people and made conversation the way most people breathe. She pulled people to her, coaxed them out of themselves, and embraced them in all their flawed and sometimes maddening glory. And she clearly enjoyed being with them as much as they enjoyed being with her. She was capable of intense and detailed conversations about anything with anyone. It was amazing to watch.

Her gregarious nature completely took over our social calendar. Although Chris had only a few truly intimate friends, she seemed to know hundreds of people. She had a gift for remembering names, relationships, personal preferences, and other details about the lives of virtually every person she met. It was an ability I couldn't match, but I reaped the many benefits of being with the woman everyone loved to see arrive at the party.

And she was beautiful.

Just beautiful.

Her magnificent hair will always be fixed in my memory. I had never been around hair like that. It was long and thick, dark and heavy, healthy and strong. We had a ritual that Chris loved at the end of a long workday. She said it lowered her blood pressure and smoothed over any bumps she had inadvertently brought home from the office. She would sit on the floor in front of the couch and I would perch behind her brushing her hair all over—rhythmically, constantly, first to one side and then the other, the brush raking gently across her scalp—until she was so relaxed that her head dropped to her chest and her long hair covered her face. It became the way we separated the office from home, stress from rest, work from play.

I loved the way her hair blossomed onto the pillow when she lay down in bed at night, like a dark and beautiful flower framing her face. I loved seeing it blow every which way in the wind and her attempts to try to wrestle it back under control. She would often just have to give up. And I will always remember the way she looked when she would peek out at me from under that familiar, tangled dark curtain and smile.

Someone in her family told me that her great-grandmother had been a Spaniard, a woman with long dark hair and striking blue eyes. Wherever her physical gifts came from, Chris's ancestors had given her lush dark hair, warm olive skin, and blue eyes that went on forever.

For a long while, our lives together had seemed extraordinarily blessed. Then in 1983, our son, Eric, was born and our lives changed in a much different way than life does for most new parents.

Eric had serious health problems—a hole in his heart that prevented him from getting enough oxygen—and doctors told us that we needed to keep him alive until he was old enough and strong enough to survive the drastic surgery that would save his life. They said he had to be at least three years old or weigh thirty pounds before he could endure the lengthy and complex operation.

From Eric's birth onward, our focus changed. Every moment of our lives was dominated by fear for him, the demands of his stringent medication schedule, and the struggle to keep him alive.

When he exerted himself too much—something that happened frequently—Eric turned blue and our own hearts would nearly stop. We learned how to bring him back from the edge. We learned to measure our days by his doses of medicine, to work around what he needed and what we needed to do to keep him alive.

During that time, we were never quite able to feel at peace, knowing that we could lose him with just one misstep, one missed medication, one moment when we weren't paying enough attention. We worried constantly, wouldn't let him out of our sight, instinctively held him tightly and looked out for any danger or subtle sign that he was in medical trouble. It was hard. Although we were essentially newlyweds, it seemed we had the weight of the world on our shoulders. Nothing mattered more than making sure his little chest kept taking in air, his heart kept pumping, his body kept growing.

As we struggled toward his third birthday, we began planning for the kind of future we hoped would be possible once Eric had his surgery.

Austin was experiencing a big boom in population and real estate prices. We jumped into the market and sold our starter home for what seemed to us like a small fortune and started building another house in the far northwest corner of the city, part of a sprawling, brand-new development. We chose our house plans carefully, looking over architectural designs for hours on our dining room table, dreaming of a place that had the extras we knew would make our lives there even better.

Our new home on the corner of Hazelhurst Drive had a spacious kitchen that opened into the dining room, where Chris could cook and watch Eric play on the soft carpet just a few feet away. We had a fireplace, where we could all cuddle up on Austin's not very cold winter nights, watching the flames flare and pop, pretending we didn't live in a place where the temperature seldom hit freezing. Eric's room was on one side of the house, down a hallway. The master bedroom was on the other side, but close enough that we could hear him if he cried out. Our bedroom had a full bath, where Chris could soak in the tub, and another fireplace facing the bed that allowed us to read, lounge, or drift off to sleep while the fire danced.

For us, it was home, a real home.

And Chris made it so much better. She was a design whiz, and I was always proud to have people over. It seemed that even though we had no more money than any of our neighbors, Chris's ability to dream up ways to decorate our living space made our home look rich. She did it all by squeezing a dime till it begged for mercy, always able to find a deal, a real buy, or a castoff treasure that elevated our home into something better.

She ruled the house—food, décor, party planning, and home shopping. I was the master—or slave—of everything outside. I mowed, weeded, chopped, planted, and generally crawled around our property on my hands and knees, trying to make everything better. I dreamed up a deck/pergola area and built it myself while Chris watched encouragingly from the kitchen window.

I so wanted to please her.

Our backyard dream deck was designed for entertaining, even if we were just entertaining ourselves, and we could cook out, dine, and drink wine as we watched the sun go down and the shadows grow in the evening.

Our home was close to work for both of us, but quiet enough to seem like we were in the country. We could hear dogs bark in the distance, kids play in our neighbors' backyards, and sometimes the sizzle of steaks on the grill next door, but we never felt we were at the mercy of maddening traffic, too many people, or too much urban noise.

We believed we had found a little piece of heaven in suburban Austin.

In June 1986, Eric turned three years old. His doctors said the time had come to take him into surgery and try to create a new and healthy life for all of us.

We drove to Houston full of hope and fear and paced the hospital hallways, clinging to each other, while he was on the operating table. But the moment we saw him after his surgery, all of our worries melted away. For the first time in his life, our little boy was a beautiful, beaming pink. He was going to be okay.

And so were we.

Two weeks after his surgery, we drove home exultant and felt so proud when our neighbors gathered around the car to see our beautiful, healthy boy. Eric could now run and play just as hard and as recklessly as any other kid, and he loved it. He didn't grow exhausted or turn blue.

We practically did, trying to keep up with him.

Chris and I would watch Eric race around the yard like anybody else's kid and look at each other in amazement. We'd made it. Finally, we felt we had the future in our hands.

What we didn't know was that we had built our home in a neighborhood that wasn't exactly what it appeared to be. As the Austin suburbs spread north, city and county boundaries become hard to discern. While our new house was still in Austin, without realizing it, we were living on land that sat just outside the borders of the more urban Travis County and inside the southern reaches—and jurisdiction—of much more rural Williamson County.

Wilco, as the locals call it, boasted a legal system dominated by a longtime sheriff whose actions and opinions carried almost biblical authority for the public and the prosecutor's office. The prosecutor was a perfect partner for the sheriff, a big-fish-in-a-small-pond bully so committed to the idea of "law and order" that he was willing to break the law to win convictions. Together, Sheriff Jim Boutwell and District Attorney Ken Anderson brought a dangerously small-town approach to the big-city crimes that had begun to occur in Williamson County as the city of Austin intruded on the mean little Mayberry they had created.

It made no difference to us on a daily basis, but it would become profoundly important in the years ahead. In fact, if we had built our home one mile this way or that, I believe the next twenty-five years would have been very different.

CHAPTER TWO

TO ME, SCUBA DIVING ALWAYS FELT LIKE FLYING.

Whenever I would dive beneath the surface of the water and begin swimming farther and farther down into a freshwater lake, I felt the way birds must when held aloft by a kind wind. I loved it and relished every chance to get in the water.

I made my last dive on August 12, 1986. It was my thirty-second birthday, the afternoon before everything went terribly wrong—the last good day of my old life. Having a chance to dive on a weekday was an incredible rarity. But the grocery store chain where I worked had a generous policy of giving all its employees their birthdays off.

Chris was at work, Eric was at his beloved babysitter's, and I felt like a kid who had just gotten a snow day off from school. For both Chris and me, there had been too little playtime, too many worries about Eric's heart problem, too many fears that we wouldn't make it to his surgery.

Now that he was on the mend, so were we.

I had gone to Lake Travis that day to check out a new diving spot that a friend and I planned to explore together that weekend. Always cautious, I wanted to make sure that it would be worth the trip (and safe enough) for my buddy. I had high hopes that we might do more diving together in the future.

Liking what I'd seen at the lake, I stripped off my gear, packed up, and headed home. I planned to do something even more exotic that afternoon. I was going to take a nap.

This was living.

Chris and I had plans to go to the current Austin restaurant crush, City Grill, that night for a celebratory birthday dinner. One of our neighbors had volunteered to babysit Eric so we could have a more romantic evening, but we had turned her down. The truth was that we loved taking him along. And for us, having our boy healthy, dressed up, and sitting there, smiling beside us, slurping out of a sippy cup while we drank wine, was the height of romance.

Dinner that night wasn't solely about my birthday, it was an acknowledgment that our family had found a new kind of peace. It had been only a couple of months since Eric's surgery, but the growing serenity we felt was heady stuff for three people who had been through too much.

Before dinner, we sat outside on the restaurant's big deck, enjoying a glass of wine and a night that was warm but had just enough of a breeze to keep everyone cool. Dinner was perfect, and Eric acted like an old hand at dining out in a snazzy restaurant. Across the table, Chris looked as happy as I had seen her in a long time. She smiled at me in a knowing way.

I decided the night was going to get nothing but better.

I distinctly remember savoring the moment when the three of us were walking across the parking lot to our car. Eric was in the middle, and we were swinging him back and forth while he squealed in absolute delight.

At home, Chris got him ready for bed while I listened to the end of a presidential news conference. President Reagan was fielding questions about ending apartheid in South Africa, tearing down the Berlin Wall, and his support for the new idea of workplace drug testing—all issues that seemed to matter so much that night, and would quickly fade for me in the hours ahead.

At that moment, the only thing on my mind was romance. Chris came out to the living room by the fireplace, and we curled up on a blanket on the floor. I had poured two glasses of wine, and without telling her, I'd popped an adult movie into the VCR.

Looking back, I can't help thinking that I was not only an oaf but an optimist. Like so many moms, Chris had worked all day and, until a few minutes prior, had been taking care of an active toddler. She was exhausted.

Of course, I'd had a nap and was raring to go.

I had just started rubbing her hand when I heard tiny feet in the hallway. Eric was up. Chris said she'd take care of it and headed for his room, leaving me again, amorous and alone.

When she finally came out, I could see she was tired. Still, I continued to caress her, hoping to trigger a little interest. Instead, I soon heard her familiar soft snoring. Feeling sorry for myself, I got up, tossed back the wine, and went to our bedroom, leaving Chris on the floor.

Alone in our big bed, I finally fell asleep, peeved at what I saw as a missed opportunity. Later, long after midnight, Chris came to bed, curled around me, and whispered that she was sorry. She kissed me and said, "Next time, babe, next time."

I WAS ALREADY AWAKE WHEN THE ALARM WENT OFF AT 5:00 A.M., THE way it did every weekday. Once again, I followed my rigid morning routine—showering, grabbing a bite, and leaving the house for work at 5:30. You could set your watch by it. Chris always slept later and then dropped Eric off at the sitter's on her way to work. Staggering our schedules this way allowed me to pick him up about 2:30 every day, limiting the time he had to be out of our care.

Still smarting from what I saw as a rejection the night before, I did one last thing before leaving. I wrote a note to my wife that will haunt me for the rest of my life.

Chris, I know you didn't mean to, but you made me feel really unwanted last night. After a good meal, we came home, you binged on the rest of

the cookies, then with your nightgown around your waist and while I was
rubbing your hands and arms, you farted and fell asleep. I'm not mad or
expecting a big production. I just wanted you to know how I feel without us
getting into another fight about sex. Just think how you might have felt if
you were left hanging on your birthday. ILY.

I propped my petulant missive against something near the bathroom sink, so she'd be sure to see it when she got up. There is a small measure of peace for me today in knowing she never did read what I'd written.

That morning at work, I expected to hear from her, teasing me about the note, telling me off, something. Instead, there was nothing.

Otherwise, it was an absolutely normal day on the job—a blur of customers and demands, co-workers, corny jokes, and busywork. I left at the usual time, ran a couple of quick errands, and headed to the babysitter's to get our boy.

I knew something was wrong as soon as I got to the door. The babysitter had an odd look on her face and asked me what I was doing there. Eric had not come in that day, so why did I stop by? And Chris hadn't called the sitter to tell her that she and Eric weren't going to be there. I could feel my heart begin to pound as I dialed my home number from the babysitter's house.

Chris was incredibly efficient and responsible. She would never have failed to let me know of a change in plans. She called work regularly, sometimes just to tell me about things that didn't even directly affect us but she thought I should know. I recalled her calling me at work, terribly upset, the day the *Challenger* blew up.

I felt sick when an unfamiliar male voice answered my home phone. He identified himself as Sheriff Jim Boutwell and told me to come home as fast as I could.

I sprinted to my truck and drove maniacally home, running stop signs, swerving, sweating. My hands were shaking on the steering wheel, and I began to do a sort of involuntary emotional and situational triage—I started to accept that something had happened to Chris. Maybe our house had caught fire, maybe she had been hurt, maybe she had become sick in some way. I focused on Eric. Where was he? Was he okay? Was he hurt? Was it worse?

When I reached our house, I saw what I feared most—our home was surrounded by yellow crime scene tape, and there was a clutch of police cars parked in front. It seemed as though the entire neighborhood had gathered there, forming a line of solemn faces on the sidewalk and standing bunched in small, worried clusters across the street. They were watching me, watching the house, and whispering to each other.

I careened to a stop, jumped out, and was moving briskly across the lawn to the front door when a police officer stepped in front of me and stopped me in my tracks. He told me to stay put, and I was left standing helplessly in the yard, the only person at the scene who didn't know what was going on.

Sheriff Jim Boutwell, a rail-thin man in a huge white Stetson, swaggered toward me and demanded that I identify myself. When I did, he said nothing more, didn't explain what was going on, just kept looking at me. I was distraught and could hold back no more. I blurted out, "Is Eric okay?" The sheriff said he was, that he was at a neighbor's house.

Then I asked about Chris.

He told me simply and flatly, "Chris is dead."

Chris is dead . . .

I stood there in our yard, weaving slightly, feeling myself completely collapse on the inside. I knew that I was standing, but it felt like I was falling—falling down, falling apart—breaking into pieces under the weight of the sheriff's words.

It was almost as though I was diving again, but this time I was flailing, in a free fall to the bottom of the deepest lake in the world.

I couldn't breathe.

I was drowning.

CHAPTER THREE

AT THE SHERIFF'S URGING, I BEGAN TO MOVE FORWARD. I SLOWLY crossed the lawn toward our front door, each footstep feeling more unreal than the previous one. I was oddly weak and felt surprised that I could walk at all. My legs seemed to be made of glass, like they could shatter at any moment.

When I stepped inside our doorway, into the house that had been so familiar, the home that we had both been so proud of, it became clear that this place no longer belonged to us. That feeling was underscored by the way the sheriff was treating me—as though I were a distasteful guest he had been forced to invite into his office.

It seemed as though the house *had* become Sheriff's Department property. The rooms were teeming with officers, some of them loitering and laughing among themselves, others going through our cabinets, a handful of them smoking. A man in street clothes was covering the walls and doorframes with dirty black powder, apparently dusting for fingerprints. Another officer appeared to be looking closely at our cache of firewood in the backyard; others were going through drawers, closets, cupboards, all of our possessions. I heard a happy voice call out that they had "finally" gotten ice and could now chill drinks. I listened as the big grocery store bags of cubes and crushed ice were dumped into our kitchen sink and officers began shoving bottles and cans of soda into the makeshift cooler.

Down the hall, where our bedroom was, I heard people walking and murmuring, digging through things, occasionally calling each other over to take a look at some kind of discovery. Deep inside the room, I could hear a constant series of shutter clicks, and I saw bright flashes light up the hallway walls, momentarily turning the darkened corridor into a narrow shaft of bright, white daylight. I knew Chris must still be in there, knew they must be surrounding her, taking pictures of her, recording whatever it was that someone had done to her. I very much wanted to go back to our room, to see her, to just be near her. I was also afraid of what I would see. I was picking up cues that she may have been beaten to death.

When I asked, I was told they weren't sure about the cause of death—that there was a possibility she'd been shot. This uncertainty so early in the case was a harbinger of the police incompetence to come.

Sheriff Boutwell was close to being a caricature of an old-style Texas lawman. He stood well over six feet, wore a couple of gun belts on his slim hips, cowboy boots, and a ten-gallon hat that seemed to sit a little too high on his head. He had on a tie clip that looked like a couple of tiny handcuffs. He spoke to me in a thick, cold drawl—without empathy, without emotion. As we sat in the breakfast nook, where I had wolfed down my morning cereal, Boutwell suddenly began to tersely read me my Miranda rights, something I wasn't expecting. I told myself this was probably completely called for—they had to start from scratch on this case, right?

Then the sheriff's lead investigator, Sergeant Don Wood, asked that I sign a consent form for them to search my house and car. That seemed off, since they had clearly been here for some time, going through everything. But I signed the form, still trying to help, still hoping that these officers would find the answer to what had happened to Chris. I remember thinking that if rules had to be bent to solve Chris's murder, I would be the last one to object.

With Sergeant Wood sitting beside him, Boutwell asked me for details of my day. I choked out everything I could remember—what time I had left that morning, whether anything had been out of the ordinary, what I did at work all day, who could vouch for me being there, what time I usually got home. They were mundane questions that, on this day, took on a dark and desperate importance. What was Chris wearing when I last saw her? Had we spoken before I left? Was Eric awake when I walked out? I answered as completely as I could, eager to do what it took to help the police catch the person who had hurt Chris.

Soon, the sheriff clumsily opened a new line of questioning, asking me whether Chris and I had a happy marriage, whether I loved her, whether there was anyone else in my life, whether there had been violence between us, whether we argued, what our sex life was like. I was totally honest, wanting to share with them everything, every single detail, as transparently as I could. I told them that our marriage, like any marriage, was not all sunshine and puppy dogs, that we had our ups and downs, but that ours was a forever marriage, that we were a good match, that we loved each other very much.

Sheriff Boutwell brought up the note I had written and left in the bathroom. He didn't want to know too much about it. He just wanted me to admit to him, unequivocally, that I had written it. I groaned, aching at being reminded of what I had done, not knowing yet if Chris had seen it. I told him that I was the author and that I profoundly wished I could take it back.

As the hours of questioning went on, I could see that the sheriff and his sergeant were trying to do some kind of good cop–bad cop routine. Boutwell would speak to me angrily, his questions taking on an accusatory tone. Wood was supposed to be the good cop—acting more sympathetically, accepting my answers, encouraging me to tell them more. He did some of that, but the approach clearly wasn't working the way they had planned.

The problem was that Sergeant Wood seemed to keep forgetting his role. When the sheriff acted angry at me, Wood would explode at me as well—at least until Boutwell gave him an enraged look. Later, I realized that, even during the attempted role playing, Wood was just incapable of setting aside his sycophancy toward the sheriff, a mind-set that was rampant in the entire Williamson County system.

Boutwell had made headlines for his unique law-and-order style on two occasions, neither one of them displaying particularly good police judgment, but they were the stuff of Texas law enforcement legend.

In August 1966, a former Marine with a brain tumor, a troubled childhood, and a drug problem climbed the tower at the University of Texas carrying a small arsenal of rifles, pistols, and a sawed-off shotgun. When Charles Whitman reached the top, he began firing at the students below, ultimately killing thirteen people. Boutwell, then a reserve deputy in Williamson County, was at the airport he owned when he heard about the UT attack. He climbed into his own small plane, flew to Austin, and began buzzing the bell tower, firing repeatedly at Whitman in an attempt to distract him so police could take him out, which is ultimately what happened. Whether Boutwell's spectacular flyby shooting made a difference in stopping Whitman is unclear. But the incident did leave a lasting impression of Boutwell as a cop who would do almost anything to get his man.

Later elected sheriff of Williamson County, Boutwell again made national headlines in 1983, when he finagled detailed confessions out of the proven serial liar and self-proclaimed serial killer Henry Lee Lucas. While in Boutwell's custody, Lucas confessed to 360 murders, give or take a few. Boutwell was still basking in the glory of the Lucas case when Chris was killed.

Only later would we all learn that the Lucas confessions had been made in exchange for cheeseburgers and milk shakes, cigarettes and jaunts in Sheriff's Department cars to play at looking for bodies. Lucas may not have killed with the abandon he bragged about, but he did murder the myth of Sheriff Boutwell's infallibility. Sadly, I was in the penitentiary by the time the truth came out.

I knew none of this as we sat in our breakfast nook, going over the details of my life with Chris. By this time, we had been talking for hours and I was desperate to see Eric. I asked again to go to him.

Who knew what he had witnessed? The officers stepped away to speak in private and then came back, saying Sergeant Wood would take me to see my son. They decided we would not go out the front door but would move from backyard to backyard, staying away from the television cameras that had already gathered in front of our home.

I learned later that they wanted me outside at the back of the house so they could remove Chris's body through the front.

Eric was with the neighbor two houses away and across the street. So I slipped through our back gate into the yard next door, with Sergeant Wood following. We walked to the other side of the yard and faced the next fence. This part of the neighbor's fence had no gate.

The sergeant hesitated. Vaulting the fence was going to be a challenge for him. He ran his hand along the top, groping for a firm hold. One foot found the fence's two-by-four cross-member. He seemed unsure about what to do with his other foot.

Wood was out of practice and out of shape. I considered helping him—I wanted to get to Eric as soon as possible—but I didn't want to embarrass the sergeant or damage his ego. I didn't know what else to do, so I stood and watched.

After one false start and one hand-scraping failure, Sergeant Wood climbed to the top of the fence. He wobbled for an instant, then hurled himself over and onto the ground, landing hard. It wasn't pretty, but he made it. When I was able to follow in short order, I could see that our physical differences registered uncomfortably with him. I felt bad. It's almost laughable how concerned I was about hurting the feelings of one of the men who would do so much to destroy the next twenty-five years of my life.

WHEN I FINALLY GOT TO ERIC, THE POOR LITTLE GUY WAS WEARING someone else's diaper and some other kid's shirt. He was disheveled, and I could see right away that he had been crying—a lot. He must have felt so alone and so scared.

When he saw me, we ran to each other, collapsing against the wall and weeping in each other's arms. Finally—finally—I had the chance to hold our little boy. I didn't know what he might have seen. I didn't know whether he had been threatened. We both cried for a long time—huddled together—holding on tight to all that was left of our family.

CHAPTER FOUR

I WAS LOST IN MY OWN NEIGHBORHOOD.

I had no idea where to go, what to do, or who to ask for help. My parents and siblings were on the way, but they lived hours from Austin and wouldn't be in until morning. Chris's family hadn't arrived yet either.

And Chris was gone. Forever.

The police had finished questioning me for the day, and the forensic people were beginning to clear out of our house. It was late afternoon, and I was walking toward home with Eric clinging to me for dear life. When our next-door neighbors asked if we would like to decompress at their place—maybe get Eric a bite to eat—I accepted with relief.

It had been several hours since I learned that Chris had been murdered. I know now that I was in shock. That day, the whole world seemed surreal—familiar, yet foreign. Eric was teary eyed, playing tentatively before me on the floor. I was propped stiffly on the couch, lost in pain and disbelief.

People who lived nearby streamed into the house to tell us how bad they felt about Chris. I vaguely remember the whispered condolences, the tears, the comfort so many people tried to give us. But I very clearly recall the sense of sudden terror everyone living near our darkened home felt—the panic of knowing that someone or something evil had entered our neighborhood, broken into one of our houses, killed a person we all loved—and then slipped away.

Any pretense of personal safety had vanished, replaced by a kind of instinctual, primal fear. I could see it in my neighbors' eyes, in the skittish way they moved and acted, in how tightly they clutched their children.

When Chris's father, Jack, pulled up to our house, I felt some relief. Scooping Eric up, we walked through the neighbors' yard to our home on the corner. Jack was on the sidewalk, headed to the front door.

When something like this happens, family should be a source of healing, a safe place to express your grief and pain, a way to begin the long process of mourning and moving forward. I desperately needed to be with people who loved Chris and understood the enormity of what had happened. I was glad to see Jack, because I knew how much he loved his daughter.

I often think back to Jack's reaction to me that day and wonder if he had already begun to worry about my being involved in her murder. The police had told me that Jack had been there earlier in the afternoon (he'd been in Austin for business and just happened to stop by), and I wonder now if the sheriff or one of the deputies had said something that made him feel I might be at fault.

All I know is that Jack was brusque and distant with me. We spoke briefly and he hugged Eric, stayed for only a short while, and then left. This wasn't completely out of character for him, since he wasn't exactly an easygoing or lovable guy. But his leaving Eric and me alone that night in the house where Chris had been killed was beyond comprehension for me.

In retrospect, maybe I should have taken Eric and left, too. But the shock of the day's events left me groping for what to do, where to go. I think I decided to stay at our home that night, in great part, because I could still so much feel Chris in the house—still smell her cooking, her perfume, her hair. It was as though, by staying, we could be with her a little longer. There were traces of her everywhere—her clothes in the closet, her makeup on the bathroom counter, her favorite dish towel draped on the refrigerator door.

Eric was withdrawn and quiet, in the way children are when they have been traumatized. He wasn't crying anymore, but I could tell he knew things were very wrong. His fear and anxiety were palpable.

I tried to keep him on his regular routine and give him some sense of continuity. He had eaten, so we lay down on the floor in his room and played until it was time for bed. I snuggled up beside him and held him close until he fell asleep.

Then I did the achingly difficult thing I knew I had to do. I walked toward our bedroom, turning on every light as I passed. I could see that someone had left a light on beside our bed.

I stood in the doorway, not breathing, and looked inside.

Lit only by the bedside lamp, the room was mostly dark, but I could see that the bed had been stripped. In front of our large dresser, I saw a haphazard pile of clothing and accessories—belts, scarves, and shoes that appeared to be all mixed in with shirts and pants belonging to both of us. When I looked more closely, I could see that some of the dresser drawers had been pulled out and were turned upside down or sideways and emptied on the floor.

I flicked on the overhead light and immediately felt sick.

The ceiling was flecked with blood, and the headboard was spattered with more blood and pieces of human tissue. The book Chris had been reading was sitting on its side in the bookshelf directly above where her head had been. The title was partially covered by a spray of dark blood. It was *If Tomorrow Comes*, a Sidney Sheldon pulp crime novel that Chris considered perfect bedtime reading. It had a story line that wasn't deep enough to keep her awake.

I moved through the room as though I had never been there before. The amount of blood I saw broke my heart. The sheriff had told me they weren't sure initially whether Chris had been beaten to death or shot. And to an untrained eye, the scene was confusing. Blood splatter was everywhere—arching up along the walls, splashed onto the carpet all the way across the room, obscuring our faces in a framed family picture that sat inside the head-board bookcase.

It is not enough to say that this was hard for me, not enough to say that standing there and taking in this carnage was heartbreaking. I almost felt as if seeing this, trying to process this terrible scene, was changing me, right down to my bones, altering me in ways that would never—could never—be reversed.

I walked through our bedroom as if exploring an alternate universe. For the most part, I just looked, trying to make sense of what I was seeing. Once in a while, I had to touch something, lay my hand on it, just feel it, as if attempting to reinforce the distant fact that an object belonged to us.

I rubbed my knee against the cushioned frame of our bed. My fingers traced the edge of the lampshade on my side of our bed. I turned on the water in the master bathroom sink, trying to wash away the fingerprint dust. It was our house and our stuff.

But it didn't feel like ours anymore.

Our home looked like it had been picked up by a giant and shaken hard—then angrily thrown aside. Everything was in disarray. Our entire closet full of clothes was tangled and tossed on the floor. I wasn't sure who to blame. Had the murderer or the police made this mess? The police officers who smoked had left overflowing ashtrays all over the house. They'd made no effort to clean up after themselves, acting as if my son and I were not still living there.

Everywhere I turned, there was another sign of the dark shadow that had fallen over our lives.

I desperately wanted to talk with Chris about it, but her body now lay in the morgue and her blood and brain tissue covered the walls and ceiling of our bedroom.

I looked through the window and saw the wide yellow crime scene tape encircling our home. That was one thing I decided I could handle myself. I stepped out into our dark, quiet neighborhood and walked to the side of the house where the yellow tape had been tied. As quietly as I could, I moved along the tape, wadding it into a ball—removing the most obvious evidence of what had happened behind the walls of our home.

I WENT BACK TO ERIC AND CURLED UP WITH HIM. I STAYED THERE FOR ten minutes, then got up, walked through the brightly lit house, and went back to Eric and lay down—and then I did it all over again.

Again and again.

All night long, I glided like a ghost through our glowing house, looking for someone who wasn't there, looking for meaning in what had happened—searching for anything to help me wrap my head around the bomb that had gone off in our lives.

As morning broke, I was still moving through the house, aching with grief and lack of sleep. I knew I had to pull myself together for Eric's sake. I brewed some coffee, sat down, and began making the kinds of phone calls I never dreamed I would have to make—notifying far-flung friends and family about what had happened. I hadn't even thought about making initial inquiries about funeral arrangements, or trying to figure out where Chris would be buried. It is one of the ironies of losing someone to sudden death that those hurt the most have to begin immediately making big decisions at a time when they are least able to.

I felt like a zombie, and I would for weeks. It seemed everyone had questions for me and I had very few answers. What were Eric and I going to do now? No idea. Would we sell the house? I didn't know. Did I have any idea who had done this to Chris? None. Were the police making progress? Who knew?

The day after Chris died, my family came in full force, and I was so grateful. Eric loved them all, and they were great distractions for him when he badly needed something other than darkness and despair around him. My mom and dad were hugely helpful in squiring Eric around, playing with him for hours, and keeping both of us fed, dressed, and moving forward.

Chris's brother John and his wife came. They were actually beginning their move from Houston to Oregon, but they stayed through the funeral. John was the oldest child in their family. He had a bachelor's degree in marine biology and an overwhelming love for his little sister Chris. Mary Lee, the youngest of Chris's siblings, had lived with us for a while. Chris was an almost maternal pillar for her, someone who looked out for her, guiding her choices and giving advice.

When they got there, John and Mary Lee wanted to go to the room, wanted to see for themselves what had happened. And as hard as it was for all of us, the three of us stood stricken beside the bed, trying to do our own amateur forensic work. Where had the man stood? What had he been looking for in our drawers and closets? What had he taken?

I had already told police that I knew a pistol was gone—a .45 that I kept in a leather pouch on the top shelf of our closet.

John, in particular, was angry and frustrated. He believed the police were not doing enough to look for the killer. They hadn't been out to the house at all during the time John was there, and he was convinced they were blowing the investigation. Of course, his fears turned out to be well founded.

While I attended to the myriad demands triggered by what had happened, John told his wife he was going to take on an exercise aimed at "getting inside the killer's head." He stood in the bedroom and began to act out what he believed would have been the logical approach the killer used to get into and out of the room. And then he retraced the most likely path the killer would have traveled to make his getaway.

John wanted to check for any small piece of evidence that police might have overlooked.

With his wife at his side, John walked through the house to the dining room, then through the unlocked sliding glass door where we assumed the killer had entered. He walked into the backyard and toward the fence, reasoning that the killer could have parked near the wooded area behind our home, jumped the fence, and gotten access to the house.

Immediately, John found something police hadn't noticed—two large footprints just inside the fence. They were deep, as though the person who made them had climbed the back of the fence, swung his leg over, and jumped into our yard, landing hard and sinking into the soft ground. This was encouraging for John, so he continued his trek of the imagination, this time walking out the side gate of our yard and moving toward the place he believed the killer's car may have been parked.

One of the features Chris and I liked about the house was the greenbelt that ran behind it, a scrubby, wooded area that had not yet been developed. The secluded clump of trees and native Texas grasses was crisscrossed with small trails, superhighways for jackrabbits, deer, coyotes, and the occasional unlucky house cat. There was also an abandoned campsite, with torn-up clothes, a small blackened fire pit, and empty beer cans, a sign that two-legged varmints were regular visitors there as well. Most of the neighborhood attributed the campfires to teenagers or the occasional hobo, certainly not to anyone seen as a threat.

John was looking for something specific, however. Maybe something from our house that the killer had taken and dropped, maybe the weapon he had used to kill Chris, maybe something that looked completely innocent but held the answers all of us so desperately wanted.

That is exactly what he found.

Beside the wooded area, there was one house under construction, but work on it had been sporadic. The shell was built, but the inside remained rough and unfinished. Not far from this house, John spotted a square of dusty blue cloth clinging to the curb. It was a Western-style bandanna. John crouched down beside it, and without touching the fabric, he looked carefully at each section of the cloth. His attention was drawn to a cluster of small, dark brownish stains. He wasn't a trained investigator, but he believed they might be bloodstains.

And he was right.

So, unlike the inexperienced officers he was making up for, John took great care to keep the evidence uncontaminated. He picked the bandanna up by its corner with two fingers and held it out from his body as he headed back to the house. As he walked into the breakfast nook, John told everyone to stay back and called for his wife to get a plastic bag that he could put the bandanna in. She grabbed a clear baggie out of a kitchen drawer, and he carefully lowered the bandanna inside.

No one had touched it any further, no one had held it, no one knew it existed.

On the same foray into the woods, John had gone into the house under construction and collected what appeared to be a napkin with dark stains. This piece of overlooked evidence, too, was preserved and packaged. John then called police, told him of the discoveries, and asked that a deputy come to our house and pick up these items.

It wasn't long before an officer showed up, picked up the baggies, and disappeared again into the Williamson County Sheriff's Office. It would be twenty-five years before any of us knew the true success of John's search.

CHAPTER FIVE

SHERIFF JIM BOUTWELL AND HIS INVESTIGATORS WERE IN REGULAR contact with me for days after Chris's death. The sheriff had also been speaking with local reporters, and I opened the paper one morning to see a story on Chris's autopsy results, in which Boutwell was quoted. The article noted that the Travis County Medical Examiner Roberto Bayardo had pinpointed her time of death as 6:00 A.M.

That made sense to me. I knew that I had left at 5:30 on the dot. I also believed, naively as it turned out, that the official time of death would serve as a tool for detectives in eliminating me as a suspect. But I wasn't thinking clearly, I wasn't protecting myself—I hadn't even contacted a lawyer. Why would I? It was simply beyond my comprehension that I would be considered a suspect.

Looking back, I recognize how much I was reeling from loss.

I had been a religious person when I was young but had grown away from the church in high school. It had been a long time since I thought about the significance or power of the human soul.

The vacuum Chris's murder left in my life, though, brought some of those old teachings back. Her absence seemed to leave a gaping wound in the world, a shrieking emptiness that I had never known could exist. I believed I could feel the loss of her soul in my life.

I realized then that being married *is* very much like becoming one person. Chris had been part of me—a vital organ, a limb, a function I needed to live. With her gone, I felt like I was dying.

I experienced the kind of phantom pain amputees often report. When I sat on the couch, I could almost feel her beside me. When I walked into the kitchen, I could practically see her laughing and making dinner. I thought I could hear her in other rooms or catch a glimpse of her walking out the front door or tending her flowers in the yard. Her absence was so powerful, it was like an undeniable, tangible force. I spent time in my head talking to her, looking for her, trying to communicate with her, telling her I loved her, begging her to come back.

I HADN'T SLEPT IN WHAT FELT LIKE DAYS.

And every waking moment was filled with dark demands—from arranging Chris's funeral, even deciding what she was going to wear, to dealing with the appreciated but seemingly unending condolences from all quarters.

First and foremost, I was trying to take care of our heartbroken little boy. I was keenly aware that Eric might have seen something terrible, that he must have felt threatened, that he may even have been assaulted in some way. Spending time with both sets of extended families was good for him to a point, but we were all struggling mightily with our own crippling anguish.

Sometimes—inevitably—it got the better of us.

I remember sitting at the table one night after dinner as my mother steadfastly gathered up the dirty dishes for us, doing anything she could to try to keep our lives as normal as possible. She'd made us a nice meal, even though no one really had much of an appetite. When I glanced up appreciatively, I saw that her face was beginning to crumple, even as she struggled to continue her task. Then she gave in to her grief, falling against the kitchen wall for support, her body racked by hard, painful sobs. A few moments later, she regained control, wiped her eyes, stood, and went back to clearing the table.

It had to be a bewildering atmosphere for a little boy, first being in the house when his mother was murdered, and then being reassured and comforted by adults who every now and then completely lost it. I started looking in earnest for a therapist who might know how to work with Eric, maybe help him find some measure of peace.

Meanwhile, I felt under siege from all sides.

The media had been contacting me day and night, pestering me to sit down for an interview that I didn't want to do. This was not just another news event for me. I didn't care whether it was on TV or on the front page of the paper. I didn't care that the public "wanted to hear from me" about the terrible thing that had happened to my wife and our life together.

What I needed most were some answers.

Who had done this? Why? I believed the police were the people who would eventually deliver those answers, and I was determined to do anything I could to help them.

THE PHONE RANG AND WHEN I PICKED IT UP, I HEARD SHERIFF BOUT-well's now-familiar voice. He said he wanted me to come down to his office and chat, that he wanted to update me on the investigation.

I see now that I could not have been more helpless, more alone, or more vulnerable.

I told the sheriff that I was on my way.

He was waiting for me, as usual, behind his massive old wooden desk—surrounded by enough Western memorabilia to open a museum. There were horseshoes on the wall, gun belts and handcuffs on pegs, and a wide-brimmed Stetson, his ever-present signature hat, atop the sheriff's head.

The old wood-frame building was filled with the sound of Bout-well's boys at work—the deputies' boots clomping across the bare wood floors, the creaking complaints of heavy doors being opened and closed, phones being picked up and hung up and occasionally slammed down, and the constant low drone of their conversations, sometimes punctuated with laughter or annoyance or anger. Every sound in the place seemed magnified by the office's tall ceilings and ancient walls and windows.

I sat down in the old-fashioned oak office chair across from the sheriff with high hopes. It soon became clear that he was not going to be the one sharing information.

I was.

Once again, he led me painstakingly through every detail of the last twenty-four hours of Chris's life, questioning every one of my movements and choices, my habits and whereabouts. I had grown accustomed to this. A friend who had some police experience told me that this was standard practice, the theory being that if the sheriff and his sidekick Sergeant Wood could catch me in even one small inconsistency, then I would most likely crumble under the weight of their discovery and confess everything.

At least, that was the way it was supposed to work.

It was a theory that rested, of course, on the premise that I had, in fact, murdered my wife. Since I had not, going over the details again and again got us nowhere. I had no insight to offer, no clues that the police could follow up, no information that would crack the case for them.

But they kept digging.

At one point, the sheriff targeted the last meal Chris and I had together, our celebratory dinner at City Grill in Austin. He fixated on what side dish Chris had chosen to go with her fish entrée. Whenever I told him she had ordered the zucchini, he challenged me, accusing me of being wrong or actually lying about what she ate.

I was dumbfounded at why he was so obsessed with disputing this easily confirmed information. Why didn't they just contact the restaurant and check the bill? I wondered if this was some sort of new police ploy, an attempt to rattle me and perhaps force some kind of breakthrough in the case. When the sheriff asked me again and I gave him the same answer, he made no effort to hide his disappointment and anger.

We were at an impasse. We all just sat there, staring at each other. Sergeant Wood broke his gaze and leaned over to the sheriff, pointing at a piece of paper on the desk, apparently the autopsy report. Wood whispered, loud enough for anyone in the room to hear, "I think that where it says 'vegetable matter,' that means zucchini. Zucchini is a vegetable."

The sheriff looked momentarily crestfallen, then quickly went back to shooting daggers at me. Again he launched into a fresh challenge of everything I had detailed about my day.

That was the moment when I realized with a sad and profound certainty that these men were simply not up to the task of solving this case. They may have been able to handle day-to-day, hometown police work—sorting out domestic disputes, car accidents, and neighbors fussing at each other. They undoubtedly knew how to investigate petty theft, home burglaries, or teenage vandalism. That kind of nuts-and-bolts, small-time crime was on the menu every day for them.

Chris's case was different. It was difficult. No one had any reason to hurt her. She had no enemies or angry ex-husbands, no affairs gone south or riches someone wanted to plunder. I'd told police I believed it had to have been an intruder, someone who broke in after I left—someone who may even have chosen Chris at random. It was the only scenario that made sense.

Now, having watched these men work the crime scene and work me over had convinced me of one thing: they were never going to solve the case without help. Whoever killed Chris would never be caught, would be free to ruin another family's lives, to destroy somebody else's world as thoroughly as they had decimated mine.

It made me sick. I had been there answering the same questions for hours and I was frustrated, exhausted, and anxious about their inability to do their jobs.

I had to do something to move things forward.

When the sheriff hurled his next accusation at me, I blurted, "If I take a polygraph, then will you believe me?"

The two men lit up like kids on Christmas morning. That was exactly what they wanted to hear but never dreamed I would offer.

The sheriff told me he would schedule one for that evening at 6:00. I was to meet him back there at the Sheriff's Department and we would be done in a flash. It seemed worth it to me. I wasn't afraid of polygraphs—my employer had used them on occasion, for years. New hires and managers who handled a great deal of money or prescription drugs were regularly required to take them. I'd taken a test myself and was familiar with the science of how polygraphs worked.

I very much believed that since I had nothing to hide, I had nothing to fear. And I prayed that clearing me once and for all would lead the cops to look elsewhere before the killer's trail got too cold.

I climbed back into my truck and headed home, hoping I might be able to catch a nap, or at least collapse in a quiet room with Eric—maybe play together with his cars and recharge our own batteries a little bit.

But when I got there, the chaos that followed Chris's death was still waiting for me. Friends and family filled every room, neighbors kept knocking on the door delivering their sympathies. And the press was back in force, still refusing to take no for an answer about my doing an interview.

Finally, I agreed to let the Austin newspaper take a picture of me sitting in the backyard. They agreed that if I did that, they would leave me alone, at least for a while. I was desperate to be given some space.

I recall thinking that it seemed so unnatural to be asked to pose for a photo solely because something terrible had happened to someone I loved. I sat down in the backyard on the deck I had built for Chris, next to the table where we had shared so many meals, and marveled grimly at the unique awfulness of the moment. I felt both cornered and abandoned, heartbroken and wearing a brave face, angry with the police and totally dependent on them. I appreciated everyone who was trying to help me and fervently wished they would all go away. My stomach growled with hunger and I had no interest in eating. I was dead tired, but when I closed my eyes, I began reliving the past few grinding days, one tragic detail at a time. And I was still worried sick about our son.

Now I had the further distraction of a stranger standing in our yard, snapping pictures of me as I sat there in the heat, the constant shutter clicks punching through the drone of the air conditioner and the buzz of hungry mosquitoes. I thought at the time that the picture would be simply a snapshot of one man's grief. The police, the press—and eventually the Williamson County prosecutor—would look at the picture of me and see something else entirely.

They saw a portrait of guilt.

CHAPTER SIX

THREE FRIENDS OF MINE ARRIVED AT OUR HOME TO ESCORT ME TO THE polygraph test. They were all husbands and fathers, men with wives and lives and jobs, but since Chris's murder, they regularly dropped everything to drive me to and from places I didn't want to be. Now they were here to pick me up for what I thought would be a break-through appointment with the sheriff. I was right, but as with every-thing else in the past few days, it turned out differently than I had expected.

Bone weary, I was poured into their car and they drove me back to the now familiar sheriff's office. We got there, as instructed, at 6:00 P.M. But as soon as we arrived, the agenda changed.

The sheriff announced that I would be riding with him to the Department of Public Safety headquarters in Austin, miles and miles out of the way. We could have saved so much time by just meeting the sheriff at the DPS offices. When I told my friends we had to head back in the direction we had come from, I could see they were perplexed. But they hadn't been watching the Williamson County Sheriff's Office at work, as I had. This latest twist was a perfect ex-ample of my frustration with the sheriff and his team. Everything was more difficult than it needed to be. Everything about their op-eration seemed dysfunctional. And I couldn't tell if it was malice or incompetence that led to these kinds of decisions.

All I could do was grit my teeth and march forward.

Our caravan pulled in behind the DPS office at almost 7:00 P.M. There were a handful of deputies on hand, along with Sergeant Wood, all led by the imposing sheriff. My trio of friends and I brought up the rear. Our two posses headed for the now empty building's back door, only to find it locked. We tried another door. It, too, was locked up tight. Finally, through a series of trials and errors, we were able to get inside and found ourselves in a long, nondescript corridor.

That was followed by another empty hallway, and then another. We climbed the stairs and tramped down at least two more empty corridors. I was hopelessly lost, and I was beginning to think the sheriff was, too.

The linoleum floors had been buffed to a high gloss, and the sound of our small army of feet reverberated as if we were giants. Every door we passed was closed. Many were labeled with indecipherable acronyms, cop speak and state seals. We were in the bowels of a massive bureaucratic beast, and no one was home.

The sheriff stopped at a door and tried the knob. Locked. He knocked. No answer. And then we were off again, down more empty halls, past more empty offices, trying more locked doors. The sheriff wouldn't even look at me, and I thought he must have been embarrassed. If the moment hadn't been so sad and frustrating and deadly serious, it would have been funny.

Finally, a voice called out from down the hall. It was the polygraph examiner, who apologized for being late. He pulled a tangle of keys out of his pocket and unlocked one of the dull, unmarked doors.

Sheriff Boutwell told my friends to wait in the outer office. I followed him and the examiner, along with the deputies, into another room. Boutwell and the examiner whispered in one corner while the deputies gave me looks they must have reserved only for the guilty.

Next, the sheriff ordered the deputies to remove me so he could share the details of the case with the polygraph operator. I sighed and trudged into the next room. My friends weren't there, but there was a table and a chair. Sitting down, I told myself that I could endure this last test. I had to do this. If Chris's killer was ever going to be caught, I had to get this out of the way, no matter how tired, frustrated, and upset I was.

By now, it was clear—even to me—that I was very much a murder suspect.

I laid my head down on the table, and despite the hard surface and the rough treatment—despite all my angst and anger—I fell asleep immediately. When they woke me, it was well after 8:00 P.M. Finally, I could take the polygraph and go home.

I followed the examiner into a tiny room, where he sat down at a little desk, his old-style machine at his side. I sat in front of him but facing the opposite way, so he was looking at my back. I was staring into a large mirror on the opposite wall. As the examiner droned on about how the polygraph worked, I realized that Sheriff Boutwell, Sergeant Wood, and God knows who else were sitting on the other side of the mirror.

The examiner began asking questions—had I had any alcohol? Was I fatigued? Lack of sleep could skew the results. Was I taking drugs? I told him I was ready and that I just wanted to get this over with so the police could find the person who killed Chris, so I could go home and be with my boy.

That's when he told me that I shouldn't expect to be headed home until well after midnight.

The sheriff had told me to be there at 6:00 P.M. and I had been. But he had blown the deadline. I was sick of his incompetence. I was sick of Sergeant Wood's foolishness. I was sick of not seeing Eric. I was heartbroken about Chris's death. I wanted to be with my family. I wanted them to find the killer.

I had simply reached my limit. I told them I wasn't going to take any test that night. They would have to reschedule.

Instantly, the sheriff and Sergeant Wood came tumbling out of the adjacent room, the ruse of the two-way mirror totally abandoned. Boutwell was incensed. He said that the examiner had come in after hours as a personal favor, that he was very busy, that rescheduling would be next to impossible. He pleaded with me to reconsider.

But nothing he said mattered to me. I was tired of his swagger, his gun belts, and his bravado. I was tired of his cowboy hat. I was tired of the unprofessionalism, of always having to make allowances for what he needed. I was tired of him treating me as if I had killed Chris.

And on top of everything else, I was just tired.

I left with my friends. And after that night, everything changed. I did not realize it, but my late-night refusal to take a polygraph hit the reset button on the investigation.

A FEW DAYS LATER, I WAS NOTIFIED THAT I WOULD HAVE TO GO TO PRObate court because Chris had no will. Neither did I. We were both young and healthy and thought we would live forever.

I called a lawyer friend to talk about probate, and he suggested a day for me to stop by his office. When I told him that I couldn't make that appointment because I was taking the rescheduled polygraph test with the sheriff's office—as it turned out it had been perfectly easy to reschedule—he went ballistic. He told me probate court could wait, that what I needed right now was a criminal defense lawyer. He wanted me to see two friends of his—Bill White and Bill Allison.

Up until that point, no one in my life had ever needed a criminal defense attorney for any reason. I didn't know any defense attorneys and had no idea where to start looking, so the advice from my friend was a godsend. Very soon, I found myself standing outside the office of White and Allison in central Austin.

Bill White and Bill Allison—or the two Bills, as they were sometimes called—complemented each other well. White was quick on his feet, street-smart, and had an uncanny ability to connect with people instantly and intimately. He had been a prosecutor in Travis County some years before and knew more about the ups and downs of criminal court than anyone. He inspired confidence in me, at least in part because he drove a beautiful new Porsche. I thought he must be good to afford that car.

Bill Allison could not have been more different. Well over six feet tall, he was thin as a young sapling and sported a massive mustache. He spoke slowly and thoughtfully, and each of his comments was delivered with a world-weary authority. Most important, I immediately got the sense that he cared about me, that what happened to me mattered to him personally. I would learn in the days ahead that Allison's heart was outshone only by his intellect.

Together, they were brilliant, accomplished, and eager to help.

"Never talk to the police again," Bill White told me. "We will do that. It's our job, not yours."

That was just fine with me.

The more we talked, the clearer it became how far out of my depth I had been. Allison told me, "I'm going to cancel your polygraph tests with the sheriff. You can take a couple from independent examiners first."

What White said next was sobering. "I don't know if you know this, but no one's passed a polygraph test at DPS in the last five years."

CHAPTER SEVEN

CHRIS WAS BEING BURIED IN HOUSTON—ABOUT 160 MILES FROM OUR home in Austin—because her family still lived there. It seemed to give them some small peace to know that their girl would always be close by. And frankly, I wasn't sure where Eric and I would be in the years ahead.

I didn't know if, as a struggling single dad, I would keep my job, our house, or our plans for Eric's future. Chris had wanted him to grow up in a house on a Texas lake, a place where he would learn to swim and fish and feel at home with the water. Now, the oppressive summer temperatures and the tragedy that would be forever linked with Texas were driving me away from the place I had planned to live out my life.

But before I could make any decisions about Eric's and my future, I had to say good-bye to Chris.

As I trudged across the funeral home's asphalt parking lot, heat waves rising around my feet, I knew exactly why I was there. I needed to see her. I needed no proof of her death, but I needed something tangible, some moment that allowed me to let her go, something—anything—that would force me to concede to myself that Chris was never coming back, something that would help me figure out how Eric and I could begin moving on.

I stepped inside, and everything became soft and serious and terribly sad. Even the music seemed to whimper from the ever-present speakers. The funeral director—all obsequious concern and carefully practiced grief—met me just outside his office. When I told him I wanted to see my wife, I could tell that he had not been prepared for the request. He fumbled the moment, letting his discomfort show. The man's lack of finesse told me in an instant everything I feared most—that seeing Chris's body was going to be even harder than I'd imagined.

He said she would be ready in five minutes and silently swept out of the room, leaving me alone in the place where so many people had mourned. I was struck most by the way it smelled. The scent of flowers, of photosynthesis itself, was overwhelming. Packed with plants and blossoms, mossy baskets and massive floral sprays, rich, oxygenated air filled the rooms, as if the building that hosted so much death was simultaneously—and ironically—bursting with life. I had never before, and have never since, smelled anything like it.

Double doors off to one side opened quietly, and the funeral director motioned for me to come forward, then stepped aside so I could enter. I passed him, and as I walked into the dimly lit chamber, I heard him scurry away behind me.

I was alone at the back of an empty room, looking at my wife's steely gray coffin. It sat open at the front with rows of upholstered chairs lined up to face it. The setting felt like a small church that had been deserted by a fleeing congregation, the music left playing, the seats of the chairs still warm.

I gathered myself and began the long, painful walk to my wife's body.

As I got closer, I could see deeper inside the coffin. I couldn't see Chris yet, but I saw the creamy silk fabric that surrounded her, the handles on the side of the casket that would help us carry her to her grave, the curves of the huge box that held her. I knew that, if I kept walking, I would see her any second.

Flinching, I veered hard to the right. I wasn't ready. Standing at the foot of her casket, I swallowed the lump in my throat and thought about how much I loved her, how much I needed to be with her. I knew it was going to be horrific. I knew it was going to hurt. I knew I was going to see something I would never be able to forget.

I stood for what seemed like a long while, staring at the foot of the casket—then I began inching closer. First, I saw and recognized long strands of her beautiful hair. I saw her soft hands folded with serenity and grace—her familiar chest, where Eric had so often fallen asleep. My eyes sought her face. I needed to see her.

What had been her head came into view.

I had been through so much in the past few days—being told she had been killed, seeing the evidence in our bedroom of how brutally she had died, holding our sobbing son, all the while fearing that he had witnessed his mother's murder—nothing, none of it, came close to preparing me for seeing firsthand what the killer had done to my beautiful wife.

Her body was bloodless, and the violence that had taken her was far, far away. But even cradled in silk and dressed in her best, with her hair combed and her hands delicately clasped, the savagery of the attack that took Chris's life was shockingly evident. It looked as though her skull had been crushed, shattered, collapsed—left concave by repeated blows. The funeral home had clearly tried to put her back together. But their efforts had failed tragically, leaving my beautiful, beautiful Chris looking as if someone had partially inflated a balloon inside her head—offering only a cruel and grotesque semblance of who she had been and what she had looked like.

I lost my hearing.

The roar of what sounded like escaping steam filled my brain. My eyes watered, and I couldn't see; my breathing came in gasps. It seemed as though the room had tilted, that I was running uphill as

I bolted for the door. My senses were under siege, and in response, they seemed to shut down.

When I reached the outdoors, I noticed no difference between the heavily air-conditioned funeral home and the blistering August heat. I sensed that the funeral director was behind me, rushing toward me, maybe even extending his arms to help me. It didn't matter. I was beyond reach—no one could have calmed me, no hug from a stranger could heal me. I was as broken on the inside as Chris was on the outside.

She was gone—truly gone—and, finally, so was all the psychological endurance that was left in me.

Yanking the car door open, I fell inside. I remember cranking the engine frantically, desperately trying to turn the air conditioner on. In seconds, it was blowing full blast, right into my face, but I didn't feel a thing. All I could sense was a growing homicidal rage— a blood-red anger that built in my heart and moved to my hands, that stretched to my head and drenched my hair, that finally flooded each cell and changed every bit of me that it touched.

It consumed me.

Right there, in my simmering car in the funeral home parking lot, all by myself in a city I didn't know, I was certain beyond any doubt of what I was going to do. And it didn't matter if it happened in broad daylight, with hundreds of witnesses.

I was going to kill the man who murdered Chris.

On a trip to Houston years before, I had purchased a shotgun at a big gun shop that I remembered as being nearby. In reality, I had no sense of where it was. I was lost, geographically and emotionally, with no map to help me find my way home.

I peeled out of the funeral home parking lot, dead set on replacing the pistol that had been stolen from our home by Chris's killer. I was going to find that gun shop and buy a large-caliber pistol, a big weapon that would tear apart the man who tore apart my family.

My breathing was still shallow and uneven. My face felt warm despite the waves of icy air flowing from the car vents. But my hearing was beginning to return, and slowly, the sounds of the traffic around me started to register. It became clear that my impressions of where the gun shop was were vague at best. With each passing mile, I realized that I didn't know where I was going—and I didn't know who had killed Chris and I didn't know why and I didn't understand anything and I knew I had nowhere to turn—and that my chance of finding the target of my rage was even slimmer than the chance I had of finding the gun shop.

My breathing began to return to normal. And eventually, so did my thinking.

I pulled to the side of the road, lowered my head, and wept in frustration and pain and utter hopelessness—finally letting my tears go, finally letting my wife go.

Eventually, I pulled myself together—exhausted, humiliated, brokenhearted. I began the drive to my in-laws' house to see Eric, to be with the people who loved Chris, and to prepare myself for the funeral.

WHEN I ARRIVED, I FOUND CHRIS'S FAMILY FEELING AS LOST AS I WAS. I so wanted to be included in their grief. I wanted to be with them, to hold someone who shared Chris's DNA, who loved her the way I did. Sadly, it seemed that Sheriff Boutwell's heavy-handed tactics had already succeeded in pulling us apart.

Shortly after my in-laws had arrived at our home in Austin, clamoring for any information they could get about what had happened to Chris, Boutwell began setting one side against the other. Her family understandably wanted information. They wanted to see crime scene photos. They wanted to know what the neighbors had seen or heard. Were there fingerprints? They wanted to know what the police had found when they first walked in.

Like me, they wanted to see something tangible, something that would help explain what had happened. We were all standing to-gether, along with a few of my friends, when Boutwell told everyone he had crime scene photos he would share with her family, but only if I was not there. If they insisted on standing with me, they would have no opportunity to learn more about how Chris had died. It was a cruel and manipulative way to treat people who were wild with grief, but his ugly plan worked beautifully. I didn't know what else he had said to Chris's parents or siblings when I wasn't around, but I could feel myself being pushed farther and farther away. He divided us when we needed each other the most. He forced them to choose between learning more about what had happened to Chris and standing beside me—someone whose family membership came only through marriage.

They made the obvious choice, the only choice.

By the day of the funeral, we were thoroughly divided. Chris's burial would be our last act as a family.

The morning of my wife's funeral, the powerful bells of St. Christopher Catholic Church tolled deep and solemn as we filed into the massive sanctuary. It felt like a citywide announcement of the unspeakable nightmare that had befallen our families. No one in Houston could hear the tone and cadence of those bells and not know that something terrible had happened. Our private tragedy was now a public pageant of grief and pain.

Chris's family worked in real estate in Houston, and they had many, many friends at the funeral. I had friends and family there, too. Couples we had known in Austin, our co-workers and college buddies filled the pews.

The service was beautiful and heartbreaking. If love and tears and regret could have brought Chris back, she would have been in our midst that morning. There were remembrances of her too-brief life, stories of her courage and humor and strength, and words of profound sympathy for her family, her broken husband, and her be-loved little boy.

For me, most of it was a blur. Through all the handshakes, sobs, and embraces, no one knew what to say to me. There was nothing that could be said. I felt like I had died, too—as though this had been a funeral service for my life as well.

At the cemetery, standing beside her casket before it was lowered into the ground, I felt that it was holding not only my wife's body but also my heart and my hope for the future—that those were being buried with her.

The only reason I had to keep pushing on was our boy. Eric needed me now more than he ever had. Chris's sudden absence had yanked away the most foundational pillar of his life. She was gone and no one could tell him why. His three-year-old mind did not and could not understand it.

Not long after the funeral, Eric and I visited her grave together. He knelt down next to the mountain of beautiful flowers on the fresh soil—and asked the hardest question I've ever had to answer.

"Where is Mommy?" he wanted to know.

I told him the first thing that came to mind. "Mommy's asleep under the flowers. She's asleep under the flowers."

Miraculously, he accepted it. A shadow of understanding crossed his face. And in the weeks, even months ahead, he would repeat those words like a mantra—to me, to his grandmother, to himself as he played alone.

"Mommy's asleep under the flowers." It was the only thing he had been told that made sense, the only thing he heard that he seemed to believe as we set out on our new lives.

I didn't know much about Catholic teaching until I met Chris. I knew that she loved it all—the imagery and the ideas, the stories and the saints, the power of centuries of tradition and belief. And St. Christopher's church in Houston—her childhood church—along with its revered namesake, played a haunting and poignant role in our lives together. Saint Christopher is seen as the patron saint of travelers, the figure who accompanies us and watches over us on our journeys. And it was in beautiful St. Christopher's church that we had been married and begun our lives together.

It was fitting that here at St. Christopher's we marked the end of our journey. It was where, with broken hearts, everyone who loved Chris told her good-bye.

Five weeks later, I was arrested for her murder.

CHAPTER EIGHT

ERIC AND I WERE BACK IN AUSTIN AND SLOWLY FINDING A NEW KIND of normal. I went back to work. My mother stayed with us for several weeks, filling in as best she could for Chris. She spent time with Eric, and while she was no substitute for his mother, my mom was a powerful, generous, and loving maternal presence. She knew how to comfort both of us. And she kept our house and our lives from falling apart—cleaning up constantly, making sure the refrigerator was stocked, keeping Eric's toys where they needed to be. She cooked our meals, did the laundry, held us close, and kept us moving forward—one long, sad day at a time.

My going back to work was an imperative. Chris's salary had been vital in keeping us financially comfortable, and at this point, I faced the added burden of attorneys' fees. Sheriff Boutwell was still treating me as his number one suspect and showed no signs of moving on to find the real killer.

Between my job and our home, I spent time planning and working with the Bills, my devoted defense team. They tried mightily to keep me upbeat and believing the best about my future. It wasn't easy. The sheriff and his band of deputies were always circling, always intruding—going neighbor by neighbor, house by house—pecking away at my reputation and any remaining shreds of belief in my innocence.

I heard through the grapevine that Sergeant Wood had shown up at a meeting of Neighborhood Watch, a community safety movement that gained momentum after Chris's murder. Wood told the assembled neighbors that he had serious suspicions about me. Even worse, he called for a show of hands of residents who believed I was guilty. Based on no evidence at all, he had our friends and neighbors "vote" on whether I had killed Chris. I couldn't imagine what they felt like, knowing that local police clearly thought I was guilty—but still free—in a home just next door, a stone's throw from their bedrooms, their wives, and their children.

On a regular basis, I saw patrol cars parked in front of homes up and down the street. I knew the Williamson County Sheriff's Office had sent deputies and investigators to spread doubts about me, to plant deranged, manufactured notions about why I had murdered Chris, and to generally try turning the people who knew me and believed in me into accusers.

I knew that some of the neighbors had been convinced.

My attorneys hoped to convince the prosecutor's office not to charge me. And discussions had begun between my attorneys and the prosecutor, Ken Anderson, about my case.

Anderson was new in his job, but he'd built a tough reputation working under the previous district attorney, Ed Walsh. When Walsh went into private practice, Anderson ran for his seat and won handily. He was young—really just about my age—and though I had never met him, I knew from news reports that he had a capacity for showing outrage and disgust that registered far beyond his years. His behavior in court was colorful to say the least—a festival of fist-pounding, seemingly heartfelt pleas, moral sanctimony, and dire warnings against showing mercy.

And that was just in the small, obscure cases.

Chris's murder had made headlines. It would be the biggest case he had ever prosecuted. Frankly, my attorneys and I feared what he might try to do—it would make no difference to him that I was innocent.

One day as I sat in their office, Bill White got Anderson on the phone. He wanted me there so I could respond immediately to any proposed deal. The cavalier way they talked about my future, my wife's murder, and my own life wounded me.

Anderson, his nasal voice squawking through a buzzy speakerphone, announced that he had decided he would "consider" a deal. He said if I confessed and entered a guilty plea, he would offer me the great and generous compromise of twenty-five years in prison.

There was silence on both sides of the line. I vigorously shook my head in disapproval.

Bill White told Anderson that a plea deal wasn't going to work. I was saying flatly that I hadn't killed Chris and I was refusing any deal that involved me standing in court and taking responsibility in any way for her death. I could hear Anderson sigh deeply. He was quiet for a long time. Eventually, he said he wanted to think about it. He shared that he was going to a legal conference in Waco over the coming weekend and that he and my attorney could talk again when he got back.

They hung up on good terms. The two Bills and I actually felt hopeful. But we were all prepared to go to the mat if we needed to, and I was beginning to understand the weakness of my position.

In the days before DNA, there was little science could do to separate the guilty from the innocent. Prosecutors and defense attorneys had to rely on persuasion, characterization, and the circumstances surrounding a crime to convince a jury which person should walk free and which should live behind bars far away from civil society.

In Chris's murder, there were no identified fingerprints except mine, Chris's, and Eric's, no witnesses, no smoking gun, no motive—there was nothing. But it was the kind of case where good police work could have made a difference, the kind of case where the experience and empathy of a seasoned, fair-minded prosecutor could have led to a decent solution—a decision not to prosecute me and to expand the hunt for other suspects. I had no previous criminal record, no reason to hurt Chris, no history of hurting anyone.

We all felt that our best hope and first priority was convincing the novice prosecutor that he shouldn't go forward with the case. After hearing the phone conversation, I finally felt like that was a real possibility.

I told my mother I thought it was time for her to go back to her own life. I appreciated her help, but I had to learn to stand on my own two feet, and I knew I would never be able to do that as long as she was there, serving as our loving, effective safety net.

She reluctantly agreed and began packing for the five-hour drive home. The next morning, she left us—in a sea of tears and a flood of kisses, and with a long list of written reminders and recipes.

That night I cooked a special dinner—nothing gourmet, but something Eric and I both liked. Eric seemed to be evening out. He danced around the kitchen, doing his best to help me as I rinsed and chopped, simmered and stirred. We laughed, and for the first time in a long time, I finally felt at home.

As I stood minding the pots on the stove, I heard a knock on the front door and hoisted Eric onto my hip. I didn't want to leave him in a kitchen with full pans still boiling on the burners. We reached the door, and I opened it wide, still holding Eric at my side. Sheriff Boutwell was standing on our steps. Sergeant Wood and a handful of his deputies stood behind him, apparently as backup.

"Michael Morton," he said flatly, "I am here to arrest you."

CHAPTER NINE

I PLEADED WITH THE SHERIFF TO LET ME TURN OFF THE STOVE, AND HE allowed me to carry Eric back into the kitchen. I could feel the growing tension in my son's body as I held him. His legs began to clamp my side. He knew something was very wrong. I know he could feel my fear, my despair, and my building anger, even though I was working mightily to stay calm.

The sheriff informed me that he had made arrangements for some neighbors to take Eric—and they were not the people I would have chosen to care for him. I had another family in mind, a couple who I thought knew him better and would make him feel more comfortable. But in the end, I had no authority over where he went or with whom.

Looking at the cops in the yard, I thought about the last time there had been a full police presence at our house. It had been a really bad day. I could see that Eric was remembering that now, too, as the small army of deputies began prying him out of my embrace. He clung to me, shrieking, his little arms outstretched, his whole body trembling.

He called for me again and again and again. At that moment, Eric had to feel that first he'd lost his mother without warning and now he was losing me, too. I tried my best to be upbeat, to smile and reassure him. I tried to tell him everything was just fine, but I couldn't convince him. He knew that what was happening to us was bad—very bad.

The only thing louder than the metal handcuffs snapping onto my wrists was Eric's terrified screaming.

With my hands manacled behind my back, I saw the couple I didn't want to babysit Eric reaching for him. When they got their hands on him, the volume and intensity of his screams became unbearable. I saw a crowd of neighbors gather, gawking and whispering behind their hands. One neighbor raised his fist to me, as if to tell me to stay strong—or to go to hell. I never did know which. Most of the people I had lived next to for years looked at me as if they had never seen me before.

I was reeling as a deputy pushed my head down and helped me into the backseat of the police car. I'd never been in the backseat of a police car before. It was totally unfamiliar territory. My senses were blurred, and yet I felt acutely aware of even the smallest details—the sound of the hard-to-decipher radio transmissions, the flash of our familiar neighborhood as we sped past, the disdain of the deputies as they looked at me sitting shackled and beaten.

It was like being hit in the face in a fight you had not been expecting. I was numb and mad and afraid. I was scared of where I was going and what was waiting there.

The ride to the sheriff's office usually took about twenty minutes. This trip though felt like two minutes. I soon learned I wasn't going to be with Sheriff Boutwell in his office that night. He had ridden to his headquarters in a separate car, and I wouldn't see him again that day. I was headed to the county jail—an antiquated, uncomfortable collection of concrete cells directly above Boutwell's office—his law enforcement kingdom.

Despite my lot, some of the deputies and the jailers were surprisingly courteous, and I was truly thankful for that. They said "please" and "thank you" and every now and then threw in a "sir," just to make me feel I was still a human being.

I told myself they were doing that because they knew I was being railroaded and were trying to make my ordeal as painless as possible. In reality, they were probably being decent because they thought I was exactly the kind of crazy inmate who might explode into a dangerous, homicidal rage.

Getting booked was awful. It was hot and crowded and loud. The sounds of men arguing and shouting, the stuttered stories of the half deaf and the completely drunk, the impatience of the tired deputies—all of it together formed an ugly, inescapable cacophony.

I did whatever they told me to. I stood where they pointed, waited for them when they ordered it, and answered every question they asked. I posed for my mug shot, not knowing where to look or *how* to look. Should I try to look trustworthy?

Innocent?

Normal?

I didn't even know what normal was anymore, much less how to feign it.

As I stood by the booking desk, a street cop came over. He asked his counterparts why all the cameras and reporters were outside. The cop doing my paperwork jutted his chin toward me in a wordless answer. The street cop looked me over and shrugged. None of this mattered to him one whit. He went on to something else, someone else, one of the other tiny human tragedies that made up a typical day at work for him.

While I was inside getting a crummy photo and a case number, the sheriff was outside, doing what he did best—making people feel safe, whether they should or not. He regaled reporters with the details of his latest triumphant arrest, the skill he had demonstrated in cracking the case, and the evidence that convinced him I was the bad guy.

And the reporters believed it.

Worse, they shared the sheriff's skewed version of my story with everyone within broadcast range, anyone in the county who read a newspaper, everybody who gossiped about current events. I was hot news.

Inside, I was mostly just hot. There was apparently no air-conditioning in the crowded, lousy space that was every Williamson County inmate's introduction to incarceration. All of that changed dramatically when we got in the elevator to go up to the jail. It felt like we had stepped into a moving meat locker making its way to the Arctic Circle. As we rose higher, the jailers escorting me joked darkly about the bone-chilling cold, saying it was a sure sign that some county official's incompetent brother-in-law had gotten the contract to handle the building's heating and cooling.

Ha ha.

The whole experience was like checking into the world's worst hotel. I was handed a well-used mattress, a threadbare blanket, and a new set of clothes. The inmate uniforms had apparently been white at one time. Now, the rest of the "guests" and I were wearing pants and pullover tops that each had its own shade of not-very-white-anymore. After too many washings and too much hard wear, the clothes looked like a lot of the inmates—worn out. But the county jail's inmates weren't hard-core criminals; these were guys who got drunk, who started fights in bars, who hit their wives or robbed gas stations. Not the best company, but as I would soon find out the hard way, there are different classes of criminals. Criminal justice is a system that elevates the real pros in the same way the NFL does. The county jail types were more like high school players—inexperienced, but some of them already showing real potential for moving up the ladder. Some might make it all the way to the state penitentiary.

I was relieved when I was led to a private cell, let in, and locked up. I wanted protection, too. Looking around at my new living quarters, I saw—absolutely nothing. The walls and the floor were essentially bare. Previous residents appeared to have used mostly bodily fluids and scrawled obscenities to add to the place's personality. The only seating was a toilet in the corner and a metal bed attached to one wall. There was no one to talk to, no radio, no TV—having something to read was a distant dream, and my cell was too dark anyway. I flopped my thin mattress onto the beaten-up steel bunk, climbed aboard, and tried not to think about who had slept there before me and what he might have left behind. I wrapped my worthless jailhouse blanket around me as tightly as I could and closed my eyes. Sleep was the only way I was leaving this place tonight.

I had no idea what time it was when I woke up, but the lights were on and I could hear voices and running water nearby. My cell door was left hanging open. I stuck my head out and looked in the direction of the racket.

It was coming from what everyone called the dayroom—a multipurpose space where we ate, showered behind a dirty plastic curtain, and could sit with other inmates to "socialize." I met a kid that morning whom I really felt for. He was a handsome young African American, only nineteen years old and clearly in over his head. He told me he'd gone out drinking with some friends the night before and awakened that morning in jail—with a hangover and a pending robbery charge for holding up a convenience store. The poor kid needed someone to lean on, and frankly, comforting him helped me avoid thinking about my own situation.

My bond had apparently been set at something north of $250,000. I had to have 10 percent of that to offer as bond before I could walk out the door. I didn't have that kind of money lying around, and my parents didn't either. I certainly couldn't ask Chris's family to help—I feared their answer.

My parents came to see me. They were staying with poor, rattled Eric at our house. My mother had just reached home after her drive from Austin when she heard about my arrest. She and my dad had literally turned the car around, gassed up, and headed back to my house. I could see how upset and tired they were. I felt that way, too.

There was nothing for me to do but cool my heels in jail for more than a week, waiting for the court schedule to make room for a bond reduction hearing. In the meantime, I made friends, learned the ropes, and tried to make an unlivable situation a little bit better.

I got some surprising help from my parents. In an intuitive gesture, my father brought me a carton of cigarettes, even though I didn't smoke. "Maybe it'll help you get what you need," he said. My father had never been in jail, but he was right. My mom brought our old black-and-white TV from the back bedroom into the jail. Suddenly, we prisoners were in touch with the world—or at least as in touch as you can be using rabbit ears to find an elusive broadcast signal. TV shows faded in and out, mystery shows went to black right at the climax, local news reports dissolved into static just as the big stories started—but having a link to reality was everything. My new friends and I sat and watched the flickering, buzzing screen for hours on end, waiting to be sprung from the purgatory of the county jail.

Finally, I got my hearing, and my bond was drastically reduced. It came down to something within range—my parents ended up turning over about $2,500 in exchange for their dirty, bedraggled son. But I was keenly aware that I was one of the lucky ones. My parents had the means to bail me out, and they cared enough to pull me through. Many of the guys I'd lived with for the past week weren't so fortunate.

I was particularly worried about the kid charged with robbing the convenience store. I cuffed him on the shoulder, handed him my old TV set, and walked out the front door—finally, back in the real world.

For how long, I didn't know.

CHAPTER TEN

MY ARREST CHANGED EVERYTHING.

The life I was released into after a week in the county jail was not what it had been before I was locked up. I had changed, too.

My grief over Chris's death had dominated every day, almost my every thought, for going on two months. Now, after my arrest and my brief taste of life behind bars, survival came before everything else. I knew I was fighting for my life, my freedom, my future with Eric. I knew if I failed, I wouldn't be able to raise or protect him, I wouldn't be able to support him, I wouldn't be able to see our little boy grow up, get married, maybe even have children of his own.

I would lose everything I had been living for.

From the moment I left the county jail, I could feel an instinctual fight-or-flight response taking over. For the sake of survival, I had to compartmentalize my sorrow over Chris and put every ounce of my effort into the battle to stay free. In my mind, it was a perfectly natural response, because every interaction I had underscored how much of an uphill fight I faced.

In the Williamson County Jail, newspapers were as rare as PhDs. Despite having a half-working black-and-white television set, I had little access to news broadcasts—often I either couldn't hear what was being said or couldn't get the station tuned in at all. No one else in the Austin area had suffered that disadvantage. They had been inundated with information about Chris's death and my arrest for her murder. Unfortunately, what they'd seen on TV and read in the local papers was a fictionalized version of my life, my character, and my wife's brutal killing—but they believed it.

Sheriff Jim Boutwell, already a towering Texas law enforcement figure, further burnished his badge by presenting me as a lower life-form, a sex-mad, selfish monster without redeeming qualities, some-one who was clearly and unquestionably guilty. His version of the story had a week's lead time. By the time I knew what the public was being told, it was hopeless to try changing anybody's mind.

What's the old saying? A lie travels around the world while the truth is still putting its pants on? That's what happened in my case. Boutwell's wild stories were racing out to the public while I languished in a filthy jail cell adjusting the rabbit ears on a tiny, static-filled TV, hoping to get a clear signal for *All My Children*. Maybe it was a good thing I didn't see the coverage in real time; it might have broken me.

Now free—or as free as someone can be when trailed by cameras, cops, and a campaign of lies—I was driving back into my old neigh-borhood and seeing it with new eyes. It quickly became apparent I'd lost the public relations war—badly.

My neighbors started looking away when we met on the street. If we crossed paths on the sidewalk while getting the mail, they were icy—formal, unfamiliar. They treated me as if I were a scary stranger, either that or completely invisible.

Friends who'd once come over for dinner in our backyard now drove past without even glancing my way, as though the house was no longer standing, as though it had disappeared along with Chris. Women who lived close by would stare and whisper, clearly begin-ning to see me as a monster in their midst—the kind of man who would beat his wife to death while she slept, simply because she wouldn't have sex with him on his birthday.

What a creep. I wouldn't like that guy either.

Nor did I like being cast out by the people I had once counted on as a kind of neighborhood family.

In the weeks and months before my trial, I could feel in my bones how my every action was instantly suspicious. When a patch of marigolds Chris had planted in front of our house died from drought and neglect, my final cleaning-out of the ravaged garden bed became fodder for backyard gossip about my guilt. If I removed dead flowers from the yard, I was killing Chris all over again. If I didn't, I was letting the house go and forcing Eric to live in conditions Chris would never have tolerated. If I was with Eric in the front yard, they viewed me with resentment. If I wasn't playing with him in public, they worried about my son's safety.

I couldn't win.

There was almost a dark humor in the severity of some of my neighbors' reactions. Sometimes, I could see a once friendly neighbor struggling mightily to walk a new kind of social tightrope with me—not wanting to socialize with a murderer but certainly not wanting to insult a desperate killer with nothing to lose. Who knew what could happen if they angered me?

My arrest had given me the ability to terrify people just by saying hello, just by breathing, just by showing my face.

It was a power I wouldn't wish on anyone.

Going back to work was almost worse, although I have to respect the fact that management was at least completely up-front about rejecting me. They openly told me they didn't ever want to see me again. They said my presence on the job, coupled with all the negative news coverage, would hurt business. End of discussion.

Frankly, I was a little shocked, since I had worked at the company for eleven years, had a great record, and got along with everyone at the store. And I was a department head who didn't really have much contact with the public, but who wanted to shop for groceries or fill prescriptions in a place that employed a vicious madman?

OF COURSE, THERE WAS THE SMALL DETAIL OF MY NOT HAVING HAD THE chance to defend myself in court, but their flat, self-serving assessment was a blunt lesson in how criminal justice works in the court of public opinion.

I was guilty until proven innocent.

My attorneys sent a letter asking my employer to reconsider, to no avail. Luckily, the employees' union took on my case pro bono and forced the company to keep me on the job until the trial had ended. I wasn't even a member of the union, so their generosity surprised me. It was my first experience with someone helping me out as a matter of principle, without having to be paid.

Luckily, it would not be my last.

The company made all kinds of proposals, everything from my working only midnight shifts to being transferred to another city. But the union representative who joined me in the negotiations stood firm and let them know the union and its contingent of lawyers were eager to sue my employer for violating basic fair employment guidelines, which would have left them with a healthy legal bill and hefty fines.

In the end, the company caved. They had to. At least until the trial, I had my old job, clocking in and out at the same time I always had.

Being able to work again was a godsend—it gave my life some semblance of normalcy. Eric and I were back in a familiar pattern. And I had a chance to be working once more with people who had known me for years, some of whom were understanding and remained friendly, giving me the benefit of the doubt until after the trial.

Still it was hard, and on occasion, bitter laughter and black comedy were the only ways I had left to cope.

One day, as I ferried some paperwork to the front office, a man pulled me aside. I seldom dealt with customers, but he had initiated the conversation, so I couldn't just ignore him.

"Excuse me," he said. "Where's that guy who beat his wife to death? I heard he works here. You know him?"

"You want to see him?" I whispered.

My conspiratorial tone brought a look of perverse glee to his face. He nodded in excitement. The sick fascination of seeing a "killer" in his natural habitat clearly appealed to him.

I motioned with my head for him to follow me. He fell in without hesitation.

We walked to the far side of the building, where a tall mirror on the wall served a few purposes—part advertising, part decorative touch, part shoplifting prevention tool. When we reached it, I waved for him to stay back, slowed down, and peeked around the corner. Then I signaled for him to come and stand next to me. He did, with a look of delight at his chance to see the infamous murderer. Boy, would he be able to brag at the barbecue tonight!

We faced our reflections in the mirror from about twenty-five feet away.

I pointed to myself in the mirror and said, "Look, there he is."

It took about five seconds for him to realize what was happening. When he did, his eyes grew wide and his mouth gaped open, his horror eclipsed only by his fear and embarrassment. He bolted.

It was just another day at work for Austin's most infamous might-be murderer.

Still, I didn't miss a day on the job. My legal bills were mounting by the minute. Bill Allison and Bill White were working as hard as they could to piece together a defense for me, but it was terribly difficult. They simply had nothing to go on except Chris's time of death—and the fact that I had been at work at that point—along with my reputation as a decent guy who loved his wife. Of course, that reputation wasn't holding up so well these days.

I really wasn't much help to my defense team. I just kept repeating the same stories, the same details, the same memories that I had so many times before.

One day, Bill White offered to take me out on his boat. He knew I loved the water and must have believed that a day on the lake might be a way to boost my spirits. We climbed into his small sloop at the marina, sat down, and started talking. Hours later, we were still there—still riding the waves, still lashed to the dock, still talking—we never did take the boat out.

During our long conversation, he said something that has stayed with me ever since. He told me that an innocent man in a case like mine is absolutely useless to his defense attorneys.

And it was true—I knew nothing about the crime, had no explanation, could point to no suspects or offer any provable alternative explanations for what had happened to Chris. I was clueless. White told me that wasn't surprising, that a truly innocent man is the hardest kind of defendant to represent.

When we had first met, I was struck by my lawyers' lack of curiosity about whether I had actually killed Chris. They told me they didn't care—that innocence or guilt was immaterial—they would give me the very best defense possible whether I was a victim or a villain. Were they trying to pull a withheld confession out of me in order to get information they could use to *help* defend me? Were they letting me know there would be no shame in accepting a plea offer?

There had to be plenty of defendants who proclaimed innocence initially, then came to their senses the first time they heard the details of a deal that would avoid trial and give them certainty about how much time they'd be doing.

A deal was not an option for me—or my attorneys. So we kept working on putting a case together. We began lining up character witnesses. There were at least two men I knew I could count on to vouch for me.

David Marshall had lived across the street from Chris and me in our old neighborhood. We had stayed close through the years, and when Chris was killed, he was invaluable to me. He led the "three amigos"—a trio of longtime friends who helped me get to appointments and interviews with the sheriff; they had accompanied me on that fateful night when I refused the polygraph test. Now David was ready to stand up for me in court.

Mac and Mitch were the other two "amigos," offering emotional support and physical assistance. They even helped paint over the bloodstained bedroom walls after Chris's death.

Mario Garcia was another true-blue friend. He worked with me. A United States Marine—there is no such thing as a *former* Marine—Mario used to bake cakes to mark the anniversary of the formation of the Marine Corps. For me, he was a semper fi kind of friend, always faithful. Always. And once again he was prepared to stand by me, this time under oath.

I can't imagine the pressure on David and Mario, two men who pledged to serve as my character witnesses in a controversial trial. I don't know that I could have been a less sympathetic public figure.

As we prepared for trial, we got hints that my arrest had been a kind of coup—that Sheriff Boutwell had purposely pulled it off when Prosecutor Ken Anderson was out of town. That made some sense. Anderson had sounded like he hadn't entirely made his mind up about my guilt or innocence when I listened in on his phone conversation with my attorneys.

But you would never have known that Anderson wasn't on board once I had been charged. He was gung ho, every way, every day. I imagined him whispering to reporters that I was an unrepentant killer, hinting at a terrible dark side of mine that would be fully revealed at the trial.

The two Bills sent me to a consultant group for witness training, which was really a kind of jury profiling back when the now-popular concept was still in its infancy. Bill Allison and Bill White were really on top of their game, always at the legal forefront, always trying to find new ways to better represent their clients.

I remember meeting with two women in Austin. They put me through mock interviews and pretend cross-examinations. They offered examples of how the prosecutor might try to establish motive, questioning me rigorously about whether this had been a crime of passion or, perhaps, a killing aimed strictly at getting my hands on Chris's life insurance money.

We both had policies that paid about $200,000 in case of accidental death, and we each had additional coverage at work. I sort of dismissed the exercise on determining motive, thinking that no one would be crazy enough to claim the crime might have been driven by both passion *and* cold greed. It turned out they were right, though. I learned the hard way that nothing argued in court had to be reasonable, it just had to resonate.

My attorneys prepared me for testimony by repeating again and again, "Only answer the question you have been asked." I was to add nothing, offer no colorful anecdotes, reveal no weaknesses, or confess to even paltry moments of imperfection in my life or my marriage.

They harped on me not to start dating anyone—as if that was a possibility. It was absolutely the last thing I felt like doing. I was still deeply into the stage of grief where even spending time talking with another woman felt like cheating on Chris. I lived every day and every night with memories of her, in the house we had shared, with the little boy we had given life.

And frankly, I didn't imagine many women were interested in someone facing the kinds of charges I was.

At that point, my life was really all about Eric and fighting for my freedom.

While preparing for trial with White and Allison, I also had to work forty hours a week. I had to take Eric to day care. I shopped for our groceries, cleaned our house, washed our clothes, and cooked our meals.

With Chris gone, Eric needed me in ways he had never needed me before. I needed him, too. I clung to him as much as or more than he clung to me. We were alone against the world—together.

One day, Eric said something unexpected, something I had waited for, looked for, and feared. I was on my knees, scrubbing the master bathtub and shower. Eric stood beside me. We were in what you'd call a conversational lull while I worked on making the tub sparkle, and he watched intently.

"Daddy," he said. "Who was the man in the shower with his clothes on, the man with the blue shirt, purple shirt?"

I gaped at Eric, stunned. A thousand images ricocheted inside my head, images of that day, images of Chris, images I did not want to see. I just kept him talking, kept our conversation light.

The next day I told the therapist who had been working with him. I also told White and Allison. We talked about the significance of his comment, but they believed it would be ruled "hearsay" and could not be used at trial.

Still, the magnitude of Eric's declaration forced me to think. My little boy had seen his mother's killer—a man who had apparently stepped into our shower to wash my wife's blood from his clothes.

I tried not to, but I couldn't help picturing Eric pushing aside the shower curtain and seeing not his mother but her murderer.

Why, I wondered, had the man not harmed my son? Or had he?

What Eric said made me heartsick, but it gave me an almost taunting, tenuous lifeline.

He had seen someone. He had seen the man who killed Chris.

I had to hang on.

CHAPTER ELEVEN

PRETRIAL HEARINGS BEGAN LONG BEFORE MY ACTUAL TRIAL STARTED. Those sessions were valuable, giving me an introduction to the courtroom, the formality and ceremony of it all. They also offered me my first look at my adversary—Williamson County Prosecutor Ken Anderson.

He was not an imposing figure, sort of short and wearing ill-fitting clothes. He was struggling with a growing comb-over situation on a rapidly balding head. To counteract it, he looked to be in the process of growing a beard.

To me, Anderson seemed physically soft. But in court, with the power of the state behind him, he seemed to grow in stature, and his physique gave way to a hard and unyielding personality that clearly cared more about winning than anything else. He disputed even minor points with my attorneys, refused to agree with them on almost anything, and was very obviously preparing for the battle of *his* life. He felt dangerous to me, like someone who cared too much about his own grandiose ambitions and too little about the law. I knew enough not to underestimate him.

There were constant arguments with my attorneys about whether Anderson was turning over the information that he was required to give the defense team. He seemed to constantly try wiggling out of his obligations to give us official autopsy reports, detectives' notes, and witness interviews, always claiming that he intended to but, in reality, making us fight for every detail.

Anderson's decision to make us work so hard for the information we were legally entitled to would make a crucial difference in my upcoming trial—and the next twenty-five years of my life.

My parents arrived at our home in Austin about a week before our final face-off with Anderson began, helping me and Eric get accustomed to yet another new schedule. We bumped around the house together, cooking comfort food and doing anything we could to relieve the tension that hung over our heads like the glistening, sharpened sword of Damocles.

One night, a few days before the trial began, in another of my sometimes ill-fated ongoing attempts to make everyone feel better, I brought home a movie I'd picked up at the rental place. It was titled *Runaway Train* and starred Jon Voight. I didn't even bother to read the back of the VHS box to see what it was about. Good grief, the title *Runaway Train* pretty much gave up the plot, right?

Wrong.

We all settled in to watch it and discovered, to our horror, that it was set in an Alaskan prison that looked like something out of Dante's *Inferno*. My mother crumbled into a corner of the couch, whimpering. I felt like I had blown it again. But then, I had become accustomed to that feeling. I had become like the proverbial mule tied to the fence post in a hailstorm—all I could do was stand there and take it.

The night before the trial, I don't remember what I had for dinner or how it tasted. I don't remember how I felt, what I said to my family, or whether I held Eric especially close. I didn't worry about what I would wear the next day or if I'd be late or if I was going to be on TV again. I don't remember if I slept well or not at all.

I know I got up early enough to be at Bill White's house on time. He handed me the keys to his beautiful, brand-new Porsche and told me to drive to the courthouse. And each day after that, he did the same.

Sitting in my prison cell, years later, I sometimes wondered if

Bill's act of kindness—and letting someone drive your new Porsche is a bona fide act of kindness—was something he did because he recognized the real possibility that his efforts and those of his partner might fail and I might be found guilty. Had he contemplated a far-in-the-future scenario where the burden of my time in prison would be lessened ever so slightly by the memory of rocketing down the freeway at the wheel of a beautiful car? Maybe someday I will ask him.

On the trip to the courthouse on the first day of my trial, he did most of the talking, including telling me where to park—a few blocks away so no reporter could make an issue of me hot-rodding to court, as if I were having my last fling before prison.

When we approached the courthouse, the giant clutch of cameras and reporters from radio stations, newspapers, and TV operations was waiting outside. When they saw us, they pounced. I knew they were all essentially working men and women, people just doing what they were paid to do.

But being the focus of that kind of circus is all-consuming. We walked in tandem through a roiling, noisy mob alive with shouted questions, the whir of overworked camera shutters, and the constant presence of TV cameramen, usually adept at shooting while walking backwards, but occasionally falling onto the pavement—damaging their pride and, occasionally, their precious cameras. No matter what happened, the mob just kept moving, staying with us, staying on us.

We reached the front steps and began climbing, the media carnival coming right along. The reporters and photographers grew increasingly frantic as we got close to the front door, beyond which they could not follow. My attorneys' faces were hard and set as if they were entering an arena, ready for a cage match. I was carried along by the crowd, at the center of it all but feeling like an outsider—like a man just learning the ropes on the first day of a new job.

I didn't know what to do or where to look or, more important, how to feel anything anymore. I had become a zombie, someone who was going through the motions, almost devoid of feelings. I was in a trance—part of a public beating and completely incapable of affecting the outcome.

As our mob reached the doors and my attorneys scrambled to swing them open, I thought again of how much I missed and needed my wife.

Chris, can you see what's happening down here?

CHAPTER TWELVE

FOR NINE DAYS IN FEBRUARY 1987, I WALKED THROUGH GEORGETOWN'S historic central square each morning and past the soaring statue of the Confederate soldier who served as a stone-faced greeter for the old Williamson County courthouse.

The figure of the young infantryman—a kid holding a gun and wearing a forlorn hat—was a powerful reminder that in this place, the past wasn't past at all. It was in full swing.

The judge in my case was close to seventy years old—and even closer to being completely deaf. Judge William Lott had been on the bench for years. In deference to his diminishing hearing, the courthouse had recently installed a microphone stand for witnesses. Despite this assist, the court reporter must have struggled mightily to keep up with the judge's frequent requests that arguments be repeated, testimony be restated, and points be made again—louder, please.

The call to "keep your voice up" appears in the transcript of my trial more often than the words "call your next witness."

I had to wonder, if Judge Lott would admit needing this much help hearing, even *with* a microphone, what were the odds that he was missing more of the trial than we—or he—knew?

What I couldn't miss on the first day in court was how the whole system seemed stacked against me.

Juries seemed smitten with the prosecution. The judge often deferred to the prosecutor as well, or at least gave him the benefit of the doubt. And Ken Anderson and Sheriff Jim Boutwell were as tight as members of the same small-town bowling team. They chatted easily, felt at home in the courtroom, and were unaccustomed to judicial decisions that didn't go their way. They held an enormous amount of power in this place—they were in control and they were against me—and almost nothing else mattered.

A large pool of potential jurors had been called, and as they waited in the hallway, a bailiff literally shuffled a stack of cards, each with a juror's name written on it, determining at random which locals to question. I had a sinking feeling the deck was stacked.

That was confirmed when, in the course of questioning by my legal team, one woman in the first group of potential jurors turned out to be Ken Anderson's secretary. I recall thinking that if the pool of potential jurors was so small that it included someone that close to the prosecutor—and her obvious conflict was revealed only through close questioning—I was in deep trouble.

By the time the next group of possible jurors entered the courtroom, my attorneys were ready to try a new tack. Bill White asked for a show of hands by anyone with *any* kind of link—by marriage, employment, experience, friendship, or family ties—to the prosecutor's office, the sheriff's department, or anyone connected with the case. At least half of the potential jurors raised their hands. My attorneys turned to the judge, their arms outstretched in frustration.

The bailiff once again shuffled the cards, and another group of possible jurors filed in. Eventually, we whittled the group down to a smaller pool for closer individual questioning.

Everyone had heard of the case, through newspaper or TV, from neighbors or in church. One by one, they were called to the front if or when they voiced concerns about their ability to be fair in judging the case.

One potential juror turned out to be prescient. She told the courtroom, "I like to do my civic duty and all that. But . . . I wouldn't want to be responsible if the man is innocent."

She didn't make the cut.

Another testified that it would be "very difficult for me not to believe" police officers. She would always "take their word over someone else's, to be very plain about it." Ken Anderson told her he hoped "everyone on the jury panel feels exactly like you do."

That's what I feared most.

As I sat in my chair, watching people who worried about convicting an innocent man be sent away and other, less conscientious folks make the cut, my hope for a fair trial dwindled.

Bill White and Bill Allison did their best. At that time both were in leadership positions with area criminal defense legal groups, and the courtroom was packed every day with attorneys eager to watch them work. Still, the odds were as stacked against my lawyers as they were against me. But my lawyers would not pay as dearly for a loss.

By the end of that first day, we had a jury in place, seven men and five women. I couldn't help but think that any of them might have felt at home in the Eisenhower fifties. They were community minded and worried about crime. They admired and trusted the sheriff and believed the prosecutor represented them. I was just another of the many outsiders who had been moving into their neighborhoods in recent years and, in the process, rapidly changing their quiet corner of the world into a more crowded, more conflicted place.

Williamson County, Texas, was being pulled into the present. I was being dragged into the past, into a setting where I had little history, no family, and few friends.

Opening statements pretty much set the tone.

I listened and watched the jury as Ken Anderson launched into what was not just an assessment of the case but a histrionic point-by-point assassination of my character. With colorful language and clear disgust, he painted me as a monster—a selfish, cruel, sex-obsessed man who brutally beat his wife to death in a porn-fueled rage.

The imagery he used was as stark and as extreme as possible. I came to recognize this technique as simply his courtroom style—making statements so outrageous, so beyond comprehension, so disturbing, that juries would fill with collective anger against the defendant and the terrible things that Ken Anderson said he had done—even when the actual evidence did not support his awful imaginings.

This habit of his, along with the lurid descriptions he gave to the jury about my character, about what had happened to Chris, about what had happened in my house, left me wondering about *his* character. What the heck was going on inside *his* head?

Ken Anderson's partner on the prosecution team was Mike Davis, a former cop now armed with a law degree—a dangerous man to have against me.

The first witness the prosecution called was my mother-in-law, Rita Kirkpatrick.

She was asked very few questions, but made an impact on the jury when she told them that she could never accept that Chris was dead—that "she would always be part of the family."

Then she stepped down and asked for permission to stay and watch the rest of the trial, saying she wanted "to make my own decision based upon the evidence." My attorneys had no problem with that.

She took a seat, positioning herself right behind my chair. My attorneys told me this seating arrangement must have been planned in advance by the prosecution—so that every time the jury looked at me, they would see Chris's mother and her pain, and they would want to ease it. They would want to hurt me in order to help her.

The next witness gave them plenty of reasons to hate me.

Elizabeth Gee, her husband, and their little boy had lived next door to us for a year. We saw them often as we walked to or from the front door, and in the evenings, both couples would sit and watch the two boys play together in the yard. Elizabeth was, to be honest, not someone I felt close to. Chris and I both thought she was harmless, if a little high-strung. But Elizabeth was the person who'd found Chris's body, and her story became an important part of the narrative.

On the day she testified, Elizabeth wore a sailor dress and a bow on her head that stuck out as far as her ears on each side. She told the jury how, on the morning of the murder, she had seen Eric sitting on our front steps—going in and out of the house—and occasionally peeking around the car in our driveway to look at Elizabeth as she worked in the yard. She said hello to him but didn't think anything was amiss.

She began to wonder what was going on around noon, when she realized she hadn't seen Chris with him at all. She walked over to Eric and picked him up. She said his diaper was heavy and desperately needed changing. So she pushed the front door in and walked through the house calling for Chris. She changed his pants, then walked around and through the house a couple of times. She left Eric at her house playing with her son, then came back and looked further.

In our darkened bedroom, she noticed dresser drawers dumped on the floor, but thought nothing of it. Then she saw that the bedcovers were pulled up all around the bed and tightly tucked in. She knew that wasn't the way Chris made the bed.

At the top, where the pillow should be, she saw a pile of baskets and a blue suitcase. She felt around at the base of the bed through the bedspread. Eventually, her hands could make out what seemed to be feet and ankles. She went to the side of the bed, lifted the covers, and saw a wrist. She felt for a pulse.

Nothing.

Terrified, she ran out and called the sheriff's department from her home. When they arrived, saw the body, and found the snarky note I had left in the bathroom, she was told that I was a suspect.

And she ran with it. Everything I had ever done—or *almost* done—was now seen through the prism of my status as a suspect in Chris's killing. Elizabeth came to court with a long list of my sins—

transgressions she said she had observed from her front-row seat in the driveway, on my back deck, and in both of our homes.

I was a rampant jerk, and she had the inside scoop. She told the jury that Chris and I argued about "all kinds of things, what plants they'd plant in the yard," the cost of the deck, even the weights I had bought. She was primed to tell the jury that I didn't like our dog and had even kicked our collie in her presence. My attorneys were able to keep that bit out of her testimony.

Elizabeth did say that I had barked at Chris, "Bitch, go get me a beer," in front of others. She even recounted how I had turned on a Big Bird performer Chris had hired for one of Eric's birthday parties, saying that as I held my son—within earshot of all the other children, no less—I had snapped at Chris, "Pay the bitch and get her the f*** out of here."

There was truth to that story. Big Bird *had* been a big bust at the party. Eric was absolutely terrified by the giant, bright yellow-feathered, long-necked critter. Of course, we didn't know that until we had planned his whole party around the Big Bird theme, had a house full of kids, and promised to pay the heavily sweating performer. It happens to a lot of parents—clowns are notorious for scaring birthday boys and girls.

The Big Bird incident happened, only it was hilarious. Chris and I had to keep Eric and Big Bird apart throughout the event. Our little boy couldn't even catch a glimpse of a yellow feather sticking out from around the corner without melting down. But if I had said anything remotely like Elizabeth claimed I did, it was said with a laugh at our ridiculous predicament.

Chris and I liked to laugh, and we were, at times, a bit bawdy. The "Bitch, go get me a beer" line was an example. That was a direct quote from a singularly unimpressive friend of a friend who actually spoke that way to his girlfriend. We said that to each other because it was *so* ignorant and *so* awful—it had become a running gag. Chris *never* got me a beer—or anything else—when I said that. It was, to us, a reminder of our long history, our shared belief that no one should ever be treated that way, a secret laugh that had started when we heard that jerk say it the first time.

As for our late collie—I wished for nothing more desperately than that the old girl was still alive, still prowling our backyard, still protecting Chris and Eric the way she had for years. If Leisha had been at her post on the morning of August 13, no one would have dared enter the yard. She was ferociously loyal to Chris. If I had been as rotten to her as Elizabeth was now claiming, that beautiful old collie would have chewed my leg off a long time ago. And I would have deserved it.

On cross-examination by my team, Elizabeth had to concede that she had never heard me "yell" at Chris, never heard me threaten her, saying only, "Around me, he never threatened his wife."

She admitted that she had never seen physical violence between us. But I could feel that the damage had been done.

Ken Anderson put a parade of uniformed officers on the stand, sometimes very briefly, just to confirm that they had escorted me to the lab for a blood draw or that they had been present when a hair was plucked from my head. The whole point was to get as many authority figures as possible—in uniform—lined up against me.

It was working like a charm.

There was a great deal of tedious testimony about what we had eaten at dinner the night before and how long it would take a person to digest it, all part of a buildup the prosecution was constructing to turn Chris's stomach contents into a smoking gun that proved me to be the killer.

Listening to the wrangling over the exact recipes for our dinner entrees, seeing the receipts waved around the courtroom gave my memories of that night a surreal air. Now what we talked about as we ate that meal, how stunning Chris looked, beaming at me across the table, the toast we made to Eric's burgeoning good health—that last night we shared as a family—it all seemed like it had happened to someone else.

The two teams of attorneys clashed constantly over police notes, reports, and other written materials that had not been turned over to the defense, as the law requires. Ken Anderson would put a witness on the stand and then whip out a document my attorneys and I had never seen. Their exchanges would degenerate into sputtering, extremely personal shouting matches, often ending with my team objecting under the U.S. Constitution, the Texas state constitution and rule 614, and the laws of simple decency and fair play.

I recall Mike Davis petulantly announcing that if my team got a document, then "we're going to be entitled to see all the things that their little investigators and everybody else has done." Every discussion of sharing evidence was colored by the prosecution's clear distaste for me, my attorneys, and the whole notion of cooperating on even the smallest issues.

Once, the judge had to admonish the two teams of lawyers to stop shouting at each other and speak only to him.

Dr. Roberto Bayardo, the chief medical examiner for nearby Travis County, was a devastating witness against me. He was an elegant man with a graceful accent who claimed he had done close to seven thousand autopsies.

His graphic description of Chris's injuries was the stuff of nightmares. I had seen Chris after she was cleaned up. He had seen her as the killer left her. He told the jury that, on her forehead, there was a "six-inch-long, two-and-a-half-inch-wide cut through which brain, blood, and particles of bone were exuding." He said her face was so battered, "the color of her eyes could not be made out." That elicited a whimper from Chris's mother. He recounted her fractured nose and upper jaw, the way one of her teeth had been knocked out.

He said he had counted eight different blows to her head.

I felt her loss and the horror of her death all over again. The jury would not look at me—or if one of them accidentally caught my eye, they would quickly glance away.

The coup de grâce came when Anderson asked him whether he had an opinion on the time of Chris's death. He said he did, that

"Mrs. Morton died up to four hours from the time of her meal. That would be 1:15 A.M.," that "based on my experience, I would say no later than 1:15."

That estimate was a complete turnaround from his earlier opinion, that Chris had probably been killed closer to 6:00 A.M.

This new claim in front of the jury meant her murder had taken place while I was still in the house. My attorneys would skillfully show that his opinion on time of death, his technique for gauging it, his assertion that stomach digestion rate was related to the time of the crime—all of it was completely bogus, pseudo-science hocus-pocus. But it didn't matter.

I felt the noose tightening around my neck.

Sheriff Boutwell followed soon after, approaching the stand in full mournful cowboy costume and character. He sat down, a lanky, lean lawman with three decades' experience. And he came off exactly as he hoped—the jury saw him as a serious, dark-eyed soul who carried the awful burden of dealing with the county's tragedies, protecting the victims from the villains, the good guys from the bad. Boutwell acted as though he was all that stood between the good folks of Williamson County and the kind of horrible fate that Chris had met.

It was up to him to seal the deal in my case. He did not disappoint.

He told the jury that he had met me in the front yard of our home and that I had asked whether Eric was okay, then, as an afterthought, asked about Chris.

"I told him that she was dead," he intoned. As for my response to the awful news—"there was no particular reaction at all."

We all think we know how we would react to devastating news. Some of us believe we would cry, others might reason that they would feel faint. Still others believe they would scream and collapse if they were told they'd lost someone they love.

When I learned of Chris's death, I had collapsed, but not spectacularly there on the lawn. I had fallen apart quickly and quietly, completely on the inside—and that was apparently something the sheriff didn't accept as a normal reaction.

It was downhill from there. He told the jury about finding two pornographic movies in the living room. He said he had found an almost microscopic amount of very old marijuana, something Chris and I had kept for the past four years but hadn't gotten around to using.

He told my attorneys that he was the chief investigator on the case, not as we'd been told earlier, Sergeant Don Wood. We would learn years later that he said this to keep Wood's notes hidden—because they contained information that would have helped my case and hurt the prosecution.

He told the jury that he had wanted to arrest me "within a week" of the murder. When my team objected and said that was irrelevant, the jury was sent out and Ken Anderson spoke to the judge about why they had held off, in the process revealing the inappropriate power equation in Williamson County.

Anderson told the judge and anyone within earshot that he "held off because I wanted to make sure, dadgum sure, everything was right on this case before we went out and arrested this guy. The problem was I didn't see the pictures to understand what all happened there," he groveled aloud. "I was being too careful and I hadn't been at the scene myself, which isn't going to happen on another murder because I am going to get my rear end out there."

Suddenly, it became clear why I'd been arrested while Ken Anderson was out of town—Boutwell had made a unilateral decision. He wasn't going to let this novice prosecutor delay the march of justice—his justice—any longer. And Anderson, an officer of the court, a man who had sworn to head the "search for the truth" in the Williamson County system of justice, had instead decided to search for approval from the sheriff. The prosecutor simply could not run the risk of pushing back on Boutwell—not if he wanted to keep his powerful job.

I was a pawn in an intramural local law enforcement power play.

Okay, God, I thought, *you can stop now.* But the universe was not done with me yet.

When Judge Lott ruled that Ken Anderson could show portions of the sex tape I had rented to watch with Chris on my birthday in open court, I felt like I was standing there with my pants down. I felt as though my privates were being examined by a heartless clinician while images of the entire gruesome and unflattering process were projected onto a huge screen in front of everyone. In front of my parents, who sat there through it all—in front of my friends.

The notion of abject humiliation doesn't begin to capture the moment. In fact, it remains so far beyond anything I have ever experienced or imagined that it still feels impossible for me to relate adequately.

Ken Anderson walked over and popped a tape into a VCR at the front of the courtroom. He hit play, and in a heartbeat my pride, my privacy, my life, my honor, my sense of self all dissolved.

As this minutes-long portion of the tape played, not a word was spoken. No trucks or car horns were heard on the street below. The doors outside the courtroom did not slam as they had throughout the rest of my trial. No phones in the entire courthouse rang. It seemed utterly silent—except for the grunts and groans, the practiced ecstasy of the actors' cries on the video. Those sounds blocked out everything else.

I sat there hoping for an explosion, a thunderstorm, a masked gunman—anything—to break the moment.

It was like having the way you dance or the way you kiss—or the way you make love—replayed in slow motion and critiqued by a gathering of disgusted and disappointed viewers.

It was excruciating.

There was a l-o-n-g, wordless pause afterward—a threshold had been crossed, a taboo had been broken. We were in uncharted territory. It felt like anything could happen now.

Chris's murder had rocked me. My arrest was equally unexpected. The media attention was so far out of my sphere of experience that I didn't know how to handle it. Nothing in my life made sense. There were no longer any rules.

I had just watched part of a porn movie with my mother and father. I had just seen myself reflected in the flickering images that bounced off the stunned jury members' eyes. And now I heard my attorney calling me to the stand.

I had known this moment was coming. I had looked forward to it and dreaded it, and finally, it was here.

Ken Anderson looked at me with disgust for breathing the same air as the good people of Williamson County.

I walked to the witness stand and took my place. This was it.

It began easily enough, with my lawyers leading me through my life with Chris and the difficult years when Eric was so sick. My team had told me to answer only what I was asked, to speak in short, declarative sentences. I was to be straightforward—I was not to overshare. But most important, I was to hide nothing.

I was to tell the whole truth. I sat there, struggling to find my truth.

Out of necessity, I had compartmentalized my life—part of me focused on caring for Eric, part of me did my very best at work, part of me budgeted our money, making allowances for our new legal bills. Part of me was still deeply grieving the loss of my wife. Part of me wondered if Chris was watching all this, if she wanted to help.

I had erected walls between all these different parts of my life in order to handle them. One or two at a time, it was almost manageable. Taking it all together, though, I was consumed by a tsunami of despair and disappointment, fear and tragedy, disaster and betrayal.

So when Ken Anderson began questioning me, when he began launching an onslaught of verbal abuse and accusations, when he had me pinned down by his power and experience and animosity— I didn't always stick to the game plan or give perfect answers.

My attorneys' advice had been good, but it didn't take into account my inexperience, my stress, my grief, or my growing hopelessness. Anderson backed me into rhetorical corners, and I sometimes acknowledged things that didn't sound too good, I sometimes said things I shouldn't have—relying on the faith that my attorneys would be able to clean up after me.

I admitted nothing terrible. I had done nothing terrible. But I acknowledged that Chris and I often disagreed, that we occasionally spoke harshly to each other. Anderson told the court that I resented her higher income when, in reality, I was thrilled about it—her success at work was something I was so proud of.

Anderson roared that I had beaten her in a rage—again and again and again—twisting and contorting his entire body to show the force he imagined I had used. He accused me of masturbating with Chris's dead hand—once more, employing his technique of offering something so repugnant, so morbid, so ugly that the exercise of normal human intellect became almost impossible.

I really had no response. I was dumbfounded, horrified—helpless.

He held all the cards. I was just the latest joker.

The jury got the case before lunch.

I sat alone in the courtroom waiting for a verdict. I had not gone to lunch through the entire trial. I couldn't eat and I didn't want to be out and about in a world that saw me as a monster. I craved the solitude and spent my lunch hours pacing the courtroom, looking out the windows, flabbergasted that life outside was going on while this catastrophic mockery of justice was unfolding inside.

It was the last privacy I would have for more than two decades. It didn't last long.

The jury was out for only two hours.

When they filed back in, they wouldn't look at me. They appeared to be struggling to be stoic and unemotional, despite the fact that their humanity—their collective conscience—had been played like a piano by the prosecutor.

"We, the jury, find the defendant, Michael W. Morton, guilty of the offense of murder, as alleged in the indictment."

The spectators gasped. My mother cried out.

I faced Chris's mom and looked pleadingly into her eyes. I told her again and again, "I did not do this. I did not do this."

Her mouth formed a thin, straight line. She looked hard at me and turned coldly away. It would be the last time we were face-to-face for twenty-five years.

I saw Sheriff Boutwell and his team moving in and heard their handcuffs and keys, their gun belts and boots jangling and scuffling as they took their position at my back.

I heard the whizzing snap of the handcuffs opening wide.

My knees buckled, and my attorneys struggled to hold me up.

It was over.

I was lost.

IT SEEMED AS IF THE WORD *GUILTY* WAS STILL RINGING THROUGH THE courtroom when I felt the cold steel of the cuffs close on my wrists—a sensation that in the next quarter century became as familiar as wearing a wristwatch.

My mother reached out to me, holding me as close as she could. She was crying, her face distorted in despair. My father was rattled, too—a rarity for my stoic old man. I had seen him cry only once, at Chris's funeral.

Her family just watched me wordlessly. They offered nothing in their stony expressions except icy anger and an almost palpable disgust. Why had I expected more?

It had become clear to me months ago that they believed I had killed Chris. They had been talking with Ken Anderson, with the sheriff, with reporters. Everybody was reinforcing everybody else's opinions. No one talked to me. No one wanted to.

Now the people who had suspected me all along had the triumph of a jury's considered judgment to banish any lingering doubts. Chris's family watched me with righteous rage as I was being handcuffed, then turned their backs and walked away from me.

Sheriff Boutwell and Sergeant Wood led me out of the courtroom and down a series of echoing stairwells. They flanked me as we stepped into the glare of the winter sun and marched past the crowd that had gathered. The onlookers outside the courthouse gaped as though I were Hannibal Lecter, a man too dangerous to be in public without armed guards, handcuffs, and a phalanx of deputies. We didn't stop for a second, but I sensed they were parading me around, playing to the crowd.

Television cameras were jammed into my face, and the accompanying helmet-haired reporters waved microphones and fired off the kinds of questions that felt more like thinly veiled taunts. "How do you feel about going to prison?" "Why did you do it?"

I didn't answer any of the shouted questions from what felt like an angry mob, but I had come upon a single statement that summed up what I wanted the world to know. I repeated it again and again.

"I did not do this. I did not do this."

I was still saying it as a deputy put his hand on my head and pushed it down—shoving me into an idling squad car. I couldn't see anything through the car windows, but I imagined my in-laws' outrage, my neighbors' faces twisted with disgust, my attorneys' defeated looks, my family's anguish and despair.

I felt the weight of my crushing new reality. It could not be ignored. For the foreseeable future, somebody or something else would be in charge of every decision in my life. I would no longer have any input on where I lived, what I wore, what I ate, where I laid my head at night.

I had nothing.

I was nothing.

And the world thought I deserved nothing.

It was the first day of the next twenty-five years of my life.

PART II

PRISON

The one overriding emotion I experience these days is simple fatigue.
I am tired and just want to go home. What a long, strange trip it's
been. God, please get me out of here.
—JOURNAL OF MICHAEL MORTON, MARCH 4, 2006

CHAPTER THIRTEEN

WE DROVE THE FEW MINUTES TO THE WILLIAMSON COUNTY JAIL, A place that was familiar but triggered no fond memories. This time, however, I wasn't put in the general holding area—they took me to a different part of the jail, a section specifically for inmates who were on their way to prison. I was given a jail uniform, and everything I had of value—my watch, my wallet, a large portion of my pride— seemed to evaporate.

I was handed what jailers called a "mattress" but most closely resembled a long, worn-out, not-quite-filled pillow. I carried my shabby cushion to the "tank," two massive rooms holding ten or twelve men. It was dirty and dark, but I could make out a kind of dayroom, a shower, and a sleeping section. There was a communal toilet in the corner.

Glancing around, I saw that the place was packed. All the bunks held mattresses, or bodies, or both.

An older guy walked over as soon as the deputies slammed the door behind me. I was on guard, my defenses up. He told me the guys there had a seniority system for doling out bunks. He said as soon as someone left, I would get that guy's bunk. He advised dragging my mattress over to the wall in the common area and making a sleeping spot there. Another guy shared that he had claimed the same space when he came in. He'd only had to sleep on the floor for three nights.

I learned later that I had gotten good advice from the "tank" maître d'—the older inmate who served as the county jail "shot caller." Deadly serious and rational—even helpful—the older guy seemed to know his way around jailhouse rules and rituals. I found out later he was a professional—a professional prisoner, that is—having done time in several states in addition to Texas.

I would soon learn that guys like him were very much part of keeping a prison of any kind running, if not smoothly then at least predictably. There was an unspoken system controlling everything. My job was to pay attention and adapt.

I slept fitfully that first night, not just because I was tossing and turning on a filthy and painfully thin sleeping pad on a concrete floor, in a crowded room filled with violent—and violently snoring—men. The guilty verdict, the entire trial, the whole six-month saga since losing Chris played continuously in my mind, like I was stuck in a theater that showed the same heartbreaking film over and over again.

The next morning, I was introduced to another of the dubious charms that dog our massive systems of prisons and jails—the lack of effective oversight for the people in charge of the inmates' health, safety, and security. Worse, what little oversight there is often meets with hostility from the hired hands working most closely with the inmates.

Not long before my conviction, the state agency governing Texas jails had paid a visit to the Williamson County Jail. The inspectors apparently were not happy with what they found. For one thing, there was no hot water. So, they instructed the county to turn the hot water on for the inmates. In a fit of pique, the jailers did, indeed, turn on the hot water.

But they turned off the cold.

When I got out of "bed" and headed for the nearby shower, I could see a man already under the spray, soaping up and washing as fast as he could. He had expected his usual icy shower—which was what he got until the cold water ran out.

Then the scalding water hit.

He flung himself out of the shower and onto the concrete floor, with a scream and a bone-cracking landing. The man had received first-degree burns. Needless to say, no one wanted to shower after that. We went three days without bathing—until the inmates had proof that someone in the state capitol had finally convinced Williamson County to give its inmates hot *and* cold water.

It had now been twenty-four hours since I had last seen Eric. I did not know that I wouldn't see him again for a full year—or that he would go on to be raised by a family that completely and thoroughly hated me. Apparently, Chris's family had been preparing to fight for custody of Eric long before I was convicted. They hired Williamson County's former district attorney, Ed Walsh, to handle their case. The judge who made the ruling on custody was the same one who oversaw my conviction, Judge Lott.

I missed the final day of the custody hearing because the morning the decision was to be announced in court, I was on my way to the penitentiary. Like every other inmate awaiting transfer, I was moved or held back according to a mysterious schedule that was never shared with the people it would affect most—until the last minute.

Every few mornings a jailer would just walk up to the bars of the tank with a piece of paper and read off a list of names—men who were being transferred. There wasn't even a two-minute warning—you were gone.

I was amazed to learn that the guys who were leaving were actually happy about it—happy to be going to prison. They said the county jail was nothing but sitting around, doing nothing. That much was true—there was no TV, no radios, no newspapers, no make-work jobs, and very few visitors. All we could do was wait.

For me, the boredom was broken by interviews local newspapers wanted. Sheriff Boutwell said I could do them, but only if he was sitting right there. I wasn't sure if he wanted the publicity or the chance to continue his personal persecution of me, but these interviews offered the last chance I might ever have to get any of my story out.

I jumped at it.

Sitting in a small cell with peeling paint on the walls, wearing my inmate uniform—and with the sheriff a few feet away—I told reporters that my trial had been based on emotion rather than reason, that inflammatory accusations had taken the place of real evidence. The prosecutor's operatic performance—the table pounding, yelling, and crocodile tears—should not have overwhelmed rational thought. But Ken Anderson's diva act, the sheriff's malignant attitude toward me, and the community's great desire to close the case and move on all combined to almost guarantee my conviction.

The reporters, like the jury, had not seen evidence that wasn't admissible in court, so I filled them in. They didn't know I had passed two polygraph examinations. They didn't know Eric had told me he'd seen the murderer in the shower. They didn't know he had talked with a therapist about the man. They didn't know he'd said some of the same things to my mother.

The reporters wrote it all down, but none of what I told them sank in. To them—to everyone really—I was just another accused, tried, and convicted pervert. My statements were seen as little more than further evidence of my sick, twisted personality, now trying to use my little boy to gain sympathy for my cause. Everything I said and the way I said it was suspect.

The sheriff must have loved watching me lose the argument—all over again.

On the morning the jailers came to take me to prison, I protested that I was supposed to be in court for Eric's custody hearing—a complaint that could not have meant less to the men handcuffing me and pulling me into their car. Who cares? I had about as much control over my movements as a suitcase being tossed in a car trunk.

Most inmates headed for prison are chained together and piled into vans or—in the bigger counties—into buses for the long drive. For some reason, I was stuffed into the backseat of a squad car and escorted by two deputies—sort of the penal equivalent of flying first class.

We did almost fly. From my perch in back, I could see we were averaging about eighty miles an hour. On our mad dash to the madhouse, our unhappy little trio sped past forests and farmland, nearly deserted little towns, and long stretches of nothing but scrub brush, cactus, and coyotes.

As we rocketed past the outskirts of one tiny Texas burg, I saw a guy I will never forget. I saw him for only an instant, but in that brief moment, I realized I had never wanted to trade places with anyone more in my life.

I was handcuffed in a police car—on the way to begin my life sentence in the Texas penitentiary. He was at the wheel of a riding lawn mower, wearing a baseball cap and a headset, with a thoroughly modern-at-the-time Walkman strapped to his hip. I could almost see his head bobbing to music. I spied a cup holder cradling a cold drink.

Why couldn't I have that life—that chance to while away a morning in such an inconsequential, enjoyable way? What had he done to earn his peaceful life on the lawn mower? What had I done to deserve this high-speed race to start the rest of my life in prison?

I wish the deputies had slowed down. I wish the drive had taken longer.

The deputy in the driver's seat finally let up on the gas pedal as we reached Huntsville, a one-of-a-kind company town if there ever was one. Nestled into a leafy, historic neighborhood at the edge of the old downtown is a hulking red-brick monster of a prison with a long, dark history. Known to inmates and local workers as simply the Walls, it is the centerpiece of a sprawling facility whose satellite units stretch far beyond the main "Walls" building.

The little town is not only every inmate's introduction to the Texas prison system, it is the exit for many as well. Regularly, a side door in one of the high brick walls opens and out pour inmates who have done their time and are free to go home. Over the years they have, on occasion, been released hundreds at a time—frantic men wearing ill-fitting clothes and floppy prison shoes. Some have women friends or beleaguered mothers waiting for them in battered cars just outside the gate. In minutes the street fills with shouts of recognition, bear hugs, and long kisses—inevitably followed by speedy exits. The cars always seem to peel out when pulling away from the Walls.

The rest of the freed men often run whooping and hollering all the way to the nearby bus depot. While they wait for their Greyhound getaway, they load up on gum and cigarettes—and in an effort to look good for whoever is waiting at home, they use the few dollars that the Texas Department of Corrections gave exiting inmates to buy clothes from the limited selection on sale at the bus depot. No one wants to wear prison clothes a nanosecond longer than necessary.

The Walls is also the exit point for a different kind of release. The old Huntsville unit has always been home to the state's death chamber—the nation's busiest execution room. The clock on the outside wall above the old building's front door has counted down to the state-ordered executions of hundreds of men—and a handful of women. There is a businesslike tragedy to the place, a sense that in Huntsville the trains—in or out, bound for home or the great beyond—always run on time.

I was due to be checked in to the Diagnostic Unit on the outside edge of Huntsville. We pulled up to the back gate, getting in line behind a busload of men. Another bus packed with prisoners pulled in behind us. I felt out of place, sitting alone in the deputies' patrol car. One guard wondered aloud why I had gotten this special treatment. Was I such a madman that I needed the extra security?

Once inside the fences, I was unloaded and marched into a cavernous room with at least one hundred other felons. No one asked about my case. No one cared.

The guards were loud, unflinching, and demanding of absolute and immediate compliance. Any deviation from their expectations was met with physical confrontation, at whatever level they deemed necessary.

They told me to strip naked and stand in front of them and I did. Fast.

They looked over every inch of my body, then handed me my first pair of state boxers.

I kept in mind the advice of an old con I had met in the county jail. He told me life inside would be easier if I kept my eyes open and my mouth shut. He was right.

Guards hustled me into one of the several lines of men snaking their way to the front to pick up our state-issued boots. While I was waiting, I noticed the bare back of the man in front of me. It was covered with scars—obvious stab wounds. I counted thirteen. Either he was a hard man to kill or his assailant had been incompetent. I didn't ask him which it was.

But the way the dark red, twisted flesh marked his pale back served as a graphic reminder of how very serious my time inside the Texas Department of Corrections was going to be. People got hurt here. They got killed. I needed to adapt. My life now depended on it.

Next stop was the barbershop. While some guys walked in sporting long, scraggly ponytails or full beards, we all walked out looking the same—like closely shorn sheep. Most of my hair and my longtime mustache were gone. I sported a shockingly white strip above my lip for weeks. Many of my early conversations with other inmates began with the question "You used to have a mustache, right?"

I used to have a lot of things.

It is odd to look back and analyze my first days inside the TDC system. I can see now that in order to deal with the shock of the place and the people I now lived with, I had to push back my grief for Chris. I no longer had the luxury of worrying about the custody fight over Eric. My past quickly became a hard-to-remember dream. I simply couldn't think about it. I had more immediate concerns.

My survival seemed to hinge on my ability to blend in. I didn't want to make waves. I wanted to hide in the crowd. I vowed to obey the rules, keep my head down, and learn as much as I could about my new, dangerous world while I fought for an appeal. I figured that, even in a best-case scenario, it could take as long as a few years to get this mess straightened out.

It was a pathetically optimistic assessment.

That first night inside, though, I had no time to think about the future. I was just trying to survive till sunrise. Because the system was so overcrowded, I was assigned to a bunk in the hallway of a packed cellblock.

I didn't sleep much, but not because I spent those first nights bemoaning my lot in life. I stayed awake because I wanted to stay alive—instead of sleeping, I watched restlessly for thieves, perverts, and predators. I knew some new inmates had been beaten or raped—even killed. I was determined to avoid that fate.

So I lay there and listened—to the prison background music that never seems to change much. I heard slamming doors, buzzers, the squawking PA system, whispered conversations between cells, and the footsteps of guards walking by my bunk doing one more of their constant inmate "counts."

The counting went on obsessively, even all night. Keeping track of us—making sure heads were on pillows and bodies were on bunks—wasn't everything to the prison system; it was the only thing.

Throughout the night I could hear inmates calling out to each other by making animal noises. There were really no secret messages involved. It was just a way to mess with the moment—something inmates are very good at.

Down the line of cells, I would hear what sounded like a dog barking. From the other end would come another bark, and then the call of a meowing cat. Above me, I would hear a rooster or a cow or a crow. I would hear inmates snickering, followed sometimes by an impression of a monkey or a mynah bird or the hiss of a snake. It was like trying to sleep in a darkened zoo, complete with cages. Sometimes, we, too, had visitors from outside come to view us.

The Texas prison system's most important—and dreaded—visitor, during my early years inside, was a federal court judge with the fantastically appropriate name of William Wayne Justice. He was personally responsible for dragging the Texas Department of Corrections into the twentieth century, with the prison system administrators kicking and screaming all the way. He reorganized the entire TDC, made major changes in inmate medical treatment, addressed the issues of overcrowding, and generally made the state's prisons better—if not perfect—places to be.

Judge Justice would let prison officials know he was coming with very short notice, but he cleverly would never reveal exactly which facility he would be checking out. As a consequence, the whole prison got at least superficially cleaned up—fast.

A couple of days after I got to Huntsville, word spread like wildfire that Judge Justice was coming our way. The announcement set off an administrative panic to make sure the place was presentable. Inmates were instantly shipped out to other locations, and all bunks were removed from the hallway. It gave me a chance to worry less about being assaulted by random inmates and more about who my cell partner was going to be.

When I reached my cell, the door was open and the place was empty. There were two bunks, one over the other, a tiny sink, and a toilet in the corner. There wasn't much room. When I stood in the middle and stretched out my arms, even before my elbows locked, my fingertips touched both walls.

"Hey, cellie!"

I turned and saw a man dragging a mattress my way. I made room for him by climbing into the top bunk. He was about my size and height, and he quickly revealed that he possessed an attribute not always appreciated in the free world—he was a nonstop conversationalist.

He told me he was a drug smuggler, but for all I knew, he could have been a child molester or a murderer. Whatever he had done, he had a treasure trove of fascinating stories. He talked a lot and slept a lot, and within two weeks, we went our separate ways.

I never saw him again—but then, that's the nature of prison relationships. Whether you liked people or loathed them, you had little say in how long they'd be around you or the role they would play in your life. The person could be your cell partner or a guard, someone who threatened you in the chow hall, a bully in the shower, or a best pal in the TV room—it didn't matter. Every inmate and officer was moved at the whim of the administrators. Sometimes it was for safety reasons, but there was never anything like friendship or your wishes taken into consideration.

Each inmate stayed in the Diagnostic Unit until TDC psych workers had the chance to interview him. They needed to know how dangerous each man was, how far he had strayed from reality, or whether he could be counted on to blend into institutional life. They had a set of five or six standard interview scripts, depending on the nature of your crime, your criminal history, or your family background and education level. Some scripts were aimed at ferreting out hidden feelings that might lead to trouble inside. Sex offenders were asked about everything from their attraction to their mothers to how they felt about animals.

Hilariously, on occasion the interviewers would use the wrong script for an inmate. One guy getting ready to do time for armed robbery had to be physically restrained when he was asked if he felt sexually attracted to his young daughter.

Oops.

We all had to find our humor and humanity anywhere we could. Most days it was hard. In my psychiatric interview, the woman assigned to question me asked whether I "heard voices." In a bid to ease the tension, I laughed and told her I certainly did—I heard hers right now. She stared blankly at me, then turned again to her notes and dutifully wrote something down.

To this day, I wonder what it was.

My weeks at the Diagnostic Unit in Huntsville were just the beginning, a bitter welcome to prison life—to its lack of individuality, its regimentation, the institution's complete indifference to me as a person.

I lived on a cellblock made up completely of new inmates— prison innocents, or at least as innocent as most inmates get. We were getting acclimated to prison life together.

We knew it was time to go to sleep when the cell lights went off and only the security lamps were left glowing.

We knew it was time to eat when the "boss"—penitentiary parlance for a guard—let out a deafening bellow of "CHOW TIME, CHOW TIME, CHOW TIME."

When he did, we all began moving toward the door leading off of the cellblock. The guard stopped us in our tracks. A bunch of hungry men couldn't just charge out en masse—that would be chaotic, tantamount to a riot or an organized escape attempt. What a bunch of boneheaded newcomers we were. We had to learn to proceed in an unthreatening, under-control fashion.

The boss roared at an earsplitting level, "DEUCE IT UP. DEUCE IT UP."

I had no idea what he was talking about, and I looked at him as if he were speaking a foreign language—which he was.

"Deuce it up?"

He'd clearly seen this kind of new inmate perplexity before, so he leaned in and delivered in a stage whisper, "That means get in line, two by two."

We did, and when we reached the chow hall, we learned that most of the guys eating there were new, too. But many were veterans of a few days or even a week. My group and I were eating our first prison meal.

Prison chow halls have their own peculiar aromas, depending on the slop du jour. Eventually you get accustomed to the fact that the weird smell enveloping you is probably dinner. The chow hall is also always hotter and more humid than other parts of the prison—except the laundry. And the chow hall tends to be the place where trouble starts if there is going to be any.

Every single inmate has to go to the chow hall. So if someone is going to pass something to someone else, or if there is someone you want to attack or if someone wants to attack you—the chow hall is the obvious spot to do it. The guards know this and try to keep a tight rein on the place.

My first meal in prison was a lot like every other meal I would eat inside—mystery meat casserole, with God-knows-what sauce and a side of carbs. We all sat at long metal tables with pitchers of water and iced tea in the middle. We ate off metal trays until TDC eventually switched to plastic. The metal ones were sturdy but too often used as weapons. For all I knew, I ate my first dinner off a tray that had been used to bash someone's head in.

The guards swarmed the chow hall as we ate. Loud talking was discouraged. Table-to-table socializing could earn you a glare. We were there to eat. When the guard rapped his knuckles on the table, that meant everyone was finished—ready or not.

We were told to toss our trays in the "bean hole," Texas prison-speak for an opening in the wall where someone on the other side would take your tray, wash it, and put it back on the stack for the next meal.

A boss stood next to the bean hole and stopped anyone with food on his tray—no food was to be wasted. So the man who hadn't finished had to stand there and clean his plate quickly. The rule was "take all you want, but eat all you take."

During the decades ahead, I would learn that each meal could be quite different in its awfulness. The indifference and malice, the malevolence of the men preparing and serving the food, really represented the conscious disregard for prisoners demonstrated at every level of the system. The food was bad because they wanted it to be.

Eventually, I learned I would be assigned to the Wynne Unit, a maximum-security prison not far away. The facility housed more than 2,500 inmates—all of them men who had earned the longest sentences for committing the most serious crimes.

Would I find a way to simply stay alive?

Or would I die trying?

CHAPTER FOURTEEN

IT WAS DARK. THE SUN HADN'T EVEN BEGUN TO BRUSH THE HORIZON.

The old Texas Department of Corrections bus bumped along the rural roads outside of Huntsville, the sky so black it seemed as though we were traveling through space—pushing forward in a starless sky with no beginning, no end, no exit.

I sat there glumly, handcuffed to another inmate, surrounded by dozens of men—all of us headed to our new home at the Wynne Unit, the state's second-oldest prison.

What struck me most about my fellow passengers was their uniformity. We all wore white, making the moment seem ghostly, ominous, and otherworldly. Some of the men had shaved their heads, because with summer on the way, anything that could be done to cool off counted. And there was another benefit: in a fight, an opponent would have no hair to grab.

There were no mustaches, no colorful clothes or outlandish hairstyles. The end result of all this paring away of the outside world, the forced removal of our vanities and free-world identities, was that each inmate had been reduced to his fundamental self.

Actually, one guy did stick out. He had shaved off his eyebrows, which made him appear crazed.

He looked like I felt.

We were headed for Wynne because we'd all been judged to be

badly in need of a very secure setting. We made up a motley group of murderers, bullies, and bad guys—along with the occasional wrongly convicted, completely innocent man. Some of the inmates on the bus were assigned to Wynne because they had messed up at a lower-security prison—by attacking staff, attempting escape, or behaving in a way that made prison administrators want to make their lives more miserable.

Through the front window of the bus, I could see security lights and a gate—a glaring, bright island of concrete, chain link, and steel in a sea of darkness. Within that light stood the portal to my new life.

My name and a few others were called. We shuffled off the bus, were checked off on a list, and directed into a cage. It had no roof, only threatening rounds of razor wire glinting above our heads. There were no walls—just tall stretches of chain-link fence. Looming over us was a guard tower.

The end of a rifle poked out.

We were all totally unprotected from the elements. If it rained, we got wet. If it grew cold, we shivered. Our feelings, our comfort didn't matter. I felt like meat—like a slave, like a piece of state property—because that's what I was.

Dawn spilled streaks of pink, orange, and blue into the night sky. Clear shapes materialized as the sun rose, revealing my new world. I saw mountainous old red-brick buildings, tractors, a pasture, and the prison recreation yard. Guards moved around, sometimes barking orders. I heard buzzers and screechy PA announcements. Inmates who'd earned status as trustees went in and out of the property through a side gate.

Some of them looked at me.

I would soon learn that, in prison, nothing fascinates like novelty. I was a new face. Many of us in the cage that day were new to the system. Some of the current inmates and trustees stared at us searching for the face of an old friend—others scanned the crowd of "new boots" for old enemies.

We sat there for hours. Finally, a guard called out a list of names and escorted us in a small group into the main building. Another guard frisked each man, a process I became so accustomed to through the years that eventually I wouldn't even notice it happening. Getting frisked in prison was like shaking hands in the free world—it was simply a regular interaction, part of what the social order commanded, like having to curtsy for the queen. It was just another piece of prison protocol.

In the free world, you might be greeted with "How do you do?" Inside, it was different. "Turn around, put your hands in the air, and spread your legs."

Often, a guard wouldn't even have to say a word, just motion with his index finger, making a circle in the air—we all knew what it meant.

Finally inside the building, the guard had us sit down on long benches for more waiting. Again hours passed. It was an annoying introduction to a couple of things that were reinforced every day in the quarter century to come.

First, nothing about me mattered—my existence was irrelevant. I could live or die and the penitentiary would just do what it always did, what it would always do. I could have toppled off the bench with a massive heart attack, splitting my head open on the concrete floor. There was not going to be a stampede to help me. I was on my own.

Second, prison is, more than anything else, a bureaucracy—a state-run operation where everything takes longer than it should, requires several tries before getting it right, and keeps the people who rely on it frustrated and angry. Imagine living every day at a state driver's license office, with long lines, misfiled forms, and—too often—incompetence. Now, imagine that same scene with all the state workers carrying cans of Mace, radios, handcuffs, and—for those employees ringing the perimeter—shotguns and rifles.

I was escorted into a room where I was interviewed, assigned a job, and given a cell number. One of the men who interviewed me said he wanted to put me in the kitchen. Another leaned in, pointed out something in my file, and told me I would be working in Records Conversion, whatever that was.

My living assignment was C1-3-13T. I was on C1 block, 3 Row, Cell 13, top bunk.

Home sweet home.

I was led to the cellblock and ordered to drag my mattress three floors up to my cell. No one was home when I got there, but both beds appeared to have owners. So I dragged my mattress back down and told the block boss. He double-checked and said that was where I belonged. Back upstairs the mattress and I went, now under orders to bring down the *other* mattress and then make my bed with *my* mattress. This kind of thing was tedious, tiring, unnecessary—and constant.

When my cell partner finally showed, he said he had been keeping the bed made, hoping folks would look in, think someone already lived there, and not move anybody else in.

I settled in, fully believing that, unlike everyone else's, my days here would be relatively few—that this whole thing would get straightened out very quickly. I just had to learn the ropes and the rules and stay alive until the truth emerged and, in a flood of shame and remorse, the judge who sent me here would set me free.

In the meantime, I had to learn the rhythm of the place.

Prison is all about routine. Prison *is* routine—followed by routine—reinforced by more routine.

Lather, rinse, repeat—for life.

The unchanging schedule behind the walls of the Wynne Unit often gave its guests a schedule for the first time in their lives. If you came in without a routine, the institution's routine would be imposed upon you. If you didn't get up for breakfast, you either didn't eat or had to scrounge something up yourself. If you didn't go to the showers at the appointed time, you stayed dirty.

My routine had me rolling out of bed every morning at 3:00 to eat breakfast. I left for my job between 4:30 and 5:00 A.M. Lunch in the chow hall began about 10:30; dinner was mounded into gloppy piles on my tray sometime between 3:30 and 5:30. The gym and the rec yard opened after that. The dayroom closed and the lights were dimmed every weekday—without fail—at 10:30 P.M.

Sometimes, at night, I could hear men crying. On those battered cellblocks built of concrete and steel, men every bit as hard as that concrete and steel wept in the dark. Captivity does brutal things to a man, no matter what he's done to lose his freedom.

I never sobbed loudly or cried out in anguish the way some men did. But when it was quiet and I thought of my old life—my lost wife and my little boy—I lay on my top bunk, looking at the ceiling, crying silently, tears for me, for my family, for whatever lay ahead. I now had the time to recognize that I hadn't had a chance to fully grieve for Chris—or, now, to grieve for the loss of Eric.

I was fighting to survive, fully focused on the dilemmas I faced daily, surrounded by violence and anger, ignorance and cruelty. How do I stay alive? How can I get out of here?

During the day, I worked, kept my head down, and waited to hear from my attorneys, who were preparing my appeal. Not long into my stint at Wynne, I had gotten word that they had come across something unexpected—and, for once, it was good news for me.

Immediately after my conviction, my attorneys had joined Mike Davis, the assistant prosecutor who argued the case with Ken Anderson, for a joint interview with the jurors. This is quite common, as attorneys on both sides are eager to improve their performances by learning what worked, what didn't, and why.

During this casual Q and A, Davis told the jury that if my attorneys had seen the full investigative file and notes—Davis then held up his thumb and index finger to indicate a report that was about an inch and a half thick—they would have been able to raise much more doubt about my guilt.

Bill Allison was floored when he heard this. He knew he had never seen the full report, even though he and Bill White had worked hard to get it. In fact, the lengthy pretrial battle between

the two sides about turning over evidence that indicated I was innocent—exculpatory evidence—had led Sergeant Wood's notes and reports to be sealed and included as part of the record for the appeals
court to review. The notes my team had seen before trial amounted
to no more than a few pages. In his off-the-cuff chat with the jurors,
Davis had just let them know that there was much more to the report—and that it had intentionally been kept hidden. The prosecutor's decision not to turn over the offense report to the defense may
well have led to my conviction—that's what Mike Davis was saying.

The two Bills had immediately filed a motion to overturn my
conviction based on the Davis revelation, but the court turned them
down.

Now, Davis's comment to the jury became part of my formal
appeal.

To this day, no one knows why Davis burst out with this bit of
truth that was so damaging to the prosecution's case—and even
more damaging to the prosecutor's reputation. Hiding an offense
report containing evidence favorable to the defendant is more than
unprofessional—it is illegal.

Had Davis said that to sympathetically tip off my attorneys? Was
he just mindlessly bragging about how clever he and Ken Anderson
had been in winning my conviction? Why did he bring this up at all?
I still don't know.

When the appeal White and Allison had prepared showed up
in my mail, I took it back to my cell, ripped open the package, and
devoured it the way a starving man would eat a steak. Frankly, I
couldn't understand much of it, except that they were on my side. I
had no way of gauging the strength of their arguments or the wisdom of their approach.

I only knew I had never read words on paper that held such
power. My very life hung in the balance—my freedom, my chance
at a future. I decided to go to the prison's law library and see what
I could learn. I knew there was an underground cottage industry

of "jailhouse lawyers" inside the walls. For money, one of them would probably have read the appeal and given me his opinion on its worth. But even though I hadn't been there long, I knew most of these guys were no good. Frankly, the majority of them used their legal "expertise" simply as a way to scam the uneducated or unknowing out of the little money or extra food they had.

I decided to try to learn something myself. I soon joined the "legal eagles" in the library, reading and trying to understand opinions and arguments, case law and the odds for my appeal. I felt like a first-time astronaut, perched precariously atop a rocket while hurriedly reading an introductory astronomy textbook before I was blasted into space.

Through the years, I would file well-intentioned, carefully written, but mostly naïve motions that never really had a chance. Still, the law library gave me a quiet place to be, a setting in which to read and learn, a chance to think more deeply about what I might be able to do with my life while I waited to be free. I decided to start looking at the options I had for finishing my college education inside, a step that would ultimately help change my life.

In the meantime, my education in the peculiar mores of prison life continued apace. Privacy, I learned, was monumentally valued in prison. Since real privacy is not possible, prisoners developed small courtesies that afforded us at least the illusion of privacy. We knew when to look away, when to put on a headset, when to give each other some room. One such courtesy was the unspoken rule dictating that inmates were never to look inside another man's cell as they walked by. It was considered disrespectful. And it could be dangerous.

There was one man on the cellblock who either didn't know or didn't care about this rule. Maybe he just couldn't help himself. Whenever he passed a row of cells, he would turn and gawk inside. A few guys said something to him—warning him to knock it off— but it did no good. He just kept gawking.

One day, as he waltzed toward the dayroom to join the others watching TV, he walked slowly along the block, staring into each cell he passed. Then the gawker looked into the wrong cell. The man who lived there was waiting for him. As soon as the gawker peeped into the cell, he got a full cup of urine thrown in his face. After that, he learned his lesson.

In prison, privacy—or even the illusion of it—is important.

The other illusion all inmates work to maintain is strength, at least in some form. Strength in numbers, strength in brute force, the strength that comes from being particularly fast in a fight, the strength that comes from having strong friends inside—anything that gives you an edge, or the illusion of an edge.

This is why gangs thrive inside, because their members believe gangs give them protection, a way to convince others that taking on one of them means taking on all of them.

An inmate's personal demeanor matters, too. If you are direct, candid, and confident, opponents know where they stand. This prevents misunderstandings—so does minding your own business. An inmate's physical condition is also important, but nothing helps as much as having witnesses when you clock the first guy who gives you any grief. Because sooner or later, almost everyone fights—or they become someone's punk. And that's not good.

Prison demanded a reeducation for me. I had been taught—and wanted to teach my son—that differences can be resolved without hitting. I had never worked in a place where bloody fistfights could break out without warning. And I certainly knew that, even in the midst of the most emotional marital spat, a physical response was totally taboo.

In the penitentiary, I had to unlearn some of that. Inside, there was no prohibition on violence; in fact, there was more of a reliance on it—or there was at least an understanding that physical force occupied a prominent spot in every inmate's toolbox of responses.

On the inside, you had to deal with men who were not particularly smart. They often lacked what psychologists call "impulse control." They may have grown up in harsh environments—suffering everything from broken homes to failing schools, gang-riddled neighborhoods to dysfunctional families, low expectations to long histories of drug and alcohol abuse. Or they could be just stone-cold crazy.

No matter what their issue, though, each and every one of them—including me—understood brute force. They had all learned, as I had, that when a man has a knife at your throat or is pummeling you to death, it doesn't matter what sort of traumatic childhood he endured, whether he got the counseling or support he needed in overcoming addiction, or why he had a lower than average IQ. The only thing that mattered at that moment, was whether you could muster the physical force to stop him.

Cultural niceties, political correctness, social justice, empathy, and fear of the law—all the values we talk about in the free world—inside prison become irrelevant, inconsequential conceits. All that matters in that moment is brute force.

Like most people, I had not been around much violence. Most of what I knew—or thought I knew—about it came from movies and TV, which I soon learned bore little resemblance to reality. Fake fights had been a breeze to follow—clean face-offs with clear winners and losers, obvious motives, easy to understand morality. Not so inside.

The first few fights I saw happened so quickly that they were over before a crowd could gather. The fights began and ended with such rapidity, such ferocity that many of their finer points were lost on me—at first. Only after seeing them close up, again and again, did I begin to understand what was happening.

The good guy–bad guy dynamic was mostly a theatrical dream, particularly in a place populated with very few truly "good guys." There were almost no one-punch knockouts. Speed and agility often trumped size and strength. And experience and skill meant everything.

I learned there were unwritten rules for prison fighting—a ritual to it. These were usually just fights, not attempted murder. If a guy went down, the fight stopped. If someone stepped in to break it up, it usually stopped. Usually.

If someone in the fight picked up a weapon—a tray, a chair, a book, a bench—everything changed. When a weapon entered the equation, so did the guards.

Probably the first difference I noticed between real fights and TV fights was the sound—in Hollywood, fights are always punctuated with a sort of high-pitched smacking sound, like a fist hitting the inside of a palm, which is how I suspect that sound effect is made. In a real fight, what you hear is the unforgettable pounding of meat on meat. When you hear a fist hit someone's face, you will remember it forever. Nothing else sounds like that. The thud of flesh colliding with flesh, the brutal snap of a bone being broken—this awful, unforgettable audio will stay with me for the rest of my life.

And fights are not tidy affairs—there is always blood. When hit, faces tend to rupture and bleed. Blood gets on clothes, on fists, on the floor, on the walls. It gets on the people watching the fight.

Another revelation for me was the aftermath of fights. In the movies, a combatant seems to come away with a shiner or a cut on the cheekbone, which quickly clears up, leaving the hero's face as pretty as it was before he took a pounding. In prison, I learned the human face is an incredibly fragile commodity. A fight would leave it damaged for days, if not weeks. Sometimes, a fighter's face would never look the same again. Split lips and cracked teeth don't heal easily. Even the winner comes away wounded—your hand can hurt for days from the beating you delivered to someone else.

In some ways, I was lucky. When I came to prison, I was thirty-two years old—I was more mature, more grown into myself than many men who land behind the walls. Most of the younger guys were sent to what we called "gladiator farms," prisons for those in their twenties, where the fights and face-offs were constant. They would fight to establish dominance, to avenge insults (real or imagined), to defend themselves, and sometimes, simply for entertainment.

The Wynne Unit housed men closer to my age—from their late twenties into their mid-forties. A lot of them just didn't have the stomach for fighting the way they had years before. In other words, my prison held a lot of "professionals," men who had been in prison before. This wasn't their first rodeo.

After only a few months, I understood in my bones what every inmate does—that prison is not just a place, not just stacks of cells with bars for walls, not just a collection of old buildings where everyone inside is angry. Prison is a different planet, a world turned inside out. It has its own kind of oxygen and gravity, its own powerful rulers and hopeless slaves, its own distinct wars and martyrs, rough morality and sin. It is a warehouse filled with broken souls we don't want to look at or live with—people whose addictions, abuses, ignorance, or rage we need to be protected from.

Prison is where society puts its problems, its rejects, its mistakes. In my case, the mistake was that I was there at all.

CHAPTER FIFTEEN

I HAD WAITED AN ENTIRE YEAR TO SEE ERIC. NOW THAT THE DAY WAS at hand, I didn't know what to expect, or even what to hope for. I simply wanted him to recognize me.

The night before, I lay on my bunk and began pulling myself out of the day-to-day grind of penitentiary life. For the first time in ages, I allowed myself the luxury of thinking about my son. I fully conjured the sensation of holding him—I could almost feel him in my arms. The way he would drape himself around my neck, lay his sleepy head on my shoulder, or how he'd dig his little legs into my side to hold on tight—thoughts like that brought my old life rushing back. I hadn't forgotten that his soft hair always seemed to smell of baby shampoo and sunshine, or the way he would light up when he saw me walk in after I had been gone for the day. That's what I was hoping would happen when I saw him in the visiting room.

Once again, reality was more complicated.

Custody of Eric had been awarded to Chris's younger sister, Mary Lee. She was single, lived in a small one-bedroom Houston apartment, and had no children. In the past, she'd had bouts of unemployment and periods when she seemed adrift. She had lived with us for a while, but after Chris's murder, I had felt Mary Lee pulling away from me. Now, we were completely estranged.

Twelve months after my conviction, I wasn't sure whether Mary

Lee had a job or who took care of Eric if and when she worked. I didn't know if she was dating or whether her dates spent time with Eric. I didn't know the day-to-day details of his life. There was no legal order requiring Mary Lee to share that kind of information with me.

The custody agreement simply ordered that she bring Eric to see me—in prison—once every six months until he turned eighteen. Since I had very much preferred Eric to go to my parents or sister, I wondered if this visiting schedule was some kind of compromise by the court after giving custody to Mary Lee. Or was it simply Williamson County's way of rubbing my powerlessness in my face? I would never know.

Still, my parents and siblings saw Eric regularly, and despite our estrangement, I knew that Chris's family would never try to hurt me by mistreating him. They loved him, too. I knew he was safe, at least physically. But I also knew Chris's family detested me. They believed with all their hearts that I had beaten my wife—their daughter, sister, niece, cousin—to death. I saw the loathing in their eyes in court. I feared I would someday see that same anger and disgust on Eric's face. His spending a lifetime with people who hated me did not bode well for our long-term father-son relationship. The only way I had to fight back was to make these twice-yearly visits as meaningful as I could. I was determined to try.

I walked to the central desk in the visiting area, where all the inmates expecting someone would check in. The person behind the desk would then send them to either the contact or the noncontact visiting area. *Contact* means exactly what you think—the inmate is able to touch his visitor—they can kiss, hug, hold hands; a child can sit on his father's lap, a husband can cradle his wife's face. Contact visits are close to sacred for inmates—so many of us would go months, even years inside without anyone touching us in kindness or with compassion. For inmates, the opportunity to hold or be held by another human being was like a heavy rain in the desert. Sometimes, it meant the difference between survival and being pulled down by the pressures of penitentiary life.

The noncontact visiting room was split down the middle by a thick sheet of glass and a kind of room-length table. Inmates sat on one side and visitors on the other. Guards strolled both sides of the room—always eavesdropping and looking for trouble—sometimes even starting trouble themselves.

The area on each side was open, so there was absolutely no privacy. Every inmate could hear what the inmate next to him was saying. The visitors could all hear what the families or friends next to them were saying. In that room, voices were loud, often crude, occasionally angry and ugly with rage.

The noncontact visiting area was where violent inmates got bad news from their attorneys or heartbreaking brush-offs from girlfriends grown sick of waiting. It was where an inmate could learn his wife was pregnant, count backward, and realize he was behind bars at the conception.

I was expecting a contact visit with Eric—that was what the judge had ordered. But the guard at the desk had listed me as meeting visitors in the noncontact area, a hard place to comfort a four-year-old boy who has lost both his parents in the past eighteen months.

I protested to the guard that my court order had specified contact visits. He didn't care. So I ran the distance back to my cell to get my copy of the order. Panting when I returned to the visiting area, I handed the paper across the desk and looked around. I wondered if Eric or Mary Lee could see me, or if I could catch a glimpse of them. I knew they had been waiting. I imagined Mary Lee sitting impatiently with Eric, a look of disdain on her face. It was bad enough that she had to come to this awful place to see me—now I was making her wait.

The guard handed my court order up to a captain, and he came out and shot the paper back at me across the desk. He said the Texas Department of Corrections did not care what "some judge" thought; the TDC would handle the visit the way the TDC wanted. He told me it was going to be "this way or not at all."

I went into the room, still protesting the captain's decision.

Mary Lee did not stick up for me. And I know I looked upset and angry, because I was.

She sat quietly beside Eric across from me, letting us talk as best we could. The glass between us was filthy from generations of dirty, sad hands pressing against it on both sides. It looked like it was superficially cleaned once every few months. I didn't want Eric to touch it or even be near it—that glass probably had diseases on it biologists have yet to discover.

At the base of the glass was a three-inch opening with thick wire mesh across it, a crude sort of conduit for sound. Still, it was very hard to hear. Even laying my face down on the table and talking directly into the mesh didn't help much. When I looked through the glass, I saw a scared four-year-old boy who seemed to only vaguely recognize me. Eric was simply too young, too battered, too confused, too unmoored to know what was going on. He lost interest in my indistinct image behind the dirty glass. He kept his head down and played with his tiny cars.

They left early.

I was crushed. I felt like smashing the face of the first person I came across.

I didn't.

I brooded over the loss of my son and the powerlessness of my lousy new life. I couldn't blame Eric; he was sort of in the same boat I was—a victim of circumstance, bad luck, and overwhelming loss. The only solace I could find was in the friends that I'd made inside, many of whom shared my frustrations and anger the same way we shared everything else—from showers to bad food, dull-witted guards to unfairly meted out discipline.

My first real friend inside was Gary Stinnett. We'd met in the Diagnostic Unit. Gary was a former police officer whose wife had been beaten to death. He would be released in 1997 after revelations that prosecutors had hidden exculpatory evidence in his case.

Sounds familiar.

We were two of the only three inmates at the Diagnostic Unit that day without tattoos. The other guy was a firefighter turned arsonist—bit of an odd duck, needless to say.

Gary and I hit it off.

He was assigned to the Wynne Unit as well, although I got the better cell. I was up on the third row, far above the clatter and chaos of the dayroom. Gary's cell was right across the hall from the dayroom. Every day and every night, he had to endure noise blasting from two TVs always set on different channels and at full volume. Plus there was the relentless shouting and bellowing bombast from ill-informed sports fanatics. There were verbal confrontations and the occasional—and inevitable—outbreaks of violence. It was like living at the world's loudest and most violent sports bar during a big game that went on for years and years.

Compared to Gary, I had a penthouse suite.

Gary always believed he had been given his cell assignment because of his "bad attitude" toward the guards. He loved making fun of them and constantly corrected their speech and grammar. Maybe they were getting back at him.

Both of us had studied just enough psychology to be dangerous, and we used to sit around the dayroom analyzing our fellow inmates and trying to identify the issues we thought bedeviled them. We fancied ourselves the intellectual giants of the prison dayroom—something akin to being the state's prettiest armadillo.

Gary and I were given virtually identical jobs in what we called the "Typing Pool," the Records Conversion Facility, where we entered state paperwork digitally, photographed and developed microfilm, and generally pushed paper.

There were about two hundred of us who were lucky enough and experienced enough in clerical work that we got the enviable assignment. It beat the heck out of churning out new Texas license plates eight hours a day—or sewing together an unending number of shapeless uniforms and boxers for the other unlucky souls who lived in the embrace of the state. The finishing work on our clothing was hopelessly crude. But then what would you expect from a group of indentured tailors forced to stitch together the most visible evidence of their imprisonment? Our uniforms were handmade for angry people *by* angry people—and they looked it.

Gary and I worked together in the prison darkroom, developing microfilm for state agencies ranging from the police to public universities. I was lucky. Gary was one of the relatively few inmates I felt comfortable being with for hours, alone in the dark.

Like me, Gary had family who visited and a little money in his prison commissary account. The majority of men inside had nothing and no one to care about them. Some inmates, for other reasons, were particularly vulnerable to attack or exploitation.

Every prison has a "protection" wing for men who would not fare well in the general population. There, you would find the child molesters, the convicted police snitches, the "out" gay men who, if they didn't have protection, would be savaged by other inmates. They lived separately, ate separately, and died separately. The protection wing at Wynne had more suicides than the other wings. Even if a person is isolated for his own safety, being denied the same small freedoms and camaraderie other inmates had must be crushing.

There was homosexual behavior in the general population, usually by men who would describe themselves as "straight." While they might introduce another man as their "girlfriend" or their "lady," they would protest loudly if you mistook them for being gay. They would say they always "pitched" and never "caught," which in their minds made a difference.

Okay, then.

And there were rapes in prison, but just like sexual assaults in the free world, rape behind the walls is an act of power rather than sexual desire. Most inmates are able to fend off attacks by maintaining their ground the first time they are confronted, something that gains respect from other dominating prisoners.

But woe to the poor soul who doesn't strike back or curls into a ball and cries rather than standing up for himself and fighting. He will be taken apart like a character from *Lord of the Flies*.

We all saw it happening and we heard it happening. And there was nothing anyone could do—and very little the guards could, or would do. Violence, whatever form it took, was just part of the natural habitat. You couldn't stop it, you could only decide how you were going to react to it.

RANDY WAS A GUY WHO WORKED IN THE DARKROOM WHEN I FIRST GOT there. Like me, he was sentenced to life. Unlike me, Randy had served prison time twice before.

Everyone has something they do well—for Randy, it was teaching. He was born for it. He could take the most complex task and break it down into small, simple steps. That's how he taught me everything I know about microfilm.

One morning as we were getting ready for the day, another inmate stepped in. I didn't recognize him, but I could see from Randy's body language that they knew each other. I turned around and went back to work. Before I realized anything was wrong, the guy whipped out a shank—a kind of homemade knife—and held it to Randy's throat. Since Randy stood about eight inches taller than his attacker, the inmate looked up to him. The knife was touching the soft flesh of Randy's throat.

The inmate spat out an insult in Spanish. I froze, expecting blood on the floor at any moment. With his fists balled at his sides, Randy glared at the intruder and leaned hard into the blade. I was frozen in place. Randy called the man something unprintable—and then took a step forward.

In a terrifying battle of wills, Randy dared the guy to cut him. He stepped forward again. Instead of slicing Randy's throat open, the man backed up. Randy kept pushing him and cussing him, eventually marching the man backwards toward the door—at least twenty-five feet from where they started. After another insult, the guy slipped the blade back inside his pants and vanished.

I realized I hadn't breathed since the attack started. I had been sure I was about to see my first prison killing.

"Randy," I hissed, "you okay?"

"Pussy," he muttered about the other inmate—and went back to work.

In prison, how you handled a direct challenge was everything. You stayed alive by acting like you weren't afraid to die. You stayed safe by being reckless. And you were able to live in peace by acting like you were always ready for a fight.

But every inmate had to accept a certain amount of abuse from the guards. Many of them were what we called "state raised," meaning their families had lived off the prison system for generations. Their fathers had been guards and they had grown up knowing they, too, would become guards.

As little boys, they had been regaled with stories of the power their fathers or grandfathers had over the roughest inmates in the state. Too often, they looked at inmates the way a mean farm kid looks at cattle—as a source of income *and* entertainment—props available around the clock to be bullied, demeaned, or disciplined, whichever seemed like the most fun.

One day as my fellow Typing Pool workers and I were making our way to our jobs, a guard once again took the opportunity to show us who was boss. We all had to walk down a narrow sidewalk flanked by chain-link fence, stopping midway at a gate until we were buzzed through by the guard looking down on us from the tower. On this day, it began to rain lightly just as we started out. We broke into a jog to get to the gate, go through, and head onto the path that led inside. But when we reached the locked gate, one inmate made the mistake of yelling for the guard to "open up."

The guard did not like being told what to do by a lowly prisoner, so we all had to stand there while he asserted his authority. We were trapped as the rain grew stronger and the wind whipped it into our faces. It became a downpour, and still, we stood there unprotected and waiting.

More inmates started to yell. Some cursed. Still, the guard wouldn't open that gate. There was nowhere to go and no way to avoid getting drenched. We could see his silhouette in the tower—holding a rifle, looking down on us dispassionately as we huddled together.

Finally, the gate buzzed and we shuffled through. There was no point in running now—we were all soaked to the bone and feeling homicidal. But most important, from the guard's point of view, we had been reminded again that we were powerless—that he held the keys, that it was his hand that hovered over the buzzer, deciding whether or not to hit it. The guard hadn't acted that way because he was required to or because he needed to.

He did it simply because he could.

It was just another in an endless series of demonstrations of how prison is a hate factory—where inmates go in bad and come out worse, where men go in ashamed and come out angry.

I decided I would try to come out smarter. I read everything I could get my hands on—all the books I had intended to read, all the books I knew I should read, all the books I would probably never have read in the free world.

A group of like-minded inmates joined me for what had to be the world's roughest book club. You practically had to kill someone to get in. Literally.

We devoured everything from the classics to Stephen King, and we passed each ripped and dog-eared copy from cellblock to cellblock, bunk to bunk. As quickly as I read one, I would be handed another. We would wave each other on to or off of a planned selection. We critiqued each author's work with the clarity and strength of opinion that could come only from never having written a book ourselves.

Reading was the only means of escape available to us. With a book, we could climb over the walls, walk on the beach, meet new friends, and mourn the loss of someone we felt we had gotten to know. We got books from the library, ordered them through friends or family, and eagerly anticipated mail deliveries with book-shaped boxes. We were intellectually starving, and each new read was a feast.

My parents visited me as often as they could. They also sent me a little money for my commissary account, so I could purchase the occasional extravagance. You know, the real luxuries in life—shaving supplies or a pint of ice cream.

While my mom had been terrified during my first days in prison, the fact that I was still alive months later helped calm her down. When I related to my parents that I had seen an inmate in the shower with tattoos on every inch of his body, my small-town, churchgoing mother had been shocked. But not so shocked that she didn't ask, "Even down there?"

I told her, "Yes—even down there."

Her eyes were the size of dinner plates. "What'd it say?"

"Good God, Mom. I'm trying to stay alive in here. I didn't bend down and read it."

Seeing my parents—or anyone from my old life—was bittersweet. I desperately wanted to have visitors from the free world. But when they left, I felt more alone than ever. When we hugged goodbye, it was a reminder that I wasn't going to get another hug until they came back, that I couldn't leave with them, that I had lost virtually everything of value in my life. I had lost Chris. I'd lost many of my friends. I had certainly lost my reputation. I'd lost any property I owned, my car, my savings, any chance I'd once had to make any money. I had lost my freedom.

And I was now losing the most precious thing in my life—my son.

By the time our next visit came around, six months later, it had been a year and a half since I'd touched him—since we had really talked, since we'd hugged or played or laughed together.

By this visit, the TDC had determined that they had to obey court orders and let me have a contact visit. We sat outside at a wooden picnic table—behind double chain-link fences topped with razor wire—under the watchful eye of a guard cradling a rifle in the tower above us. Other inmates were having visits with their families all around us.

As we talked and I tried to engage him, I realized that he really felt no connection to me. A year in the life of a four-year-old is an unfathomable eternity. I was no longer even a memory. I was a slightly disheveled man in an ill-fitting white uniform, desperately trying to make conversation by asking too many questions about the specifics of his collection of Hot Wheels cars.

I don't know what Eric felt that day—or if he felt anything at all.

But I held on to every word he said for dear life. I was fascinated by his every move, by what he did, by what he chose to eat, by the way he was dressed. I could see that he was growing. He was literally growing away from me. I wasn't there to see his milestones or create new memories with him or fall asleep on the couch watching TV or the other things that parents take for granted. I wasn't there at all.

I asked him about school and sports and his friends. And I memorized his answers to replay in my head, again and again, until our next visit. To the guards, to the other prisoners, even to Mary Lee, it probably looked like Eric and I were having a conversation. It was all a charade, of course.

He was my son—but he didn't know me. I hadn't been part of his world for so long. As I watched him play with his cars at the prison picnic table, I wondered whether he remembered Chris at all.

Or were *both* of us forgotten and forever gone?

CHAPTER SIXTEEN

```
Merry Christmas.
    I have a new toy—courtesy of my mother's Sunday
School class.
```

When I received the envelope with a return address from her church, I thought it would be just another one of those "praying for you" sentiments we inmates often get close to the holidays. Instead there was a small note written in careful cursive, telling me I had a gift waiting for me on my commissary account.

Apparently, the class had raised enough money to purchase the typewriter I had been craving.

And they'd thrown in another hundred dollars for toiletries or whatever else I wanted.

I was overcome with emotion—as though I were a little kid who'd accidentally caught a glimpse of Santa Claus in the living room, setting up a toy train under the tree. Instantly, I felt "Christmas" wash over me—in all its almost forgotten, childlike glory—transporting me to a table overflowing with Mom's cooking, a comfortable chair in a familiar place surrounded by people who loved me. I could almost hear the music of the whole family in the kitchen laughing and cleaning up after dinner. I could almost feel the peace of sitting on the couch in the living room—coffee and a plate of cookies at my side—bathed in the twinkling lights of the tree, basking in the warmth of a crackling fire.

I almost wept.

The lovely, big-hearted ladies at church had held a bake sale to raise money for me. I'd been telling my mother for months how much I wanted that 100 percent plastic, prison-approved, no-parts-that-could-be-turned-into-weapons typewriter on display in the commissary. It was cheaply made, but for an inmate like me, it was expensive.

I had been saving my money, stretching my deodorant and toothpaste to last for months and months, so I could afford it. I wanted the typewriter for my legal work, but I also wanted to try my hand at writing.

Inside, I'd been reading so much I felt like I was doing time with Mark Twain, sharing a cell with John Steinbeck, and sitting in the dayroom with Kurt Vonnegut and John Irving. Occasionally Tom Robbins would pop in. Stephen King was always lurking around a dark corner, motioning for me to join him someplace terrifying. They had all become my friends—men I could count on to keep me distracted at night and entertained in the lonely hours when I couldn't find anyone to talk with who knew *how* to read.

Their books felt like gifts, as though they were written specifically for me. I wanted to write back.

With my new typewriter, I could.

I began keeping a journal and mailing pages to a friend, Jack Anderson, for safekeeping until I got out.

Whenever that would be.

Somehow, typing out a record of the day's activities or awful spectacles allowed me to maintain a healthy distance. I could laugh at how darkly *hilarious* everything was. I could tell the story of prison in my own voice, in my own way, at my own speed.

Or in the future, when and if Eric ever asked me what prison had been like, I could hand my bulging journal to him and say, "Here, Son, read this."

Reading that journal now, I am reminded of the long-forgotten details of deaths, transitions, and traumas. I can remember where I was when I wrote a particular entry. With the distance of years, and the safety of being outside prison, I can now acknowledge that the bravado with which I wrote these stories did not always match the mood of the man who sat hunched alone in the dark of his cell, feeling hopeless—tapping out entries.

I plinked away, one letter, one finger at a time, typing up poorly thought out legal appeals, novels, and short stories I could tweak and tinker with until I was happy. Or I worked on them at least until I was satisfied—or convinced I shouldn't continue. A few of them were published in small, obscure magazines, sources of triumph for me.

The days passed.

The months slid by.

The years melted together.

And the clock just kept ticking.

Behind the walls, you learn that you can fight the clock—but you can never win. I was determined to do something with my time.

From inside the penitentiary, I went back to college—but this go-round I was living in a particularly restrictive dorm and newly committed to getting my degree. God knows, I had fewer distractions than I did when I was younger. There were fewer women, of course, less booze, and not nearly as many drugs as on most college campuses.

There were other disruptions—constantly being frisked, sleeping poorly because the guy in the next cell sobbed all night, or worrying about being stabbed in the neck at dinner—you know, the usual. But I soldiered on.

Sam Houston State University offered prisoners degrees in psychology and sociology. Psychology became my major. My classes were paid for through a Pell Grant. One night a week, I attended a three-hour lecture taught by one of the professors from the university.

It was a real treat—an oasis of sanity in an intellectual desert. Sometimes the two opposing worlds collided and we'd hear a fight break out between two "students" in our "schoolhouse." One professor found the juxtaposition of violence and higher learning morbidly funny. When he heard the familiar thuds and scuffling outside his classroom, he would look up appreciatively. "Ah, academia," he would muse with a knowing smile.

All the professors seemed to like the arrangement. They could get in an entire semester of teaching by lecturing only one night a week. And inmates were different, in some ways better students.

I took school seriously, as did most of the men in the program. We were older than college kids and had no hesitation about challenging our instructors if we didn't agree or didn't understand—or wanted to know more.

Many of the inmate students were, however, terribly emotionally needy—always feeling inadequate and wanting affirmation from outsiders. They would ask the instructors how their work compared to that of students on campus. The profs would say honestly that often inmates were better prepared than full-time students—because inmates did their homework, read their material, and came to class ready to talk about it.

I told myself it was embarrassing that the other inmates needed all this reassurance. In truth, though, I was curious, too—and happy with the answer.

As I climbed the educational ladder in college classes, I was simultaneously getting a PhD in penitentiary life—the unique rules, rituals, and language of "Slammerland." I had to catch on to the lingo fast. Words and phrases that meant nothing when I arrived quickly became part of my vocabulary.

- A chain bus or Blue Bird is used to transport inmates, who are chained together. Blue Bird is a brand of bus.
- A house is an inmate's cell.
- Punks are weak-willed inmates who would do anything to

avoid a fight or, alternatively, gay men. In the penitentiary, *punk* is an insult.

- Restriction is when the administration takes some "thing" or some activity away from an inmate for a rule infraction. Sometimes, it meant you couldn't leave your cell, sort of like being grounded if you had very strict—and possibly demented—parents. It also has unofficial and profane applications. Use your imagination.
- *Ride* is a word believed to have biker origins. It was used in all kinds of ways. "Who you riding with?" could mean "Which sports team are you backing?" Or "Which gang are you with?" Or "Who's your man?" Riding on the back of a motorcycle is sometimes called "riding bitch."

Prison patois went on and on—colorful and coarse, singular in its subject matter, brutal and unfathomable to outsiders.

My early years in the penitentiary were a dualistic experience. Part of me adapted to prison, while part of me tried to hang on to the person I used to be. I fought the insidious creep of prison slang and mannerisms into my personality. I struggled against the crudeness that comes from living in state-sanctioned internal exile. I took no small amount of pride when someone asked me, "What are *you* doing here?" The inference was that any fool could see I did not belong behind bars.

But despite everything I tried and all the good intentions in the world, prison wore me down. Things came out of my mouth that made me cringe. The casual curses, the prison language, the hateful posing—it all oozed out when I didn't watch myself.

During one visit with my parents, my mother told me to do everything I could "to stay out of trouble." As is the prison way, I tore her head off. "Don't tell me how to behave," I barked. "You don't have the slightest idea what goes on in here." She could see her son was changing, and so could I. Neither one of us liked it.

I hated how easily I had lashed out at her. I'd done it without thinking, without feeling, without mercy. My rough edges became a coping mechanism.

But then prison is where coping mechanisms go when they grow up—when a person's ability to survive psychologically requires a complex system of rationalization and denial, pretense and posturing, the creation of new standards for acceptance and rejection.

If my family had known what one of my favorite coping mechanisms was, it would have broken their hearts.

For many of my early years inside, I had crafted elaborate, carefully planned fantasies of how I was going to take revenge on each and every one of the people responsible for putting me behind bars. I knew exactly how Ken Anderson was going to be killed and how Sheriff Boutwell was going to go down. I knew how I was going to do away with anyone who had testified against me. I knew how I was going to get away with it.

No one knew anything of my plans. But many of my fellow prisoners had the same kinds of plans for the people who had crossed them. Plotting revenge is a common way for inmates to try to stay warm locked in a cold cell, living in a cold world.

Once someone has seen hatred or has been treated with cruelty, it is easy to respond the same way. That's what my murderous plans were really about—I wanted those people to learn firsthand how they had made me feel. I wanted them to hurt the way I had. The heat of that hate was what kept me going—at least for a while.

Inmates *had* to find ways to get through because they were not going to get out, at least not for a long time. So each of us in our own way learned to find peace in an ugly place, to find love in a dark world where no one really cared about us. We did what most lonely, loveless Americans do—we got pets.

Now, the prison rule book will tell you having a pet behind bars is a ridiculous fantasy—nothing like that would ever be allowed. The truth is that prisons are teeming with animals that give inmates comfort and love and something to nurture.

We had cats who lived inside and outside the penitentiary, who wouldn't emerge until all the lights in the cells were turned off and only the unearthly yellow glow of the security lights on the sidewalks was left.

Rangy, feral "convict" cats that would have been turned down by even the kindest shelters stalked the prison grounds, unneutered and unafraid. They would chase cockroaches and moths, dancing in the near darkness outside our cellblocks for hours. One inmate, a guy everyone called Catman, would give them food he had taken from the chow hall or purchased at the commissary. They knew him on sight and responded instantly to the sound of his voice, knowing that his presence meant sustenance. In return, they gave him something to care for, something to look out for, something to love.

One spring Catman branched out and began feeding the skunk families who roamed freely around the edges of the prison. Unfortunately for the rest of us, the skunks quickly learned that a white uniform worn by a man walking alone outside meant dinnertime. Countless inmates were accosted by baby skunks on the rec yard or when walking between buildings. The worst part was that we couldn't yell or scare them off—because they had the power to drench us in a toxic stench that would take weeks to wash off. We had to remain calm and softly explain to the beady-eyed skunklets toddling toward us with their tails held high in the air that they had mistaken us for someone else—and then we ran like hell.

One guy had a collection of live spiders in various containers in his cell. He was referred to—of course—with the eternal clarity of prison wit, as Spiderman. This inmate would appear every evening on the rec yard—not to work out but to lunge and leap, catching flies and mosquitoes to take back to his hungry eight-legged friends. Kind of a weirdo, but well intentioned, I guess.

We also had a mouse trainer in the house. True to the prison name game, he was known as Ratman. He taught the mice to respond to his calls or chirps by feeding them treats—and then selling them to other inmates who, for some reason, seemed to want semitrained rodents as cell mates. These mice would even trail their masters around the prison, or ride along in a pocket to the rec yard, where inmates would show off their little partners' abilities by getting the mice to waddle-run toward them at the first sound of their human counterparts' voices. It was as heartwarming as you might imagine.

The rest of us had to make do with the animal pals we could see through our thick glass, screened, and dirty windows.

Every spring, we would watch the birds outside make nests, with varying degrees of success. Pigeon families broke our hearts by building homes that we knew would be directly in the sun come summer. The little squabs born there didn't have a chance in the pounding Texas heat. They hatched and thrived, withered and died right in front of us. Every year, we'd see another couple of inexperienced birds try to use the same spot, and no amount of shouting or angry pounding on the windows seemed to deter them.

One time we became fans of a bird clan that had built in what we all deemed a smart, safe spot. Their babies were growing and almost at the point where they would be able to fly away on their own when a monstrous Texas thunderstorm kicked up. We sat helplessly inside, watching through heavy rain as the creatures we had seen evolve from eggs to babies to fuzzy teenage birds were beaten to death by sharp clumps of hail as big as golf balls.

The comparisons to the lives of the men inside were so obvious even the unschooled could see them. Most of the inmates had grown up with parents who built their nests in precarious places—who didn't realize, until too late, that their children simply didn't have a chance. Most of the men inside had been scorched early on by experiences from which they could never recover. They suffered from inattention and abuse, drug use and hopelessness and, sadly, simple ignorance that seemed to go all the way to their DNA. Now, they were all grown up and had no place to go except the penitentiary.

And I was in there with them—every minute of every day. I was with them in December 1988, when the district appellate court rejected all my pleas for relief.

I was still with them in September 1989, when the Court of Criminal Appeals gave me its final rebuff. I was beginning to worry that getting out might take longer than I had thought—much longer. The days and months continued to pile up. My prospects were bleak.

I worried about my son. By this point, I had been in prison almost five years. Eric was about nine years old. I was watching him grow up on the installment plan, with visits every six months. Each time he came, it was like meeting a different kid. He would be taller, or rounder, or more talkative, or less. He would be happy or as peeved as his aunt Mary Lee. He would share peeks at his life with me—or not. And nothing I could do brought him closer.

When he was very young, I could entertain him with lemon drops and questions about his cars. As he got older, he began to look around and didn't like what he saw. I could no longer convince him that the inmate with the eye patch was a pirate. He was harder to distract in the visiting room, when some families' moments together dissolved into tears or anger. He knew that nobody else's dad lived this way. He knew I was powerless to meet him anyplace else.

God knows what my in-laws had told him about me—it couldn't have been good.

I began to feel more and more diminished, more and more distant from him. I sensed that seeing me had just become a distasteful duty he was being forced to carry out. I didn't know who to feel sorriest for—him or me.

I knew that, if I didn't get out of prison, I would lose him entirely. And he was really the only thing I was living for.

My newest efforts in the federal courts were floundering. So I tried another approach. I contacted one of the handful of actual attorneys who served as staff counsel for inmates. Most people didn't know that the state paid a small cadre of lawyers to work with inmates on legal issues that came up during imprisonment. Wives abandon husbands and file for divorce, child custody fights become vicious, relatives die and their wills need to be carried out—those were the kinds of cases these attorneys addressed.

I asked the attorneys to help me file for DNA testing. I'd been reading about advances in technology that were increasingly allowing forensic identification based on blood, semen, even hair. I hoped against hope that science held some answers for me. I knew it was a long shot, but it was all I had.

It was August 1991 by the time the court finally granted my motion. The attorney who filed it for me made all the difference. He told me prison writs were rarely given serious consideration. The lawyer's bar number on my paperwork elevated it above the typical penitentiary fare. It was actually looked at, read, and ultimately, approved.

Williamson County issued a bench warrant for me, and I was soon on my way back to Georgetown, Texas, in the company of a sheriff's deputy.

My exit from the penitentiary summed up everything anyone ever needs to know about the Texas Department of Corrections. They bid me adieu by giving me a set of *lovely* free-world clothes— electric blue parachute pants and a too-small T-shirt with hearts and flowers on the front, surrounding fancy script spelling out FRIENDS ARE FOREVER.

I must have cut a dashing figure as I was marched out the front gate, which was an odd experience in itself. Walking out was something I had dreamed of for years. Of course, in my imaginings I was never dressed as I was that day—like an oversize eight-year-old girl who needed a shave.

We sped off to the Harris County Jail in Houston to pick up another prisoner. To my surprise, the inmate turned out to be a woman, wanted for writing hot checks. As an added bonus, she appeared to be terribly sick—she was staggering and weaving on the way to the car like a Saturday night drunk. Of course, for security reasons, I was handcuffed to her. I feared she was going to pass out, fall to the ground, and drag me down with her. Fortunately, the cop decided to let her lie down in the backseat, while I sat in front.

We stopped in the middle of nowhere to grab lunch, and I experienced something I'd heard other inmates talk about but had never actually felt—sensory overload, overstimulation, too much, too soon. Call it what you will. There, in the middle of the restaurant, looking at the massive menu board, I simply couldn't make sense of it. The writing was too colorful, there was too much conversation and clanging going on at the tables, there were too many choices available. There was music playing. Everyone was happy. I felt overwhelmed, weak in the knees, lost.

The cop helped me order—chicken tacos and an iced tea. I didn't cry when I bit into the first taco, but I must have moaned with pleasure, because the woman I was handcuffed to passed me a few of her steak fingers out of pity.

It was the first real food—the first meal cooked well enough that people would actually *pay* for it—that I had tasted in years. I was in home-cooking heaven at being reintroduced to some of the powerful flavors and freshness I'd been missing out on.

Back in Williamson County, I was pleased to see there was a new jail. I was alone in a cell, and it was spacious compared to what I lived in back "home" at the Wynne Unit. It was also air-conditioned, almost too cool. I feared I would catch pneumonia. The food there wasn't bad either.

The company, however, was. I was locked up with inmates who watched nothing but wrestling or cartoons. There was a coup under way in the Soviet Union, but no one except me cared. I almost got into a fight when I tried to explain to the hostile and uninterested throng the relevance of what was happening on the other side of the world.

My blood was drawn early in my stay. Then all I could do was wait—and wait—and wait—for the results. Still, it took weeks for me to get back to Wynne, even longer before I was back on my job with the Typing Pool. I learned later that the woman who supervised me at work had actually called the Williamson County Jail and told the sheriff's department that she needed me on the job and wanted me back immediately. It was nice to be wanted—even by a prison supervisor.

I felt optimistic that finally I might be on the way to getting this terrible mess worked out. Maybe I would be home with Eric sooner than I thought. Maybe I could pick up life where I'd left off.

I had no idea how long it would take or how much more I would lose before I would finally walk out of prison—before I would finally be free.

CHAPTER SEVENTEEN

THE GUARD SHOUTED OUT MY NAME FROM THE DAYROOM.

I had mail!

I leapt out of my bunk like I'd been shot from a cannon. I had only a few minutes to catch my TDC "mailman" before he moved on to another inmate eager to be remembered by the U.S. Postal Service.

For a man in prison, getting mail is like having daylight shipped in. An envelope with an inmate's name on it illuminates, at least briefly, a dark and limited world. Even junk mail takes on magnified importance. It's more than just a break from the everyday. To those on the inside, mail is a reminder that they are still alive—tangible proof that someone out there in the free world knows we exist. I loved getting news from home or reviews from a magazine or book editor who'd been reading my work. Sometimes, a sainted friend would send me a new book that would keep me busy for a few nights.

When the guard bellowed my name for mail call, there was even the outside possibility I would finally get some word on the DNA testing I'd been waiting months and years for. I jogged to the guard in time and got handed a small envelope. I recognized the handwriting on the outside instantly. It couldn't have been more familiar.

The letter was from Eric.

I held it tightly as I made my way back to my bunk. I sat down and turned it over and over in my hands. I looked around to make sure I was semialone. Inmates never opened important mail in front of anyone else.

I wanted to absorb the news without anybody around—because I knew it might be bad. Prisoners are accustomed to getting dumped, denied legal appeals, and disappointed through the mail. We'd learned to take the bad news by ourselves, so we'd have time to paste on our faces the necessary expression of indifference. None of us wanted other inmates to see us cry or give up or waver—even momentarily.

I liked believing that Eric had written me during my incarceration, even though I knew he hadn't done it on his own initiative. Over the years he'd signed a birthday card, or scrawled his name at the bottom of a letter my mother sent. Most of the mail I got from him had my parents' home as a return address. I knew they encouraged him to write when he stayed with them. This note, however, had been sent from the home he shared with his aunt Mary Lee.

I took this development as a good sign. He was fifteen, after all— maybe it was a sign of growing up. Maybe he had finally chosen to reach out to me on his own.

I opened it carefully and began reading. The youthful imperfections of his penmanship could not soften the hostility of his message. Eric wrote that he didn't want to see me anymore—he didn't want to make the twice-yearly visit to the prison to talk with someone he barely knew. He didn't want to wait through the complicated prison check-in or check-out process, and he didn't want to sit for hours in the visiting room—surrounded by ne'er-do-wells and the needy, loud, messy families who clamored to see them.

I knew our visits had begun to feel like an annoyance, a duty he couldn't get out of. And I certainly knew my former in-laws didn't appreciate Eric's continuing connection with me. My parents and siblings were undoubtedly the only people in his life who wanted him to keep making the trek to Huntsville.

Still, Eric's letter stung—it was like a knife slashing at the meager measure of pride I had left—it cracked my brittle belief in my own future. His rejection of me mocked the glimmer of optimism I had so carefully nurtured—that someday, somehow, something decent would come out of this nightmare.

Frankly, Eric was all I had left. He was really all I was living for—the only remnant of my life with Chris. In the past decade, I'd lost too many pieces of myself—my freedom, time with my family, the company of my friends. But I had always been able to tell myself I still had my son, even if everything else was gone. And now, so was he.

I crumpled onto the bunk and just lay there, clenching and unclenching my fists, feeling hot tears forming and then falling, clutching the letter to my chest as if I were trying to squeeze all the hurt out of it—as if I could change its message by crushing the paper it was written on.

Then I did what I always did when things got too tough. I thought back to Chris and the way she calmed me, the way she could make everything better. I thought back on the difficult things we had gone through together. I thought back to the years before Eric was born, to the time when Chris and I had lost a child.

We'd just begun trying to get pregnant, and for us, conception happened quickly and easily. We took it as a sign that it was meant to be. Chris felt good and looked beautiful. We'd already chosen names—Nicole for a girl and Eric for a boy. She liked me to come along for her regular checkups, sonograms, and talks with the doctor. And I loved being able to see our baby growing and know that, with every visit, we were getting closer to the moment when we could all say hello in person.

We went in for a standard checkup one day. Chris stretched out on the examining table and bared her tummy. It was big and round and taut—she was close to twenty-two weeks along.

The technician smeared the now-familiar goop on Chris's belly and began running the sonogram wand back and forth. She was trying to find our baby's heartbeat. She moved the device lower and then higher, and then off to either side. She didn't say anything was wrong; she simply said there might be a problem with the equipment—she would get the doctor to help her. Still, there was something unnerving about her demeanor—about the way she left the room so quietly, without smiling, without any laughter or words of reassurance.

Chris and I waited in stony silence—frozen silence. We didn't breathe a word to each other about our growing sense of panic. It was as though we could keep bad things from happening by refusing to speak of them.

Finally, the doctor came in, exchanged pleasantries, sat down, and took over the procedure himself. He pushed the device back and forth and around and then back again—searching for something that wasn't there. After a long, terrible silence, he lifted the apparatus off her stomach, laid it on the table, and said flatly what we had dreaded most.

"I am so sorry. There is no heartbeat. I'm afraid your baby has died."

It was as if the floor had fallen out of the room. Chris was shattered. I was lost. It seemed impossible. We'd been walking on air when we came into the office. We left in mourning.

The doctor made arrangements to have our baby "delivered" the following Monday—leaving us with a lost weekend that seemed to stretch on forever.

Chris did not want to be around family or friends. She felt too fragile to handle breaking the news or answering endless questions. She told me she just wanted to go away. We decided we would drive down to San Antonio and just be alone—together. We wanted to absorb the loss privately. So in one of the sunniest, happiest cities we knew, we spent the weekend in darkness. It was as if there had been an eclipse in our lives. We roamed through stores and never bought anything, went out to dinner and didn't eat, stopped for a drink and stared in silence at the table.

Each of us braced in our own way for Monday. I knew it was going to be terribly hard on Chris and there was really very little I could do for her. It was difficult to know what to say—or what not to say. I just stayed close and prepared for the worst day we'd ever had together.

Monday morning at the hospital, we were assigned a room in the obstetrics wing, a brightly decorated area that seemed filled with flowers and balloons. There were doting grandparents around every corner, dads handing out pink- or blue-banded cigars, and proud, tired mothers being wheeled out carrying carefully wrapped infants—everything we had hoped would happen for us.

I was with Chris as she was given sedatives and labor was induced. In the quiet room and the low light, amid a sea of tears, our beautiful, lost little girl emerged. She was weeks too early, but far too late to be saved.

The doctor let me see and touch her tiny, still body. In another room, I stood beside her for a long while, taking in her almost eerie perfection. She had Chris's thick dark hair and beautiful skin. Her petite hands were flawless and graceful. Her little feet fit into my palm. In that moment, she became real to me—in the way she had been for a long time to Chris. A father never has the instant intimacy of pregnancy that a mother does. I hadn't felt our little girl kick or sensed her growing, talked to her at night or embraced her with my entire body, the way Chris had. But now I felt as if I knew our little girl—I knew who we had lost.

The doctor pointed out a place near her tiny abdomen where the umbilical cord had twisted into a tight little knot. Her lifeline—her connection to Chris—had been choked off.

Chris mourned Nicole profoundly. She quit her job and began working in a small office where she didn't know anyone. She didn't want to be around people for what felt like a long time, a real change for someone as outgoing and exuberant as Chris. She blamed herself. She blamed her body. Chris simply could not accept that as her little girl was dying inside of her, she had felt nothing, had suspected nothing, and had done nothing.

Chris didn't know she was losing Nicole until she was gone. Now that had happened to me with our other child—Eric was gone, too.

For once, prison routine gave me comfort. Nothing had changed in my life on a daily basis—and work, college classes, and the brutish, tragicomic carnival always under way around me gave me a place to hide the emotional turmoil I felt.

There were moments inside when I flashed back on everything I had lost—moments when a sound or a scent or a muscle memory would remind me of the life I used to have. The smallest things could take me back.

Once, lying on my bunk listening to the hissing *tsssts-tsssts-tsssts* of the prison sprinkler system spitting water on the newly cut grass, I closed my eyes and was transported to my old backyard. I could feel the familiar lawn chair I used to sit in on our deck and smell the neighbors' grill heating up next door. If I reached down, I felt certain there would be a cold bottle of beer waiting there, sweating in the heat the way I was. To my right, I saw a flash of movement from inside the house—Chris was walking past the glass doors of our bedroom. She had gone in to change. I watched as she removed her blouse and let it fall to the floor. She looked up, saw me, and gave me a delightfully wicked smile—then faded away.

I missed her. I missed the man I used to be. I missed our son.

I missed my life.

The courts were certainly giving me no relief. My petitions to the federal courts went nowhere. I felt like a drowning man who finally caught the eye of the lifeguard—and he looked straight at me and then turned away.

Every time I lost a round, I had to go through the ritual of breaking it to my parents. I had to watch them gulp and grow quiet and absorb the latest bad news. I knew how much it hurt them, how high their hopes would be with every court argument—only to have me, once again, throw a big bucket of ice-cold legal reality on them.

My appeals journey taught me that it is perfectly legal to imprison a man for a crime he didn't commit. As long as every *i* was dotted and *t* crossed, no higher court could—or would—intervene, particularly in Texas. I had to find another way out. I believed new technology was my best hope.

There had to be some evidence somewhere that would help me.

During the 1994 O. J. Simpson trial—"must-see TV" in the prison community—I watched as a young defense lawyer named Barry Scheck explained DNA, and how it could affect investigations, with more clarity than anyone I'd ever heard. I knew that Scheck had started a group called the Innocence Project to work on cases of people in prison who were actually innocent. Unbeknownst to me, one of my attorneys at trial, Bill Allison, was a friend of Barry Scheck. Bill told me he had contacted Barry on my behalf. I was elated. But I had no illusions about anything happening quickly. For me, getting help from the Innocence Project became my birthday wish, my Christmas hope, my bedtime prayer—the Holy Grail of good luck.

It was part of how I survived. Getting through the day is easier if you believe help is on the way. I chose to believe. That belief that someday, everything would be okay again kept me going when inmates on my unit killed themselves because they couldn't take life inside anymore. Or when a guard committed suicide in the tower where he stood watch over us. Or when another inmate cleanly sliced off his penis while he was alone in his cell—suffering from untreated mental illness, untrained observation, and uncaring staff.

That hope that I would someday be free kept me standing tall when a tour group came through and I locked eyes with a visitor, hoping to communicate to her that not all the men in here were awful—that we were human beings. She visibly recoiled at the dirty intrusion of my gaze.

That hope kept me going when I saw one of the inmates who

lived close to my "house" get set free because he was innocent. He had been railroaded when the police hid vital evidence in his case. When his attorneys gathered documented evidence, he was handed the proverbial Get Out of Jail Free card. What I hated was how I felt about his release—jealous, resentful, and angry. I had been inside longer than he had. I deserved to leave, too.

At the Wynne Unit, I saw elderly prisoners brutalized by guards and, sometimes, by other inmates. I saw men die of easily treatable illnesses. I saw them treat themselves because they were afraid—or too stubborn—to go to the infirmary. One man I knew used fingernail clippers to remove the wounded tip of his tongue. Another finally had to be dragged to the doctor for a toe amputation—he had waited too long and gangrene was beginning to spread up his leg.

I prayed for my continued health.

And I took advantage of anything good the prison system had to offer. Beginning with my education.

I finally got my degree in psychology—a mere twenty-three years after leaving high school. Chris would have been proud of me. We had both gone through a couple of years of college and taken jobs when we learned we couldn't transfer our credit hours to the University of Texas. We were already living in Austin and figured we could work for a short while, then take turns going to school. We both had hoped to graduate. I would never have dreamed of the circumstances under which I would get my degree.

Of course, my actual college graduation ceremony was a typically troubled Texas prison system production. Everyone graduating from anything was brought together in our non-air-conditioned chow hall, where we could sip punch, eat cookies, and sweat with our lucky invited guests.

The state hired a motivational speaker to stroke grads' egos, telling some of the least disciplined people in the world that "if you would only put your minds to it, you can be anything you want to be."

Of course, many of them had already achieved that goal. They had wanted to grow up to be tough guys—and here they were. Some inmates simply didn't have a chance. Some took every opportunity to make the wrong decision. Some couldn't help themselves. Some didn't know any other kind of life was even an option.

Guys who had struggled to get GEDs made up the largest group of graduates. Some of them had gone through the program two or three times. And these men typically weren't getting a high school diploma as part of a newfound ache for education. The TDC mandated a GED as a condition for parole. Everyone wanted parole—even if it meant they would be forced to learn to read and do basic math. "Class time" also kept the "students" from having to go to work at a prison job.

The GED students and their guests were the rowdiest part of the graduation group—and the reason we had extra guards on hand. There were also students getting degrees from junior colleges; often they were the cream of the GED crop. Most of them, having already performed at peak educational capacity in their extended families, would now retire from scholastic competition.

Those of us getting bachelor's degrees felt a little like an afterthought. But I had loved the classes, the instructors, and the atmosphere. School was a haven of sanity and reason in the heart of a madhouse. It had helped me survive psychologically. And I wanted more.

Now I had my eye on graduate school—something that would require more of me than all my previous classwork put together. I knew I could handle the academic work. The problem was that, as always in the Texas prison system, everything good came with a heaping helping of bad. Going to the University of Houston graduate school required moving off the Wynne Unit and onto Ramsey I, a facility about a hundred miles away. The unit was built in 1908 on land that had once made up five old plantations. The state had taken over the farming, with inmates doing the field work.

I would have to do hard labor in high heat and humidity, under an unforgiving sun.

With inmates half my age.

Every day.

I began training hard to make sure I was up to the task. Lifting weights, jogging, even spending increasing time in the sun so I wouldn't get dangerously burned when I hit the fields. It was the only way for me to get a master's in literature—and I wanted it badly. I knew it would help me when I finally walked out of this nightmare.

I had been behind bars for more than eleven years. I had lost everything. Even my son had told me he never wanted to see me again.

It was time for a change.

I met with Eric one more time before I left the Wynne Unit. I had written him, asking for one more visit. I told him he didn't have to come to see me if he didn't want to. But that if he wanted to cut off contact with me, he had to tell me to my face.

And that's what he did—sort of.

Eric and Mary Lee came for their next scheduled visit. I walked into the visiting room not knowing what to expect. I sat down and looked at Eric, sitting there next to Chris's sister with his head down, a nervous fifteen-year-old boy. He was withdrawn and unhappy and uncomfortable.

Join the club.

We exchanged greetings. Looking right at Eric, I asked him if this would be our last visit. "Yes," he whispered, still not looking at me. I told him if he ever changed his mind, I wasn't hard to find.

At that moment, I was profoundly hurt—deeply, deeply wounded—and I reacted the way men sometimes do when their emotions are overwhelming.

I got mad. In prison, it was safer to be angry.

I stood up and told Mary Lee to take care of my son—and I walked out. The visit had lasted only a few minutes. My hot anger didn't last long either.

But the hurt went on.

In the years ahead, I would send Eric cards on holidays and

birthdays or special occasions in his life. He never wrote back, nor did I expect him to. It was like writing to Santa Claus—he was almost an imaginary figure. He was someone my family saw, someone I knew was out there somewhere—growing up, growing older, and growing further and further out of my reach.

I told myself things would change when I got out, when I was proved innocent, when everyone knew this was nothing more than a terrible, terrible mistake. What I wouldn't admit to myself was that some of what had happened to my relationship with Eric was irreparable. The tear had been too traumatic, the years of bad information and bad advice and bad feelings had left ugly wounds and deep bruises—on both of us.

All I knew was that I would always love him—that he would always be the living embodiment of a marriage that ended too soon and a mother who should still be here. Eric would always be part of a small, shattered family that didn't deserve any of what fate had handed out. And he would always be my son.

I hoped that, someday, I would get the chance to be his father.

CHAPTER EIGHTEEN

I EMBARKED ON MY NEW LIFE BEFORE THE SUN WAS UP.
The guard had come to my cell without warning, as is typical with inmate moves. TDC didn't want anyone to be able to plan any kind of shenanigans. It was pitch-black when I walked out of the Wynne Unit for the last time in the early morning hours of Halloween Day 1999. I left as I had arrived, in the dark.

The guards began handcuffing prisoners together in pairs, but when they got to me, there was no one left to handcuff me to. I was handcuffed, but I felt a weird sort of freedom not being shackled onto someone else. In the world of a prisoner, incremental, relative freedom is often all there is.

We got on a bus loaded with other men cuffed or chained together—some from other units, some going to other destinations—and off we went to the Ramsey I Unit, a hulking old monstrosity south of Houston.

It was my first look at the free world in years, since I had tasted those chicken tacos on the way back to Williamson County to begin my fight for DNA testing. I felt like a blind man who suddenly had his sight restored. As we sped along the freeway deep into the city's massive sprawl, I stayed glued to the bus window. The color and novelty of the shopping centers, car lots, fast-food chains, and gas stations mesmerized me. It was so early in the morning that there were very few people up and about, but the sides of the interstate were packed with a riot of new development.

As we drove through the endless stretch of what passed for progress, I was surprised at how quickly the color and flash, the big and the brand-new grew old. Strip malls were thrown together with no forethought, fast-food joints had all the beauty and textured history of plastic silverware, and the many lots selling house trailers and used cars ultimately made me sad.

The gaudiness and never-ending concrete had me longing for the rural greenery I had been looking out at for so long. Luckily for my scenery sensibilities, it turned out I was headed right back into the middle of nowhere—only this time it was muggier, buggier, and in many ways, a step back in time.

Ramsey I sits in the heart of miles of farmland, some of it cultivated, some of it given over to the various creatures of the South Texas ecosystem—a humid, almost tropical place filled with head-high grass, angry fire ants, giant mosquitoes, and snakes of all descriptions, plus the occasional alligator. These critters became as much a part of my life as the inmates I would be living with. That's because all of us—men and beasts, bugs and swampy bush—were going to spend a lot of time together.

My first day in the fields was instructive. We were up at the crack of dawn, piled onto wagons, and driven to what felt like the edge of the world, finally stopping at a series of very long, very deep drainage ditches. The banks were steep, muddy, and slippery—and home to the tallest weeds I'd ever seen, a small forest of greenery, taller than the men in my squad. Just maintaining a footing was tough. Our job was to scrape off the thicket of tangled, tall grass and brambles, leaving behind only bare earth.

It seemed almost doable, if not necessarily survivable. Every single creature we encountered bit or stung or was eager to fill a person with poison. Sometimes, they could do all three.

I made a good impression with my squad when I killed the first snake after lunch—a writhing water moccasin four feet long. I cut its head off with my "aggie," a medieval-looking hand tool used to cultivate the land when it wasn't serving as a way to kill the field vermin we confronted every day.

The work was harder than I had dreamed possible. At the end of the day, I felt as though I'd just done ten hours of aerobics while carrying weights. I'd never known such exhaustion. At times, I thought I wouldn't make it. I sweat so much that my clothing couldn't have been more soaked if I'd jumped in a swimming pool.

The heat, the humidity, and the crushingly hard physical work were the price I was paying to get a graduate degree. I just had to survive in the fields long enough to be selected for another job—preferably something inside and air-conditioned. I was trying my best.

There were some elements to life on Ramsey I that I liked. The food was better—then again, maybe I was just so spent by the time we ate that it simply *seemed* better. Because the building was so old, it could not be retrofitted with the new, legally required dayroom where inmates could gather to watch TV. So each cell had its own little black-and-white TV—a flickering, fuzzy link to freedom. Finally, I could watch all the PBS and National Geographic I wanted, without having to fight the mob that insisted on tuning in to reruns of shows that were awful the first time they aired.

I entertained myself by watching as much of the Clinton impeachment proceedings as possible—a story with more twists than any soap opera would dare attempt. When Robert Livingston, the blink-and-you'd-miss-him Speaker of the House, resigned his position after his own dalliances became public, I was left roaring with disbelief on my bunk.

I had always been a fan of newscasts and following world events. Now I had nothing but time to indulge my interests—and my own TV! Kosovo, Columbine, the theater of presidential politics—every hiccup on the world stage became a kind of background music for my incarceration.

I joined a Sunday morning talk group with a handful of other

inmates, specifically to discuss world affairs. Our circle of penitentiary pundits was made up of bright men who had done dark
things—sexual indecency with a child, aggravated assault, break-ins,
armed robbery, murder—you name it. I learned in prison that these
charges and crimes represent only one aspect, one element of an
inmate's life. But sometimes, that criminality is a powerful urge they
cannot overcome, that will be played out again the first moment
they get a chance. Sometimes, though, a crime was simply a one-off,
a lapse due to drugs or alcohol.

Our prison Meet the Press was a welcome diversion, a chance
to talk about something other than field work or horseflies, professional sports or who was going to "whack" whom.

My graduate classes in literature got under way a few months
after I arrived and I was happy as a clam. I had someone new to
speak with about what I'd been reading, someone to help me with
my writing, and a new distraction to take away my prison blues.

One of my professors, Elizabeth Fields, insisted on a great deal
of creative writing from her students. After only a few weeks, I could
see a difference in my work. She taught me to add personal and telling details to my remembrances—the squeak of the boss's saddle as
he rode his horse closer to check on our work, the all but audible
difference we felt when the shadow of a big cloud passed over the
squad and the temperature seemed to drop ten or fifteen degrees.
And of course, the Pavlovian response I experienced whenever I
heard the tractor drawing close. I knew the tractor pulled the water
wagon, and I knew I would get some, and I physically responded to
it with each rev of the engine as it bumped its way across the uneven
ground toward my squad of parched workers.

Reading classic and contemporary literature and learning how
to analyze it helped me "see" my own life—and my own limited
world—differently.

The inherent cruelty and occasional beauty of working in the
prison's fields was striking. One morning, as my squad sat on the
wagons headed for a day of God-knew-what, one of the guys called

out, "Damn! Am I having a flashback or what?" He pointed to the sky. Not fifty feet above us was a flock of perfectly neon-pink flamingos. We watched in silence, gape-mouthed at the tragic and ridiculous contrast in our lives.

I remember returning to the fields once after a few days of rain, when the weather was not too hot and the work was not too hard. I knelt on the ground, moving along—weeding or something—and the smell of the earth was wonderfully overpowering. Compared to the ever-present bouquet of disinfectants, human waste, fear, and bad food that filled each prison building, the dirt seemed to be real and right and a place where people belonged.

On that day, the near silence, the soft soil, and the breeze were a balm.

Nature, of course, was not always so kind. A few days after our fabulous flamingo sighting, we suffered one of our worst critter attacks. While chopping weeds that were higher than the tallest man in my squad, someone disturbed a hive of ground-dwelling bumblebee-like creatures. The enraged hive roared up and out of the ground with such fury that they looked like a huge black snake shooting out of a hole and high into the air. I stayed low enough to the ground that I did not get attacked. Most of the others were not so lucky. The field was alive with yelps of pain, men leaping and running, swatting anything that moved. A friend of mine got stung six times on the side of the head and ended up in the infirmary.

Our boss, who watched us every day from his lofty position on horseback, had seen this sort of thing before. He and his steed stood calmly off to the side, watching the shrieking, slapping, and running. He gave us time to calm down and share with each other our stories of trauma and injury. He made sure none of us went into allergic shock. Mostly, though, he and the guards who always sat on horseback ringing the perimeter made sure no inmate used the madness of the moment to slip out of sight.

Their guns weren't for show.

I had also seen the guards behave less than kindly.

Not long after I started in the fields, I saw a man collapse and appear to pass out from heat and exhaustion. I knew how he felt. Some of the men moved toward him, but one of the bosses waved them away. After handing his pistol to another guard also on horseback, he dismounted and walked over to the rag doll figure. He grabbed him up by the collar and dragged the inmate's limp body to a nearby fire ant bed. He let go, watching as the man's face hit the bed of vicious fire ants, which promptly started stinging him ferociously. Immediately, the inmate yelled with pain, leapt up, and began brushing off the stinging insects—a clear indication he had feigned the collapse.

That was how the guards separated the fakers from the fainters. If the inmate woke up, he would be immediately put back to work. If he lay there, being bitten by hundreds of the world's angriest ants, he would get to go to the prison infirmary—disfigured but forgiven.

I wanted out of there. So I began shopping for new jobs everywhere inside the prison, going from job site to job site, trying to cajole, charm, check on openings, make myself seem like a good hire. It was like looking for work in the free world—only much more desperate. I wasn't sure I could survive more field time. And I was so physically spent at the end of the day that I wasn't at my best with my schoolwork or reading.

Finally, I was told I would be going to the commissary to work "soon." Some guys in my squad took to calling me Mr. Last Day because I believed every day was going to be my last on the job.

Finally, mercifully, I was called inside one day at noon and told to report to the commissary. This was it.

That morning, we'd been on hands and knees, gathering potatoes from the freshly plowed ground. I stood there sweaty and filthy when they opened the commissary door after I knocked. The instant I stepped inside, everyone took an involuntary step backward. I was dirty, and I reeked of hard labor. The commissary supervisor winced and ordered me to the showers.

From now on, I was going to be able to stay clean. I was going to be working in a more civilized, clean, and air-conditioned section of the prison. I had made it. Once again, I'd survived.

That night, I celebrated alone in my cell with two pints of Blue Bell ice cream and the growing sense that I might make it out of this hellhole intact after all.

Just as my life inside began to make sense, the free world seemed to jump the tracks. I had been in prison more than fourteen years and would spend more than another decade inside. It was a typical day on the job at the commissary the morning of September 11, 2001, and I had stepped outside with another man to unload an eighteen-wheeler full of products for prisoners. As we were heaving boxes back and forth, somebody walked by and asked us if we had heard about the Twin Towers. He flatly stated, "They've fallen over." Both of us brushed off his comment, considering it implausible. But even in our locked-down world, news began to bleed through about what had happened. Most of it came by word of mouth. We didn't have a TV or a radio in the commissary.

It happened on one of my short workdays and I was back in my cell by afternoon, to watch TV and try to figure out what was going on. Like the rest of the country, I was transfixed. It felt—as it did for so many in my generation—like the day Kennedy was shot. There was a forbidding sense that *anything* could happen now.

Of course, this being prison, there was always some twist that made everything worse. On this day, of all days, the running water on the cellblock was suddenly gone. Stuck in my cell with a tiny TV as my only window on the world—surrounded by the mounting smell of human waste—I heard the growing drumbeats of war, I saw the fear and confusion among Americans, and for the first time in my adult life, I felt part of a vulnerable nation.

For once, I actually felt physically safer inside.

The world had gone *crazy* outside the walls. But everyone I loved was out there. I worried about eighteen-year-old Eric and the possibility that this attack would lead to a draft and he would be sent off to fight in some unfamiliar corner of the world. I worried about my parents and my inability to help them. I worried about my siblings and their families.

I worried about my country—the country that had locked me away despite my innocence was still the country I loved.

Inside, everything got back to normal—or what passed for normal.

Every now and then, a mentally ill inmate would blow up or break down. In the chow hall one day, a man already known as "mental" (he had been caught drinking out of the toilet in the education building) had a full-blown "freak-out." He stood up from his table, poured a pitcher of punch all over himself, stormed outside, stripped naked, climbed the fence, and threw himself into the razor wire at the top.

The entire episode was witnessed by one of the inspector-enforcer types sent from Huntsville to make sure our unit was up to snuff. The sad part was that even though he'd seen how bad it was here, nothing would be done to provide decent mental health care to prisoners. Instead, the imperative became to keep the inspectors from ever seeing that kind of thing.

The beat went on.

I got results from some of my DNA testing—not bad, but not what I had hoped for. The testing of the semen stain on the bed showed what could be found in a lot of married couples' beds— evidence that the man and woman who slept there had had sex. It wasn't enough to spring me, but it did destroy the baseless and perverted theory prosecutor Ken Anderson had described in filthy detail to the jury—that I had masturbated over Chris's dead body, using her dead hand. What kind of person could even think up something like that?

I was deep into my graduate work, studying the literature of early Western civilization—an era and a sensibility that couldn't have been further removed from the setting I lived in. But studying another place, another time, another world gave me a sense of freedom I found nowhere else in prison.

For me, the last measure of freedom was found inside my head. It was my last hiding place, my last means of escape.

I would need it. My life was about to change more dramatically than it ever had—in a number of ways.

CHAPTER NINETEEN

FOR THE FIRST TIME SINCE MY CONVICTION, I FINALLY HAD EVIDENCE the cavalry was riding to my rescue.

One morning in July 2002, I was summoned to the captain's office to take a phone call. When an inmate gets a call—which is rare—the guards never give a heads-up about the topic or who's on the line. So the long walk to the office can be an exercise in terror—a panicked listing in one's head of who might be sick or dead or what might have gone wrong.

Once there, I found out I actually had good news—there were three women from the Innocence Project on the line. They told me they were going to be filing an all-inclusive writ in my case sometime in the next few weeks.

I felt like I was high on some kind of new happy drug. Maybe I was just drunk on the only good news I'd had in years. But there was something else about the call that made me giddy, which had nothing to do with my legal case and everything to do with my long isolation. I had actually had the chance to speak with three intelligent, educated, polite, *compassionate* women. They chatted and laughed and were friendly and asked questions. They did not yell at me or issue orders or speak coarsely. It was embarrassing for me to realize, in that moment, how deprived of normal conversation—normal human contact—I had been.

I floated back to my cell—high on life—for the first time in fifteen years.

It wouldn't be long before I hit bottom.

It was spring, a time for new beginnings, new growth, and high school graduation. This year Eric was getting his diploma from the private Jesuit prep school he attended. I had been looking for the announcement for some time. Finally, on one day's mail call, I got the fancy envelope. I carefully opened it, determined to preserve it in all its pristine beauty.

I read through it.

Something was terribly wrong.

Eric's name had been changed. He was listed as Eric John Olson, not Eric Morton. I knew what had happened. Chris's sister Mary Lee and her husband had legally adopted him and he had taken their name. Since Eric was over eighteen years old and had obviously gone along with this, there was nothing I could do. There was no requirement that I even be notified.

It was done.

I thought back to the beginning of Eric's life, when Chris had wanted to name him Michael Wayne Morton, Jr., and I had argued against it. I'd known enough "Juniors" who hadn't been thrilled with their monikers. I didn't want my son ever to resent being burdened with his father's name. We compromised by naming him Eric Michael Morton.

After my conviction, the court had decided to give our little boy to Chris's sister, even though my sister and her family had desperately wanted to take him, even though my mother and father had hoped against hope he could live with them.

And nature took its course. He grew up hearing the worst about me.

As time went on, the get-togethers between Eric and my family grew fewer and farther between. Then whenever a visit was *finally* coming up, it seemed that there would be some last-minute demand on Eric's time—Mary Lee had "forgotten" about a long-planned trip to the West Coast—or Eric's summer camp "unfortunately" co-incided with the promised trek to see my family. There were apologies and promises to try again, but in the end, it all worked out the way I feared most.

Eric's aunt was now his mother. His uncle was his father. His cousin was his brother. I was nothing more than a bad memory—a dangerous, misguided man who lived far away, locked up and locked out. I was unaware of Eric's life, out of every loop, deemed undeserving of the most basic inclusion.

This news left me absolutely broken. My long-hoped-for life after vindication and release was gone—irretrievably gone.

I hit rock bottom.

And I went down angrily blaming everyone and everything: fate, my sister-in-law, Chris's entire family, my family, *myself*, the legal system, the universe—you name it.

When Father's Day followed a week or so after I learned of the adoption, it ripped me open again. It felt as if my guts had been yanked out and all I could do was stare at them on the ground before me—a helpless, mortally wounded fool.

I WOKE UP EARLY EVERY SUNDAY MORNING WHEN I WAS A YOUNGSTER, because I had someplace I needed to be.

Carefully, I would put on my dressiest clothes—a gleaming white short-sleeved shirt, my good pants, and my best shoes. I'd brush my teeth, slick my hair down with water, look in the mirror, and add that last sartorial touch every twelve-year-old boy in the 1960s needed—a clip-on tie.

We went to church almost every week, and I enjoyed the ritual and semiformality of it. My mom would put on her Sunday best—hose and heels, maybe a string of pearls, always a pretty dress. My younger sister would get all gussied up, too, and we'd all step out of our home, shiny and polished, and head for the First Baptist Church of Bakersfield, California.

We weren't living in Texas at the time, but the state and its Baptist traditions were still very much part of our lives.

In Sunday School, the children learned Bible stories, and in the church service, we all learned how to apply those traditional lessons to our lives. There were no deep theological discussions, no complex academic searches for underlying messages or comparative religious theory. There was only right and wrong, heaven and hell, walking with God or walking off a cliff.

The choice was easy. I knew which path I wanted to follow.

One of those Sunday mornings, amid the music and the prayer, I felt the unique longing to make my allegiance to Christ public. I couldn't explain why, but I felt it. The minister had called for those who were ready to accept Jesus to come to the altar.

I had sat there uninspired through these kinds of outreaches many times before, but on this day I felt different. I felt called—driven—determined in some way to go up front. I felt profoundly pulled to accept the prayers of the adults and the promise of eternal life.

There were tears.

My mother was proud.

I felt cleansed and whole and included.

It all felt so right.

But years later, about the time I turned seventeen, like many young men, I rebelled against religion, against conformity, against the comforts faith had once given me.

A teenage friend had teased me when we were talking about something naughty—probably sex or beer, the two main temptations faced by teenage boys back in the day. He told me I couldn't possibly know what I was talking about since I was a good church-going type.

At that moment, in the stranglehold of peer pressure and with all the "wisdom" acquired in my short life, I decided that I would spend the coming summer "off the leash." I would walk on over to the wild side and dabble in the things mothers dreaded—the acts my church warned against and the practices my faith frowned upon. I reasoned that I'd come back and pick up where I left off—wiser, more experienced, a "man of the world."

Thirty years later, I had not yet come back. And now, I was sitting in prison. Finally, for the first time in decades, I began to think about the role of God in my life.

When Chris was killed, people told me they were praying for me. I took no comfort in that. I didn't even know what it meant—and I was in no place to try to figure it out.

I was too stunned, too rocked back on my heels at the low blow life had dealt Eric and me. I was simply trying to process losing Chris, trying to participate in the investigation, trying to keep my head above the dark, swirling water that was washing me away.

When I was wrongly convicted, I grew angry at everything and everyone. I was enraged that fate had compounded the cruelty of Chris's murder by taking my life as well. In prison, that anger may have actually helped me. My rage kept me strong; it kept me from looking back. My righteous anger protected me and comforted me and shielded me from my awful surroundings; it kept me hard and cynical about what had become of the man—or the little boy—I used to be.

My anger kept me from looking deeper.

I was certainly familiar with—and disdainful of—jailhouse conversions. The running joke was that these guys left their Bibles behind when they walked out the door. I felt the same way about inmates who talked about profound conversions that always seemed to conveniently happen just in time for their parole hearings. To me, it seemed like bargaining with God—finding faith only when you wanted something, only *because* you wanted something.

I had never done that.

I had never prayed for help when Chris was killed, or when Eric had his dangerous but lifesaving surgery. I had never prayed to be found innocent—even when my liberty hung on the outcome of a court decision or a DNA test. I had never promised to live a better life if God would only take care of some of the rather large blocks on my road to a more comfortable existence.

But I did struggle mightily with all the bad turns my life had taken.

When Eric decided he didn't want to see me anymore, the blow was so profound that I felt it *physically*. When he changed his name from mine to that of a man I didn't even know, when Eric so completely moved on, I felt the blow emotionally, psychologically—and ultimately—spiritually.

Suddenly, the only anchor I had was gone. Eric was the only safe place I'd had left. He had been the receptacle of all my hopes and dreams. He was the light at the end of the tunnel.

He was my idol, my religion—my reason for living. I believed in *him*. He was everything. He was the only thing.

And he had vanished.

I felt so bad, so hopeless and so defeated and so broken, that I did something completely out of character for me.

I cried out to God.

I begged for a sign, for a reason to go on, for a way out of my abyss and my pain—for some deliverance, some reassurance, some relief.

Something.

Anything.

I got nothing.

Only silence and emptiness—further proof that I'd been right all along: there really was no one there.

I truly was alone.

So I plodded on, day after day.

Every twenty-four-hour stretch was filled with familiar tedium—working, working out, eating, and sleeping. Then doing it again, and again, and again. Each day was just another gray day in prison. There had been thousands like it for me in the past, and it appeared there would be thousands more in the future.

At the end of yet another tiresome and typical day, I pulled myself onto my bunk. It was late and I was worn out. My cell partner was already sound asleep and snoring. I put on my radio headphones and switched off the small light beside my bunk. I tuned in to a classical music station, closed my eyes, and began listening—preparing to be carried away into another night of dark and dreamless sleep.

What happened next changed my life.

With no warning whatsoever, a bright, blinding, golden light burst into the room. The light swallowed up everything; it enveloped me. I felt wrapped in that light—a warm, wonderful, comforting light. It was a sensation different from any I had ever known.

I felt like I was floating above my bunk—fearlessly, effortlessly, blissfully.

My ears were filled not with music but with an incomprehensible roar. I didn't know if it was the thunderous roll of a massive wind or the crash and rumble of great, rushing waters. I felt I was being lifted by a monumental power—by something mighty but gentle, formidable and yet more forgiving than anything I had ever experienced.

But most of all—more than the beautiful light or the roar of unseen winds or the pure pleasure this experience gave me—I remember the infinite peace and joy, the limitless compassion and the intense love I felt aimed right at *me*.

At that moment, this power was not meant for all of the world or for all of humanity—it was being shared directly and specifically with me.

Only me.

And I knew without being told that it was nothing less than God's perfect, boundless love.

After so many years in prison, after being rejected by virtually everyone—after being bounced out of courts and kept behind bars; after losing my wife, my son, my life—this was the moment when everything changed.

Finally, at long last, I felt peace—real peace—and I reveled in it.

I escaped into the beautiful moment.

The next thing I knew my alarm was going off, the lights were on, and I was back in my same old cell, in the same place—in the same prison. I had the same problems and the same limits.

But for me it was a new day.

I had no recollection of my supernatural encounter ending—no memory of turning off the radio or hanging up my headphones or setting my alarm. I couldn't remember these things, but they had obviously taken place.

I didn't know what had happened or why it had happened.

I felt I knew "who" had reached out to me, although it would be years before I fully understood or embraced what had taken place that night in my cell.

As part of my graduate work, not long after this event I was assigned to read about the Christian mystics of the Middle Ages. They were described as individuals who had a direct experience of the divine in *this* life—people who had literally found themselves in the presence of God. The experiences recounted by the old mystics mirrored mine in startling, important ways. It gave me comfort to know I wasn't the first person to have had an encounter like mine. I wasn't insane. I was blessed.

That night in my cell I hadn't sensed an individual vision of Jesus or seen the traditional icons of Christianity. No disembodied voice told me to build an ark because it was going to rain. What I had seen and felt and heard was divine light—and divine love—and the presence of a power that I had sought, in one way or another, all my life.

I explored the possibility that something else had triggered this—what had I eaten that day anyway? What had I done? But after months of questioning, after analyzing and reanalyzing everything I could, I found nothing concrete that would have induced that moment, nothing that could provide a reasonable earthbound explanation for what had happened to me.

In the end, I fell back on Occam's razor—the old philosophical theory that the simplest explanation is probably the best.

In other words, I realized I had cried out to God—and received exactly what I had asked for—a sign.

Nothing more, nothing less. It was that simple and that profound.

I didn't change overnight. I was—and still am—a human being with deep flaws. Like everyone else on earth, I still have the capacity to make unfair judgments about others, an inherent tendency to make mistakes of pride, an ability to unthinkingly inflict casual cruelties on others.

I am a work in progress. But I want to be a person who *deserves* to be in the presence of God.

I still don't know exactly what happened to me on that dark night in prison. But I do know this—after the night that my cell and my soul filled with light, I am a different man, a better man, a more forgiving man: a man of faith.

That light has stayed with me through years of challenges and disappointments, through fresh heartaches and the settling of old scores—through the discovery of new love and the letting go of old hatreds.

That light has found its way to the center of my life. And the center is holding.

Back then, I didn't know how much I would need that solid base to survive all that was yet to come.

CHAPTER TWENTY

THERE WASN'T A PRISON IN TEXAS I COULDN'T ESCAPE.

After close to two decades in maximum security, I knew all the tricks. Just minutes after I entered my cell, I'd vanish. Without a sound, without suspicion, without a sign that gave away my plan—I would be on the other side of the world before anyone noticed I was gone.

I disappeared into different countries and centuries, other lives and faraway places. By keeping my nose in a book or a magazine or an unfinished novel of my own, I read my way out of prison every day. It did more than keep me amused. It kept me sane—and safe.

My literary life kept me from being pulled into the unending ugliness of prison—the fistfights, the petty tyrannies, the mindless repetition of spending years and years doing the same thing and desperately hoping for a different result.

Stacked in my cell, there were always books and authors, characters and adventures—real or imagined—waiting to sustain me intellectually and emotionally, to give me a place to play out my anger, nurture my hope, and indulge my ache for escape. As soon as one book ended, another began. Sometimes, I read two at a time, jumping back and forth from one universe to another.

It was the only freedom I had.

I was an insatiable reader, always seeking writers and stories that expanded and explained my claustrophobic world.

Homer's *Odyssey*, with its constantly changing litany of physical and psychological challenges, rang true. Odysseus's son—living so long without his father—felt painfully familiar. The epic gave me perspective. It reminded me that there have been injustices since the dawn of time. It helped me survive the monsters I faced behind the walls. Some of those monsters were other inmates, but some lived deep inside me—inflicting terrible wounds, feeding on years of accumulated indignities, self-doubt, and despair.

Over time I had internalized a toxic amount of the shame and undeserved guilt associated with Chris's murder and my conviction. Once in a while, when I would reveal to another inmate—or a free-world prison employee—what had happened to me, I found myself automatically offering whatever external support I had for what I was saying. Even for me, my truth was no longer enough on its own.

"I passed two polygraphs," I'd say. I'd kept the paperwork, verifying the results.

"The prosecution withheld evidence of my innocence," I'd tell them—not knowing that even I was completely unaware of the most dishonest and illegal of these omissions.

I assured my audience that I knew Chris was killed by someone else—probably someone who had broken into our house—because "my three-year-old son told me he saw a large man taking a shower with his clothes on."

I sounded, even to myself, like an old con—itself a kind of awful evidence—further proof that my circumstances had diminished me, made me doubt myself, made *me* want to get away from me. I hated it. It was so easy to feel hopeless.

Books like *The Odyssey* and authors like Cormac McCarthy and Aleksandr Solzhenitsyn reminded me that even the longest journey has a finish line, that someday I would close the book on this chapter of my life. Reading reminded me that finding justice in the end *was* possible.

In the meantime, I still had to survive.

Not long after receiving my master's, I was promptly and unceremoniously transferred off the farm and onto the Michael Unit, yet another maximum-security facility.

This place was closer to my parents, which made me happy. I'd been behind bars for nearly two decades, and in that time, I had seen them age too much. They were bewildered by what had happened to me—they simply couldn't comprehend it—and I could offer no comfort. Knowing they would be able to visit me without making a lengthy and draining cross-state drive made me feel a little better.

But as usual, this new setting was a mixed bag. The cells were larger, but they seemed to be filled with an unusually high percentage of psych patients—dayroom screamers, men yelling at the TV (as well as at imaginary people), prisoners in desperate need of medication, prisoners catatonic from too *much* medication. There was also more than the usual quotient of flat-out crazy people who really didn't belong in prison at all. They should have been in a mental institution.

Unfortunately, one of them was my cell partner.

At first, I judged him to be a tolerable sort. But after a few days, I realized how misguided first impressions sometimes are.

I began to notice that he brushed his teeth, showered, and washed his hair with Bippy—a crude abrasive prison cleanser, a lot like Comet or Ajax. Odd practices, sure—but I figured, to each his own.

The topper came when I saw him adding it to his drinking water. He was actually ingesting it. Soon he shared with me his firm belief that his clothes were bugged. Then he said he *knew* guards came into our cell every night to search through his belongings. He said he knew this because, in the morning, everything was "suspiciously" sitting there, *exactly* as he'd left it before falling asleep.

Good eye. I'd noticed the *same* thing.

He told me he was planning to kill the guards who went through his stuff at night—just as soon as he was able to wake up and catch them. He said he had written federal dispensation to do that.

Furthermore, he was a secret agent. I knew that because he told me so.

Ironically, in prison, none of this was considered evidence of mental illness or any serious indication that this guy could be a danger to himself or others. It all would have been darkly hilarious if I didn't have to spend every night sleeping—completely unprotected—just a foot or two away from him. What if he mistook me for a guard one night?

We both slept lightly.

Difficult as it was at times, the Michael Unit was, for me, a place of great possibility. It was here that the Innocence Project finally made progress on my DNA testing request. Along with the team in the New York office, an attorney from Houston agreed to represent me pro bono. I wouldn't meet him for months and months, nor would I meet the angels from the New York office for ages. But we talked by phone, exchanged letters, evidence requests, updates, and their deep thoughts on strategy.

Despite the delays, I knew my file was flying across time zones, that the pounds of paperwork and peculiar details of my case were being absorbed by smart lawyers, looking at it all with fresh eyes. And I knew that these generous souls were doing this—without having any real reason to believe me.

I wanted to be worthy.

So I waited patiently—and felt grateful to get the attention of anyone this late in the game.

The Innocence Project, on my behalf, was asking for permission to test all the autopsy swabs taken from Chris's body—everything from scrapings under her fingernails to the tiny hairs found clutched in her hand. The testing would include evidence that would tell us with certainty whether Chris had been sexually assaulted in any way, something I dreaded learning.

Furthermore, we were asking to test for DNA on the blue bandanna that Chris's brother had found behind our home. If we found evidence that the square of fabric had been in contact with Chris—if it carried her blood or her cells or her hair, intermingled with that of some unknown third party—it would change everything about my case.

It could very well tell us who had killed Chris.

I prayed it would at least reveal who *hadn't*: me.

So I sat in prison, through seasons marked by the changing color of leaves on the big trees outside my windows—spreading oaks that I fantasized about sitting under with a beer.

In winter, with inadequate heating and inadequate clothes, I learned how to keep my hands from getting too cold by making tight fists, then changing the grip every minute or so. I would tuck my thumbs under my fingers and squeeze tight—then reverse it, then do it again. I learned to pull my hands as far up into my sleeves as I could, then cross my arms and hang on tight. I would keep moving and keep hoping someone would turn up the heat inside the building.

At the time, I was working in the prison slaughterhouse, which was every bit as pleasant as it sounds. We had no heat in much of the slaughterhouse. In fact, it felt like a meat locker inside—since it was. The buildings we lived in were not much better. Everything was off by at least a season. It felt like heat was running all summer and the air-conditioning was set at full blast in the winter. Eventually—after decades—I stopped being surprised when the guards, year after year, handed out wool blankets as soon as summer temperatures reached the nineties.

Still, just as I had done on the outside, I looked forward to the holidays. Every Christmas I tried to tell myself I was being spared all the mad shopping, crowds at the malls, and tough decisions about what to buy for someone I loved. Instead, I carefully signed Christmas cards in my scratchy script—trying to always include an upbeat message to reassure my handful of friends and endlessly frustrated family—and sent the whole bundle out in a bulk mailing. In one day I was done with my Christmas social obligations—at least for another year.

One Christmas I got a surreal glimpse of Eric's life. A Houston TV newscast was showing off pictures of decorated homes around the city—and I saw Mary Lee's address highlighted under a full-screen photograph of a colorfully lit house. Through the windows, the rooms glowed amber. I imagined Eric in one of those rooms, maybe sitting at a loaded Christmas table—laughing, oblivious, lucky to be getting on with his life.

I felt like an astronaut, watching the proceedings on earth from my outpost on the moon.

My holiday meals were not so cozy. One Christmas Day, the chow hall ran out of turkey. Then they ran out of its replacement, chicken—an *unforgivable* institutional sin. Of course, the near riot that ensued was equally uncalled for, but it did give me the unforgettable gift of seeing a corrections lieutenant race into the chow hall, sweating and angry and wearing a disheveled Santa hat—while holding high a gas grenade, ready to be launched into our laps.

Ah, memories of Christmas past.

But from the time I moved to the Michael Unit, my imprisonment was always buffered by the possibility of my exoneration—an up-and-down belief that the seemingly impossible might just happen, that my team might just pull this off.

I knew that my attorneys had reached out to John Bradley, the man who was now district attorney for Williamson County. By then my old nemesis Ken Anderson had become State District Judge Anderson, a singularly unsettling thought. Still, in the DA's office Anderson left behind, little had changed. Bradley was cut from the same win-at-all-costs cloth. He had worked under Anderson for several years and, in the process, seemed to have absorbed a powerful dose of the self-importance and arrogance that Ken Anderson brought to my original trial.

When the attorneys on my side asked for a meeting with Bradley to explain their case for DNA testing and fingerprint analysis—*and* offered to pay every penny of the costs—they were turned down flat. Bradley made it clear that there would be no support from his office for anything of the kind. A court would have to order it done—and he was not going to make it easy for us.

In February 2005, eighteen years after my conviction, I got a copy of the rough draft my legal team was working on, and it was a revelation. I sat for hours in my cell, reading and rereading the motion requesting DNA tests. It was an incredibly powerful document that left me exultant and—for the first time in many, many years— truly hopeful. The motion painstakingly laid out the legal reasoning for testing to go forward.

The Innocence Project team had even found an unsolved murder that happened just blocks from our home and was eerily similar to Chris's killing. Six years before our tragedy, it appeared another family in Williamson County had gone through nearly the same thing.

Mildred McKinney was an older woman who lived alone, with a doting daughter and son-in-law who kept tabs on her and visited often. On Election Day 1980, the couple voted in their precinct and then made the short drive to Mom's house to check in. When they knocked, there was no answer.

Walking into the backyard, they found a sliding glass door to the house unlocked. In the back bedroom, they found Mildred McKinney's body. She had been savagely beaten to death, like Chris. Furniture and items from the house were found stacked on the body, just as they were piled onto Chris's body in our bedroom.

The case had never been solved.

For a time the murder had been suspected to be the work of Henry Lee Lucas and/or his horrible cohort Ottis Toole. Incompetent investigation by the Williamson County Sheriff's Office had already pointed the finger at the pair for dozens of killings around the country. The sheriff's office appeared to have added the McKinney case as an afterthought. Ottis Toole helpfully regurgitated a terribly contrived and inadequate confession in exchange for jailhouse privileges.

Most of those cases fell apart due to lack of evidence, contradictory information, and revelations about how shabbily and unfairly the confessions were obtained. In fact, the police work had been so inept—if not corrupt—that Lucas won a rare-as-hen's-teeth commutation from the Texas governor.

The brutal murder of Mildred McKinney got tossed back into the files as a cold case. Her family had to live without answers. Whoever had killed the much-loved, gentle mother in her bed had gotten away with it.

Noting the uncanny similarities in the case, the attorneys helping me wanted to test the evidence in the McKinney murder against any evidence found on Chris to see if there might be a connection. It seemed like something that should have been considered standard, thorough investigative work.

But John Bradley and Williamson County fought the request for months—first by putting off a hearing for procedural reasons, then through a series of legal delaying tactics. Finally, nearly eight months after our motion for testing was filed—most of another year in prison for me—John Bradley's office got around to responding with their best case against testing. It was staggering in its irrationality and unfairness. The DA's response offered up a healthy heaping of legal boilerplate—along with shallow arguments that showed complete disregard for the search for the truth that all prosecutors are supposed to carry out.

Bradley wrote that we couldn't do the testing now—because we hadn't *proved* it wasn't *my* fault that DNA testing hadn't been done years ago. He said we couldn't test now because we *should* have done it earlier. He said we couldn't test now because Sheriff Boutwell had died. He said we couldn't test now because it wouldn't make any difference anyway.

Bradley went on to say that even if the bandanna was found to contain Chris's DNA and that of an unknown suspect, there were simple explanations for how that might have happened. The response went on to list a number of inventive ways that the bandanna bearing Chris's DNA might have gotten there. Bradley argued it was possible I had taken *someone else's* bandanna and worn it while killing Chris. After the murder, he claimed, I could have ingeniously placed it behind our house to throw investigators off the trail.

He said that I could have conveniently stumbled upon the bandanna *after* the murder, then coldly carried it into the house and carefully dipped it in Chris's blood before returning it to the construction site behind our home.

Bradley wildly theorized that the bandanna might show evidence of Chris's blood because she had somehow injured herself—long before her murder—perhaps while working in the yard, then inexplicably chosen to stanch her wounds with a filthy bandanna she found in the street, and thrown it back over the fence.

The bizarre response reminded me of what I had always been up against in Williamson County.

Our motion to test the DNA also examined anew the record of Dr. Roberto Bayardo, the Travis County medical examiner who had testified at my trial that Chris's stomach contents *could* indicate that she had died before I left the house. He had initially said that Chris had probably died after 6:00 A.M. After conferring with the sheriff and Prosecutor Ken Anderson, he rolled the time of death back to 1:15 A.M., testifying that he couldn't be "scientifically" certain, but indicating that this was his best judgment.

In the years since my conviction, Dr. Bayardo's work had come under increasing scrutiny. Our motion contained the opinion of a nationally recognized pathologist who had examined Bayardo's work in my case and found serious flaws in his methods, reasoning, conclusions, and testimony. The motion also outlined a number of other cases where Dr. Bayardo had grossly erred—including one case where he came to the jaw-dropping conclusion that a man who had been stabbed in the back had *committed suicide*. It would almost have been funny if this indifference and incompetence hadn't cost me two decades of my life, my future with my son, and the answers we all needed about who had murdered my innocent, beautiful wife.

When I started this process, I paid lip service to the idea that I understood that this could take a while, that I knew the wheels of justice moved slowly. But the truth is, I was unprepared for just *how* long it takes to right a legal wrong. More than a year after we filed our motion asking to test those autopsy swabs, the judge hadn't ruled and there was no indication that the decision would be coming soon. Nevertheless—ever the eternal optimist—I began psychologically preparing to leave.

I wrote letters to friends and former inmates telling them how I was "lightening my load" behind the walls, getting rid of the extra baggage I knew I would not need outside. My plastic penitentiary typewriter had finally died of old age and overuse. I threw the rickety remains away, convinced that I would soon be tap-tap-tapping on a fancy new computer. I sent all my finished and unfinished manuscripts to my family. I persuaded myself that the goings-on inside the prison didn't bother me anymore because I had one foot already out the door. I began to fantasize regularly about catching that last "chain" home, leaving prison for the last time—on that last bus. I felt certain the ride would be swift and sweet.

My dreamworld grew as I actually began to consider how very different life was going to be on the outside. I realized I had never been online, never stepped into a Wal-Mart or walked past—much less *into*—a Starbucks.

I had never used a cell phone or owned a CD, a DVD, or an SUV. I told myself that these things were minor inconveniences, small hurdles that I would sail over soon enough.

But I wondered how much prison life had changed me. I wondered if my "big house" eating habits—wolfing food down like a starving dog—would be hard to shake. So I consciously practiced eating slowly, lifting my prison spork—that ingenious hybrid between a spoon and a fork—to my mouth gradually and casually, trying to remember not to speed or slurp or slop anything on myself. I certainly didn't want to embarrass anyone who would actually agree to eat in public with me. Nor did I want to embarrass myself. I was not proud of having spent two decades in prison, even if it had all been a terrible misunderstanding.

I wanted to go back to real life with my head up. I wanted to fit in. I felt as though I was sixteen again and trying to prepare for an all-important prom dinner at a fancy restaurant. This must be what it is like to be a middle-aged citizen of a faraway country desperate to make a decent impression on the people in his new land.

Finally, in August 2006, we got an answer—and it was at least partly good news. We would be allowed to test all the items taken from Chris's body. The McKinney evidence and the blue bandanna, however, would remain off-limits. We would have to continue to fight to test those.

Now began the long wait for test results.

During this tedious stretch, I had a chance to meet with John Raley, the attorney from Houston who had been working on my case, for years, with absolutely no payoff—financial, emotional, or professional.

John drove to the Michael Unit with an associate of his, the always-helpful attorney Jackie Cooper. I believe they came to see me because John knew I would soon get a decision from the Parole Board on whether I would be granted release. My chances were slim to none, since I would not "admit" my crime or express remorse, but I'd written John asking whether, on the off chance I *did* get parole and get out, he would still represent me in attempting to prove my innocence. His participation and the Innocence Project's belief in me were a big part of what kept me going.

Our meeting was John's opportunity to take my measure—face-to-face—to see whether he trusted me, to see whether he wanted to commit to an even longer haul on this maddening monster of a case.

John had worked so hard, spending evenings and weekends going over my file—sometimes ignoring his family and his practice to rack his brain over a way to force a decision, to win a chance to get the DNA testing that we all believed might shake loose something new.

It was a revelation to finally meet him, though.

John Raley was a collection of wonderful contradictions—a massive former football player at the University of Oklahoma, he now wrote with delicacy and exquisite precision in court documents. He was a kid lucky enough to have been born into privilege but talented enough to win success on his own—and he spoke with unusual passion and eloquent understanding about the burdens and unfairness faced by others less fortunate. He had never handled a criminal case before—his practice focused on medical malpractice and commercial litigation, often representing little guys going up against big guys. John helped level the playing field—he was an excellent "big guy" to have on your side.

Long before our meeting, John had told me he was a Christian— and that part of the work he was doing for me came from that conviction. Reading his words in the legal briefs, motions, and appeals over the years, I could see he had a touch of the evangelist. Talking with him underscored that. He had a unique combination of righteous rage against the legal system's flaws and profound reverence for its ability to finally bend toward justice. He recognized the abject failings and inherent good of our courts, our judges, and our police. He knew that I had been a victim of the system's weaknesses. But John always believed its strengths would set me free.

After we met, John told me he believed I was innocent. I knew what a profound acknowledgment that was on his part. For him this was no longer a case of a bad verdict, an unfair trial, or shoddy police work. After all this time, he had realized I wasn't just not guilty. I was truly innocent. They had gotten the wrong guy.

Near the end of our visit, John stepped away to use the restroom before the long drive home. He left his things behind, a simple act of trust I had not been expecting, something I had not experienced in decades. I sat with Jackie Cooper at the table, transfixed by the presence of John's sports jacket. It was all I could do to keep from touching it. It looked soft—impossibly soft, as though it were the finest, smoothest, most well-made article of clothing I'd ever seen. At least it seemed that way to someone who had been wearing ill-fitting, scratchy prison whites for two decades.

The meeting—and that moment—meant the world to me.

Not long after, I found out I had been turned down for parole, something I had expected. What I did not anticipate was the board's decision to set my next try at parole back another three years. It seemed like forever. And I had been a good inmate—no trouble, no violence, no serious problems inside—but I was lumped in with the worst of the worst. I figured it actually didn't matter that much—I knew I would be living outside by the time my next parole date rolled around.

I was wrong.

In October 2007 I received crushing news—the DNA analyses drew a complete blank. None of the samples taken from Chris's body showed any evidence that she had been sexually assaulted. There was no DNA to test further, no profile to try matching to anyone else, no sign that anyone else had been there at all—at least not on the evidence taken from Chris's body at the time.

There had been setbacks before, but this was big. I sat in my cell and stared at the floor—stunned. I felt numb when I sat down to write my parents with the news. I knew my seventy-two-year-old mother would cry her eyes out. She had been making a list of restaurants she wanted to take me to when I came home.

For me there was some small measure of peace in the result. At least Chris had not been sexually assaulted. The awful possibility that she had been abused by her murderer had haunted me. Now I knew she hadn't really known what was happening. She had simply been sleeping. She'd died very quickly. Even in death, she was not violated. And that meant something.

But the news brought an abrupt halt to my fantasies about leaving prison anytime soon. I began to wonder if I would die inside—or if I would be freed as an old man and spend the rest of my life on parole.

My lawyers soldiered on, pushing for testing of the McKinney material, fighting hard to get permission to test the blue bandanna for DNA. I'm not sure I was much help to them. They were crucial in keeping me from falling into despair. Their belief in me—along with my faith in God—was all I had left. I had exhausted my lifetime supply of optimism. Every day in prison left me tired—tired of the grueling sameness, tired of the coarseness and cruelty, tired of the dehumanization of being locked up like an animal.

John Raley and Nina Morrison, from the Innocence Project's New York office, argued eloquently before the state court of appeals. Reading the transcript gave me a lump in my throat. I copied pages from the proceeding and sent them to my mother to try to keep her spirits up.

Raley thought it went well. "Seriously, Michael—we think we're finally getting somewhere here," I heard again and again on the phone.

His reassurances aside, parole remained as a last-ditch way for me to get out, a possibility that grew nearer and nearer with each bad court decision. As a condition of parole, however, the state required me to express remorse for Chris's murder. When I told John I would not lie to get out, he was moved.

"As long as I'm breathing air," John swore, "I'm trying to get you out."

It's an oath I've never forgotten and never will.

Just as important to me personally was the help and encouragement of Nina Morrison. Nina had been working on my case for a long time. She had advised other attorneys on avenues to pursue while she handled countless other cases of wrongful convictions all over the country. She told me how long this could take and kept my hope from fading when rulings went against us. She would recount the setbacks and eventual triumphs she'd seen in other cases.

She sent me long, chatty letters sharing the news of her

pregnancy—"It's a girl!"—interspersed with detailed analyses of the grisly evidence sexual assaults left behind in murder cases. She always broke bad news in the kindest way possible, saying, "The results were not what we hoped for." Then she would invariably follow up with "We're not quitting yet—not by any means."

She was part cheerleader, part little sister, and pure, unadulterated brilliant legal tactician—a lawyer who could take apart a bad conviction, find the truth, set the record straight, and be on to the next crisis several times a day. She had to be able to do that. All she did, every single day, was work cases like mine. I knew she must have had thoroughly smitten wrongly convicted inmates all over the United States, all of us feverishly checking our mail for letters with her return address. We had never met, but on the phone, she always sounded happy to be talking to me, glad to be trying something new in my case, eager to share her contagious hope.

Finally, after almost five years of waiting, the state court deigned to give me an answer on my request for further DNA testing. It was something that I viewed as good news–bad news. Most important, we were going to be allowed to test the bandanna. But we would continue to be denied the opportunity to test any of the evidence taken from the Mildred McKinney murder. I had feared the connection was a reach, but I had prayed for any explanation that could offer insight or help that might make sense of my last twenty-three years.

By 2009, I had become used to bad news. If the blue bandanna proved useless, there might be nothing else. I knew John and Nina had finite resources. If they had to cut me loose, I told them I'd understand.

I was now fifty-five years old. Eric was twenty-six and married. My mother's hair had turned snowy white and my father's walk had slowed. Sheriff Boutwell had died of cancer seventeen years before. Sergeant Wood had suffered a series of debilitating strokes. Ken Anderson was now a respected judge. The population of once sleepy little Williamson County had quadrupled.

The world had gone on without me. All I could do was keep waiting.

I thought back to the time, years ago, when our motion had first been filed. There had been some local newspaper and TV coverage of my effort to clear myself. One news story contained an interview with a member of the jury that convicted me. He said he feared that, if I got out, I would come looking for him—and kill him. I wished I could reassure him that nothing like that would happen.

But I wondered at the time who else might have seen the articles and TV coverage. Had the man who killed Chris seen them? What did he think? I wondered where he was and what he was doing. Had he killed again? I wanted to know whether he felt regret or pain, fear or anger. I wondered if I would ever know his name or get to talk to him.

I remember thinking that if I could only ask him one question, I would ask him, Why? Why had he done this? Why had he entered our home? Why had he chosen Chris? Why had he needed to kill her?

I knew I would probably never get a satisfactory answer, if I got any answer at all. It was terrifying to think about the profound emotional disconnection required to break into a home, beat a sleeping woman to death, and then brashly wash the blood off in our shower under the gaze of a frightened toddler.

I couldn't help believing that someone who would do that—and then watch an innocent man go to prison—was a monster indeed. But I knew this vicious, unfathomable, unforgivable man was all too real. He existed—and he was still out there.

CHAPTER TWENTY-ONE

ONCE AGAIN, WE WERE ON LOCKDOWN.

The guards had found a number of shanks on our unit, knives made out of everyday stuff—a discarded piece of scrap metal from the maintenance shop or a broken piece of a plastic lunch tray. Sometimes a sharp-eyed inmate would find a shard of glass left behind by a careless worker and meticulously fashion it into a shiv—complete, of course, with a sensible safety handle wrapped in cloth. Once in a great while, a con might whittle a wooden stick into something sharp enough to perform surgery on a person—or require surgery on a person. DIY lethal weapons—prison crafts at their finest!

The bursts of villainous innovation that constantly swept through the cells of my erstwhile friends and neighbors took my breath away. The entrepreneurs who fermented penitentiary "wine" and bottled it for sale; the crude but savvy businessmen who offered protection or punishment, for a price, to fellow inmates; the guys who ran drug rings *inside* prison while they served time for running drug rings *outside* prison—I couldn't help but think how their lives would have been different if they'd used one scintilla of their commercial in-stinct to do something legal.

Instead, they'd all opted to follow in their families' footsteps, or defy their families, or simply do the only thing they knew how.

There were many paths to prison. What was virtually certain about my neighbors inside was that the vast majority would keep doing the same thing after they got out.

For many of these guys, the possibility of serving time was just another business risk—like rolling the dice on a pricey piece of real estate and losing a fortune. For them, losing huge chunks of their lives was the price of admission to their chosen profession.

The crazy people inside—and there were many, many of them—were different.

They simply couldn't help themselves. Most of them had wandered for years through their lives unmedicated, uneducated, unwanted, and unloved. They systematically failed at everything—school, relationships, work. They couldn't even take care of themselves. In the process, they alienated family and friends—and finally, the law.

Inside, their mental health care was no better. In fact, it was arguably worse than the lack of treatment and lack of attention they got outside. But behind the walls, they had lots of company—people exactly like them, men they could commiserate with or fight with, antagonize or be bullied by.

During our many lockdowns on the Michael Unit, I would sit on my bunk with my headset on and my radio off, my not-all-that-sly way of eavesdropping on the inane chatter. The lengthy conversations were full of sad and ineffectual plans for life on the outside, the ramblings of the clinically insane, and the fantasies of the criminally inept. Their ignorance and cruelty knew no limits. These dark dreams were bandied about—and carried out—by my neighbors, my fellow travelers, the men sharing my meals and my showers and my life.

Eavesdropping helped me stay entertained during lockdown, which wasn't easy. You could read—or sleep; be forced to repeatedly pack up and drag your property down to the gym for inspection—or sleep; eat your "johnnie," a baloney sandwich sack lunch—or sleep.

Did I mention sleeping?

A lockdown created an almost narcoleptic atmosphere. Many

inmates sprawled lifelessly on their bunks all day and all night. They simply couldn't come up with anything else to do. Experienced inmates—like me—always kept special material on hand for lockdowns. Sometimes, I'd dive back into a big book I knew I would never finish unless I was locked up—literally. Other times, I would just sprawl on my bunk and torture myself by looking again and again at family photos. Many were taken at holiday gatherings, and my mom sent me a new round every year. I now had quite a collection.

I searched every scene, pulling out the smallest details. Are those new curtains on Mom's windows? Again? What is that food in the yellow bowl? Whose kid is that? I could not get enough of the faces. I feasted on the backgrounds. I could almost taste the meals. The clothes everyone wore simply fascinated me. But the way my family had changed over the years hit me hardest. In more than one picture, I hadn't recognized my younger brother Matt—and that hurt.

I had missed so much. And I longed for everyone and every element of the outside world so much it ached.

I wanted to go home. I'd had enough of prison, enough of the stiff-upper-lip life I had been living for so many years. I would put the photos away to give myself a break—and then, in a few minutes, pull them out and go through them one by one again, as though they were part of a rosary I kept repeating and repeating. It was amazing how powerful and compelling ordinary family pictures are to a man who's been locked away for what feels like forever.

And it wasn't just family photos that had that effect on me. One day I was jolted emotionally simply by looking at an IKEA catalog. I'd never seen one before, never even set foot in an IKEA store. I imagined that in some snobby, disconnected corners of the country, there were probably people who wouldn't dream of shopping at such a mass-production, mass-marketed company. I did not feel any of that when I flipped through the catalog.

I felt torn between anguish and envy. The domestic bliss and the sumptuous comfort—the livability and comparative luxury of the

IKEA line—left me weak in the knees. Everything and everyone in the glossy pages seemed to almost sparkle. The women looked capable, fun, and relaxed. The children were all smiling and were clearly above average in every way. The men looked like no man I had seen in years—every single one of them appeared comfortable and happy. They looked loved.

It broke my heart. I was nearly crying looking at a catalog—for God's sake.

The emotional instability I felt probably had more than a little to do with the fact that I was expecting word on the lab results from the DNA tests on the bandanna any day. Whatever they found—or didn't find—would determine the rest of my life. That square of blue fabric would have the final say in whether I walked free or died inside. It would decide whether I would be able to spend time with my parents in their old age. It would control whether I could even attend their funerals. Everything in my life hung on whatever the stains on that fabric contained.

Early testing had indicated there was blood on the bandanna. But whose blood was it? How did it get there? Would they find anything else? If the bandanna held no secrets, I was doomed. It was literally my last chance.

I prayed as hard as I could for acceptance of what came next. I had to consider that I might be destined to live out my life behind bars, even if that wasn't fair or right or going to be easy. I braced for bad news and told myself I simply might not be wise enough to understand the why of my life just yet, but eventually—someday—I would.

In late May 2011, I got handed a letter from Nina Morrison. In it, she wrote that she was going to be in Texas the next day (!) and planned on popping in to see me. We'd been writing each other and talking on the phone for six or seven years, and I was anxious to finally meet her. I felt I owed her so much.

But a line near the end of the letter left me unsettled—she casually mentioned that John Raley might come in from Houston to join our visit. My mind reeled at the possibilities—were they both coming to excitedly give me the great news I had waited so long to hear? Or had we become close enough, and they simply cared enough, that they both wanted to be on hand when I got the news I feared most? Both scenarios made sense.

I barely slept that night thinking over—and over, and over—all the possibilities that might be played out in the visiting room in less than twenty-four hours. I even thought about whether I might be overthinking things.

Then I forgave myself for getting carried away. At such a late stage of my life and long sentence, I simply couldn't help it. I flopped around on my bunk like a fish tossed into a boat—spending the whole night alternately praying and dreaming, hitting the pillow and holding my head in my hands, fantasizing and planning my reaction to good *or* bad news, then scolding myself and comforting myself—and then starting the whole sleepless grind all over again.

Finally, dawn came and put me out of my misery.

We were on lockdown again, and moving through the prison to do anything—especially to receive visitors—was difficult. I had to jump through all kinds of hoops and was still an hour late getting out of the dorm that morning and down to the visiting room. Once there I had to stand in a hallway for an hour. I worried that John and Nina were having trouble getting in. Finally, I saw my much-loved lawyers walk through the door.

John Raley was at least a head taller than anyone else in the room—possibly anyone else in the prison. He was moving the way he always did—like he was late for a hearing or racing the clock to meet a court date or simply rushing to deliver news of great consequence. His full-steam-ahead stance reflected his approach to legal battles—every case was the Alamo all over again.

Nina Morrison operated with an almost identical mind-set. We had never met, but I recognized her instantly. Marching beside John, matching him stride for stride, Nina looked tiny—of course, everyone did when they stood next to John. But she had a singular way of appearing ferociously on top of everything and almost sweetly endearing at the same time. I'd seen her on TV, so I knew she had long dark hair. From her years of work on my case, I knew, too, she was whip smart—almost scary smart.

But I was totally unprepared to see her smile. It was so big and so beautiful and so startlingly bright that I believed she could have been used to signal ships at sea. Her high-wattage smile that day could have turned the deepest, darkest cave into Times Square. As I watched her walking toward me through the dreary visiting room, I swore that the light bursting out of her looked like a train emerging from an inky black tunnel.

As they moved to our visiting cubicle, she and John were focused right at me. We made eye contact, and in that instant—I *knew* why they had come.

I knew!

Well, I hoped I knew.

I silently prayed.

We finally sat down together, separated by that maddening glass partition. My heart was beating so hard I felt certain they could hear it, even through the thick clear wall that kept us apart. My whole body was shaking. I pressed my legs into the chair as hard as I could—simply trying to hold them steady.

John held his huge hand to the glass. I put mine up against his. He was still smiling. He looked at me, smiled at Nina as she sat beside him beaming—and then looked back at me.

He said, "We have good news."

He and Nina excitedly passed their phone handset back and forth as they explained how the testing had confirmed that the blood on the bandanna belonged to Chris. This was big. We had always speculated that the bandanna had been dropped or thrown behind our house as the killer made his getaway. This was proof that we were right.

The next piece of information was a bombshell.

The testing had discovered other DNA deposited on the

bandanna—skin cells and sweat that were clearly intermingled with Chris's blood. The DNA belonged to an unknown male—the man who had killed my wife, the man who had gotten away with murder, until now.

Now there was a chance that, by running this man's DNA profile through a national database, we could get a hit—we could find him, have him arrested and finally brought to justice. In odd ways this possibility reawakened the suppressed hurt and despair I felt about losing Chris. Nearly twenty-five years after she died, as I faced, at long last, finding out who had done this, a new wave of almost palpable grief swept over me. I hadn't expected that at all.

I had tried to imagine how I would react if the news was bad—or good. But when the moment came, when it was no longer theoretical, I was too profoundly shaken to do anything. I had no snappy comments to make or important thoughts to convey. I was struggling simply to swallow and continue breathing. The overwhelming physical effect the news had on me was a shock. I could feel it in every cell in my body. One minute I thought I had the strength of ten men and could jump so high I would touch the ceiling. The next instant I felt weak and out of control—as though I just might sink to the floor. It was not unlike the moment so long ago when I heard the jury foreman say "Guilty"—only this time, I was stunned in reverse.

I was so lucky Nina was there. She had delivered this kind of earth-shattering news before—and had helped others who had ridden the emotional roller coaster that now carried me along. Talking with her made such a difference—she seemed to understand what I was feeling better than I did.

John suggested I take a moment to simply breathe and process the information. He was right. While I steadied myself, they both stayed right there, reassuring me through the thick glass. My eyes were brimming with tears. I could feel myself forming uncontrollable smiles that seemed to come and go of their own accord. John and Nina kept talking as I struggled to regain my composure.

They, on the other hand, were exultant—laughing about their wild drive to see me. They'd met in Dallas and made the hour-and-a-half trip together in a rental car. John joked that they'd been so happy and excited their "wheels hadn't touched the ground the whole way."

By now all three of us were bouncing off the walls.

Nina brought us back down to earth. She reminded me that nothing was official yet, that the lab report had not been issued—that would take a little while. And she soberly recalled the pitched battles we'd faced in years past—just to get us to this moment.

She said that the Williamson County powers that be had fought us all the way—and they were going to keep on fighting.

She looked at the marathon of legal wrangling still to come. And she had other worries, which she laid out in her typical "trust me, I've been here before" fashion. I was told to regard this time as not unlike the months between Chris's murder and my trial. *All* of my mail, *all* of my phone calls, *all* of my conversations had to be guarded. One slip could ruin everything. She said that she and John would inform my parents, who could share the news with my family—and no one else.

It was imperative that our plans be kept secret. She warned that a word from a jailhouse snitch claiming he'd heard me say something about Chris's murder could set us back years. I knew she was right. Many of the men behind the walls would do *anything* to get out—or to get out faster. That someone here would sell out another inmate—even an innocent one—did not require a stretch of the imagination.

Our visit was coming to an end when John brought up something that sent me right back over the emotional edge. He asked if I wanted him to try to find Eric and share the news with him. I learned anew how raw my feelings were, how much I had been holding back every day. Huge, unashamed tears welled up in my eyes and slid down my face. In my memory Eric was still a little boy—trusting me and needing me, even though I knew he was now a full-grown man. My mother had told me he was married. We hadn't had contact for years. Now our relationship would change again—I hoped.

My lawyers and I said our good-byes—full of hope for what lay ahead. Nina waved and beamed as she walked away. John stepped out of the cubicle on his side of the glass—then stepped back in. He picked up the phone and, with a big smile, told me what I already knew—"Prayer works."

I would need it to work for me again.

As I walked back into the prison, every aspect of my limited life awaited me unchanged. I felt the relentless symphony of grating people, policies, and sounds envelop me again—the buzzers and shouts, the barking guards, the indecipherable squawks from the PA system, the slamming doors and endless jangling of keys and cuffs and twitchy nerves. I was still inside.

It was as if John and Nina hadn't been there and hadn't delivered incredible news. It was as if this day had all been a dream. I had to struggle to continue accepting the constraints of prison life, to stay sane through the incompetence, the sheer stupidity, and the cruelty that filled every day behind bars. Nina had told me there would be an uncomfortable period of adjustment. She was right.

As much as I once prayed for acceptance, I now asked for the power of restraint. I had to keep myself from getting ahead of events, from letting my hurt and rage explode. I had to behave as if nothing had happened, and that was hardest of all.

To get through, I focused on the fact that, somewhere out there, a computer was searching through a massive database of convicted criminals, looking for a match with the DNA profile found on the bandanna. Thinking about that kept me sane. It made the tedium and torment of daily life unimportant.

About six weeks after I got the initial good news, it was my fifty-seventh birthday—another birthday in prison. But this time was different.

Work went well, and when the guards began one of their many counts for the day, the men in my squad sang "Happy Birthday" to me. In a little while, one of the inmates produced a masterpiece of a prison "cake" he'd made for the occasion. It was a wild concoction of crushed cookies, peanut butter, and God knew what else. Then the whole thing was slathered with melted chocolate. Our entire group almost went into diabetic shock. On my way out of work, the plant manager discreetly wished me a happy birthday, and the plant accountant bellowed birthday greetings from her office.

When I reached my dorm, I was told to report immediately to the law library. This time, I felt certain about the news.

John and Nina were waiting for me on the phone—along with someone else. Barry Scheck, head of the Innocence Project, introduced himself. Then John told me straight out: "Michael, we have a birthday present for you." He said the DNA database had found a match, a man in California. We didn't yet know his name, but we knew he had killed Chris. We would have his name—and location—within days.

I grew quiet. John told me later he thought I had fainted, and he wasn't far from wrong. I remember hearing him asking—with just a hint of concern in his voice—"Michael, are you there? Michael?" I told him not to worry, that I was just letting all of this wash over me.

The next day was going to be the twenty-fifth anniversary of Chris's murder, a quarter century since her life was lost—and mine was turned upside down. After all that time, I was finally getting the answers I had sought for so long. I felt as though I were lit from within, like I'd swallowed a big, glowing candle.

Then Barry asked me an unusual question. He wanted to know what, if anything, Eric had told the therapist I had taken him to right after the murder.

The therapist had said she felt sure Eric hadn't witnessed the killing but was simply experiencing the very understandable ill effects of suddenly being separated from his mother.

Then Barry read aloud from a transcript of a telephone conversation between my mother-in-law and the head investigator on the case. I had no idea this talk had ever happened, much less that it had been transcribed and saved all these years. My legal team had just gotten their hands on it, along with some other documents from the prosecutor's and sheriff's department files. This was the material that had been withheld from my trial attorneys in 1987, the file notes that assistant Williamson County prosecutor Mike Davis must have been referencing when he told the jury there had been much more evidence that would have created doubt about my guilt.

Shortly after Chris's funeral, her mother had called the investigator to tell him about something Eric had said. He had shared with her what he saw that day, saying a "monster" had been in the house and had hit his mother. He detailed how the man had placed baskets and a suitcase on Chris's body as she lay in bed. It broke my heart to learn that he had witnessed everything. I prayed he was too young to remember it. I feared that, somewhere deep inside him, those memories lived on. Eric had told his grandmother that I hadn't been there—just "Mommy and Eric."

To her credit, Rita Kirkpatrick had called the head investigator and told him what Eric had said—she also told him to "get off the domestic thing" and find the "monster who had killed my daughter." Why hadn't she told me? Or informed my lawyers? Why hadn't anyone in Chris's family shared with me what Eric said he had seen?

While I was left reeling by the personal repercussions of this new information, the trio of lawyers on the phone focused solely on its legal significance. This was a clean, irrefutable case of the state suppressing exculpatory evidence. It was a violation of the Brady rule—and it was illegal. Someone in Williamson County was in big trouble.

CHAPTER TWENTY-TWO

WITH THIS INFORMATION, THE FULL TRAVESTY OF MY PROSECUTION and all my years in prison became exceedingly clear. But then so did my future—I was getting out. Not right now but soon. Not today but in the not too distant days ahead—it was finally happening.

I sprawled on my bunk at night and read each and every document that had been produced by the Innocence Project's open records request in Williamson County. It was hard for me to fully grasp, but the pile of records they'd pried loose proved that the investigation and prosecution in my case was much more incompetent, more corrupt, and more malicious than I had thought.

The sheriff—with the full cooperation of the prosecutor's office—had hidden my neighbors' reports of an old green van lurking for days just outside the wooded area behind our house. They had buried witness accounts of people living nearby who saw the van's driver walk into the woods. Other neighbors reported odd noises, a man standing at one home's front door in the days before Chris's murder, footprints in flower beds, and the failed burglary of a house close to ours.

I learned that, just days after Chris's murder, San Antonio police had contacted the sheriff's office and reported that her credit card had been used in a jewelry store there. It was a lead that the Williamson County Sheriff's Department didn't follow up at all—even

though San Antonio police offered to drive the card and accompanying evidence up to them!

As the case against me came undone, as it became clear I was
not long for prison life—I found everything inside more tolerable.
It was late summer and well over a hundred degrees every day, but
suddenly I didn't find the heat so oppressive. True, the small fan I
had placed by my bunk did nothing more than blow hot air on me—
it actually felt like a tiny hairdresser was standing 24/7 with a hair
dryer pointed at my face. But I knew my days were numbered.

The judge in Williamson County who was supposed to handle
my case recused himself. Apparently, presiding over a rout of the
current district attorney *and* the former district attorney—now a fellow judge—did not appeal to him. A judge by the name of Sid Harle,
who held court in San Antonio, would be coming in to oversee what
happened next in my case.

The current Williamson County district attorney, John Bradley,
had spent the weeks since the public announcement that another
man's DNA had been found on the bandanna telling the media that
none of this mattered. He said it didn't compromise in any way the
state's case against me.

We had wanted him off the case long ago, and every day that he
remained, Bradley was proving that he had no business being on
the job—or making decisions about my guilt or innocence. It was
like watching an antique tapestry unravel. Thread by thread—lie
by lie—the twenty-five-year-old case against me was coming apart.
Everyone watching could see how this was going to end. Except, of
course, the people in charge of the Williamson County system of
justice.

In late September, even as Bradley was *still* telling the media and
anyone who would listen that I was guilty and belonged in prison,
the other shoe dropped. I got a call from John Raley and Nina Morrison saying that they now had the identity of the man whose DNA
was on the bandanna.

His name was Mark Alan Norwood, and he had a long criminal

history, including burglary and assault. Now police in Austin had matched Norwood's DNA to yet another murder—a killing that was heartbreakingly similar to what had happened to Chris.

Debra Masters Baker was killed on January 13, 1988. She had been about Chris's age, they both had long dark hair—and both of them left behind three-year-old children. Ms. Baker had been murdered in her bed, like Chris, and both had died as a result of crushing blows to their faces and heads. The similarities were eerie. I shivered when I realized they had both been killed on the thirteenth of the month.

I knew this was probably good news for me legally—but for me as a human being, it was heartbreaking. The worst thing about my being convicted of Chris's murder wasn't my long sentence, it was the fact that the real killer had been free to take another life. Debra Baker would be with her children today if the Williamson County sheriff and prosecutor had simply done their jobs.

The unsolved Baker case had been discovered by Kay Kanaby and Cynthia Hepner, two people working in John Raley's law office. They started looking for similar crimes in the Austin area and hit the jackpot quickly. Even before the DNA match was made, they were certain they had found a connected killing—Mark Norwood lived only a few blocks away from Ms. Baker at the time of the murder.

John Raley's wife, Kelly, pitched in to find an even more important connection for me. She set about seeking Eric, more difficult than it might sound because of his name change. Apparently there were a number of Eric Olsons living in the country. She finally tracked him down when she was able to find his wedding pictures online. The accompanying article mentioned that Eric worked at the Jesuit high school he had once attended. It turned out that Eric had been hiding in plain sight.

Incredibly, Kay Kanaby had once played tennis with Eric's mother-in-law. And through that woman, Kay knew her daughter

Maggie—and had at least been introduced to Maggie's new husband, Eric.

Maggie was very important in moving my relationship with Eric forward. Luckily for me—and Eric—Maggie turned out to be a person who firmly believes in the healing power of truth. I was eager to meet her and to see Eric again—so eager that I didn't really focus on or understand how world changing the news of my innocence had been for my son.

Since he was a toddler, I had been the bad guy—the man who killed his mother, the creep who broke the hearts of Chris's family, the man who was so dangerous he had to be kept away from decent people. Now, in the blink of an eye, a round of obscure, difficult-to-decipher DNA testing had turned Eric's life upside down. The truths he had been raised to believe were not true at all. A dirty bandanna found decades ago now spoke with more authority, more clarity, and more proof than the people who had raised him—the people he loved.

It was going to take a while—a long while—for him to absorb everything. I regret that I didn't understand this important truth from the start. But the fact is I no longer knew Eric at all. I knew a little boy who didn't exist anymore. To me, he was more of an idea than an individual—and I knew as little about his life or his experience or his psyche as he did about mine.

In retrospect, I can see that the better the news was for me, the more painful it became for Eric. Without meaning to, I was hurting him again. I didn't know it at the time, but rebuilding my relationship with my son meant embarking on another very long, very difficult journey.

On October 1, 2011, I was told I had a call in the law library. Since I knew the Innocence Project and John Raley were involved in heated hearings over the next steps in my case, I expected an update of some kind. I was wrong.

John and Barry Scheck told me that John Bradley, the Williamson County district attorney—the man who had fought us tooth and nail every day in every way—wanted to cut a deal.

Bradley offered to let me out of prison on Tuesday, October 4, if I agreed to a list of demands—most of them meant to spare Williamson County officials any fallout. He wanted me to agree not to sue anyone, to agree I would never call anyone to testify, and to sign documents affirming that I would never require anyone to admit any wrongdoing. For good measure, he wanted me to agree I would never contact my son or my former in-laws without their written consent. He wanted me to promise that I would take my state-offered compensation and simply disappear.

It was not much of a deal or much of a decision.

There were hearings coming up that week that would lead to the arrest of Mark Norwood, something that was more important to me than walking out of prison.

I wanted to know why I had been sent to prison. And I cared about making sure that what happened to me did not happen to anyone else. I had spent years thinking about how my life and my plight could make a difference to others. I wanted to get out and be able to talk about what had happened—and what could be done to prevent it from happening again.

I told Barry to play hardball, to tell Bradley no. He said he'd get back to me as soon as he had a counteroffer.

John and Nina were on the phone with me again in less than three hours. Bradley had caved—completely. He agreed to everything we wanted and made no demands of his own. I would be bench-warranted to Williamson County and freed on Tuesday the fourth.

I simply had no words for how I felt.

Standing by my bunk, I began deciding what I wanted to take with me when I walked out the front gate. I had very little and needed less. I figured I had two days to sort through my property and give away the things other inmates could use.

While I was still waiting for word that a bench warrant had

been issued to call me back to Williamson County, a guard came and told me to pack up—pronto. He said I was moving to "seg"— segregated housing where inmates were kept for punishment or protection, or simply because they found themselves in a kind of penitentiary no-man's-land. That's what happened to me—I didn't belong anywhere anymore, at least not inside the system. And just as I had been pushed and hurried to get into prison, I was now being rushed out.

I packed what little I was taking—family photos, toothpaste, toothbrush, deodorant, a comb, and the Bible my sister Vicky had sent me. Everything else—food from the commissary, some novels, writing supplies, my radio and accompanying headphones, thermal underwear for the winter, a pair of almost-new running shoes, my big dictionary, and extra hygiene items—I wanted to give away. It filled two large commissary bags, and I gave them to the two men on my dorm that I trusted most. My friends Steve Martin and Rick Vieira would have to distribute my worldly goods—I had to leave *now*.

Guys began congregating near me. A couple of them prayed over me, others hugged me hard—and a few spoke to me with voices cracking. There were tears. Two men pressed letters into my hand. I was touched by the tenderness with which these tough guys said good-bye.

I heard the guard calling for me. I grabbed my mattress and pulled it onto one shoulder, the way I had when I first carried it up to my first bunk, on my first day in prison. Picking up my small bag of belongings, I headed for the door.

Before I could cross the threshold, I heard a commotion in the dayroom—whoops of delight, full-throated, all-out, old-fashioned hollering—good wishes and good-natured mayhem. Inmates raised their fists and pumped them. They pounded on tables and stomped their feet. I looked up at the upper tier. It was lined with faces, every one of them looking at me—clapping and cheering, waving and woo-hooing.

The heartfelt good-bye I got from the men I had lived with and sometimes loathed, the people who drove me crazy and made me mad or made me laugh, the guys with whom I had shared so many holidays and hard times—stunned me.

I got chills and began to choke up. I waved and kept on walking.

Prison had given me such a great send-off—I almost wanted to stay.

Almost.

PART III

PEACE

What I want to do is make sure this doesn't happen to anybody else.
—MICHAEL MORTON, APRIL 28, 2012

CHAPTER TWENTY-THREE

OCTOBER 3, 2011, WAS MY LAST NIGHT IN PRISON—MY LAST TIME locked in a cell, my last restless sleep on a plastic mattress and a steel bunk. I had spent 8,980 days of my life in prison for a crime I did not commit.

Early the next morning, two Williamson County sheriff's officers came to take me back to the county where I had been wrongly convicted. By that afternoon my legal record and my life would be set right—or at least as right as they could be after so much time and so much loss.

The cops brought me a set of clothes from the county jail—dark blue scrubs. I looked more like a disheveled male nurse than an inmate, but even that was a step up. Besides, my parents, now in their late seventies, were bringing me new clothes to change into before I would appear in court.

As I dressed to leave, I got one more reminder of just how incompetent the Williamson County system of justice can be. One of the cops handed me a set of shoes—Crocs, of all things. The kicker was that they were both left feet. *"Really?"* I asked the county cop. He just shrugged. I didn't say another word. I simply slipped them on and kept them on, even though my right foot ached all the way to Williamson County.

Just before I was led to the car, one of the Williamson County cops prepared to shackle me for the drive home. He pulled out the full complement of big-house hardware—handcuffs, belly chain, and a short chain between my ankles. Before he strapped me up, though, he told me, in great seriousness, that when all this happened to me, he had been only twelve years old. He wanted me to know he had nothing to do with my conviction—or the mistakes and offenses the county he served had made in my case. While he told me these things, I noticed that he stayed just outside my reach.

He seemed worried that I might try to exact some kind of crazy revenge during the drive to court—which was the furthest thing from my mind. These cops were my "freedom ride." *No way* was I going to mess that up.

The trip was uneventful—for the officers. For me, once again the man in the backseat of a police car, it was a sightseeing revelation. I felt torn between constantly looking left and right, drinking in every detail—almost tempted to hang my head out the window like a dog who finally got to ride in the car—and trying to behave with some measure of dignity. I did not want to look like an out-of-touch, institutionalized goober.

My plan worked until we pulled into a gas station to fill up.

I hadn't gassed up a car for twenty-five years. There had been some changes. The gas pumps I'd once used no longer existed. They'd been replaced by something that looked like a cross between a computer and an electronic billboard. There were flashing digital numbers, glaring ads, and what seemed like no focus to the design. I looked close, trying to decipher where to put the money or how to free the nozzle.

One of the cops laughed with me. "I guess they've changed a bit, huh?"

No kidding. I was going to need my mother to gas up the car till I got the hang of it.

I also saw the other people at the gas station staring at me—still handcuffed in the cop car—just another bad guy getting what he deserved, I imagined them thinking. They only saw the worn-out jail clothes, the shackles, and the funny prison haircut. They didn't know I was on my way to a very public exoneration and sweet freedom.

They would know soon enough.

Throughout the ride I was handled the same way any other inmate would have been. But when we pulled in to the new jail in Williamson County, everything changed. I got very special treatment. The cops cleared out the entire booking area for me. All the drunks, hookers, and other unfortunate souls waiting for their jailhouse check-in were herded into glass-enclosed tanks, where they watched me being processed into—and then right back *out of*—jail.

The entire event was videotaped by a sheriff's deputy—probably so the powers that be in Williamson County could prove I had been treated fairly. A young woman jailer handling my paperwork asked me a series of unanswerable questions.

"What is your occupation?"

What was I supposed to say—"professional prisoner"? I looked to the sergeant accompanying me. He shrugged.

"What is your address?"

I didn't have one. The sergeant shrugged again. I finally gave the address of the Michael Unit—a place I never wanted to see again.

It was an odd sensation. I was being set free but possessed none of the grounding elements that are part of a normal life. I had no job, no home, no phone number, and no plans for the future. I was simply bobbing along between prison and the free world—at this point, not truly belonging in either place.

Eventually, I was led into a small room between the jail and the courtrooms. The clothes Mom had bought for me were delivered in a small, neat stack, pressed and gently folded. I yanked off my crummy jailhouse blues and began dressing. I slid into my brand-new free-world clothes. By the time I pulled the underwear and pants on, I was in emotional trouble.

This was a possibility that had worried me. I didn't want to become so overwhelmed that I wept openly or collapsed in a heap or embarrassed myself in public. I hadn't expected that a new set of clothes would trigger my first big fight to control myself.

But I was completely unprepared for the softness, the comfort, and the fit of clothes that had been designed to look good *and* feel good. It had been so long since I had felt soft fabric against my skin, since I had worn a shirt with buttons. It seemed like a lifetime since I had last pulled on pants that fit—and felt as smooth as silk. These were not wildly expensive clothes by any means. My mother had picked them up at the last minute at Kohl's, a department store I hadn't even heard of.

For me, these new clothes were a revelation—but then, I'd spent the past twenty-five years wearing clothes designed to further my punishment. The prison uniforms were meant to strip a person of individuality, to take away the smallest comforts, to crush any bit of personal pride that hadn't been destroyed during a trial or a plea deal or a crime or a conviction.

I got a catch in my throat when I thought about the last time I had worn khaki pants and a button-down shirt. Who was that guy? That kid? That man who'd had no gray hair or laugh lines? And that was certainly an ironic phrase in my case—I hadn't laughed nearly enough in the past twenty-five years.

The last time I had seen myself dressed like this, Chris and I were dancing to Fleetwood Mac and the Eagles. On TV we were watching Denzel Washington on *St. Elsewhere,* back when he was not yet a big movie star. I remembered dressing something like this when I saw what had then been the brand-new hit movie—the now timeworn *Top Gun.* Culturally, I had missed so much that I didn't even *know* what I had missed.

I was like some kind of modern Rip Van Winkle—a man who fell off the face of the earth in 1987 and groggily reappeared nearly twenty-five years later. I had a lot of catching up to do, and getting through this first day was a big step.

Finally dressed, I was ushered into a small hallway somewhere behind the judge's bench. The area soon filled with the people who had fought selflessly every step of the way to get me here. John Raley wrapped me in a massive bear hug. Nina Morrison and her unforgettable smile enveloped me, too. Barry Scheck was waiting there to introduce himself—this time, in person—and to lead yet another lucky Innocence Project success story back into the real world.

I looked up and saw the tall, lean figure of my original attorney Bill Allison walking toward me. If he had not preserved the record, if he had not handed my case to Barry Scheck, if he had not cared— I might still be in prison. I hugged him.

I owed him.

I owed them all. I owed them my very life.

When we finally walked into the courtroom, I was stunned at how packed it was. Standing room only! Was I *that* great a curiosity?

My family was sitting in the front row—beaming. There, as always, were my long-suffering mother and father, who had been through so much, who had done so much, for so long—for me. My sister Vicky and her husband, Mike, were there, too. So were my uncle Ron and aunt Jackie and their son, my cousin Greg. I walked over and embraced them all, trying not to cry before anything had even happened.

It was hard.

I took my seat at a table in the front with Barry, John, and Nina. The bailiff called the court to order, and Judge Harle began to speak. I wish I could say that his words were moving and meaningful and I would never forget them. But I don't remember a thing—not a word, not a sentiment, not a syllable. Once again, I was in a court-room—and in shock.

Barry Scheck, on the other hand, was in his element. He guided me through the performance like a generous and experienced ring-master, at every point making sure his half-trained circus act didn't misstep during the big show.

The hearing ended when the judge issued an order that I be re-leased on personal recognizance. I do remember hearing the gavel pound and knowing that in that instant my prison life had come to a close.

I could breathe.

Barry addressed the throngs of recorders, cameras, microphones, and media members straining to get what they needed for their stories, blog posts, articles, and editorials. Apparently those people packing the courtroom were *all* covering my case—a big change from the last time I'd been in a Williamson County courtroom. The other startling difference was that, this time, they were friendly. After Barry answered their questions, I took a few. And I actually saw people tear up in sympathy. It was the beginning of my understanding that the real world had been waiting for me—that life out here was going to be okay.

I did notice—with amusement—that every time I smiled or moved, it unleashed a torrent of shutter clicks. My every word and expression was being examined under a massive moving, whirring, and jostling microscope. It was intimidating, but this kind of pressure was *nothing* compared to the perils of prison. It took more than a bunch of reporters to scare me.

My legal team had told me just to speak from my heart, which helped me find my words. I simply tried to tell the people writing about my life what I felt at that moment, what this day meant to me and to my family. More than anything, I wanted what had happened to me to *mean* something, to make a difference. I remember finishing up by saying that all the colors seemed extra bright and the women were real good looking.

Everyone laughed. I was still trying not to cry.

John Raley pushed me through the crowd like the University of Oklahoma lineman he'd once been. Just before we stepped through the courthouse doors, he whispered, "When you step outside, breathe freedom, Michael." We left the building, and I turned my face up to the sun—a free man in the free world, finally.

It was a perfect fall day—sunny, cool, and beautiful. It reminded me of the gorgeous fall days I had once taken for granted—the days

I would from now on treasure like the precious and priceless gifts they were.

We piled into my brother-in-law's truck and were pulling out of the parking lot when I saw Barry walking toward us, holding a woman by the arm. She was crying.

She had been on my jury.

She was a former high school teacher, who for twenty-five years had told her students how she'd done her civic duty and sent me to prison. Now she knew that everything she had believed for so many years was wrong. This poor soul was standing outside our truck, tear streaked and aching with remorse. My lawyers were eager to get me out of there, and frankly, I was ready to get on with my life, too. Still, I felt I couldn't just leave her. I knew too well what it was to hurt all alone. I reached out the window and did the only thing I could at that moment. I cupped her cheek in my hand and tried to reassure her that it was okay—that I understood, that it wasn't her fault.

It was time we all began putting our pain behind us.

When we drove out of the lot, someone yelled for me to look up at the courthouse. There, lining the railing was a row of uniformed cops and courthouse employees—all waving and applauding me.

Gerry Goldstein—a San Antonio attorney and friend of Barry's—was dumbstruck. He said he'd never seen anything like it in his life—cops applauding a defendant. God knows, it was a much different send-off than I got the last time I left a Williamson County courtroom.

Our whole team reassembled at a secluded restaurant where the Innocence Project had reserved a private dining room. This wasn't just for me—it was for them as well—people like Diana Faust who wrote all of the early briefs asking for relief in my case. Because of all the overtime hours, all the pressure, and all the hard work this group had put in to get to this day, they needed to celebrate, too. And they deserved it. There were people there I'd never even met or heard of but whose hard work had helped set me free.

The wine was really flowing, and the food was incredible. I ordered trout. It was the first time in twenty-five years I had eaten fish that hadn't been smashed into a square and tasted like chicken. It was the first time in twenty-five years I shared a table with people who had never stabbed anyone—so I was finally able to use a knife and a fork. Good-bye, cruel spork.

The silverware felt wonderfully heavy and solid in my hands. The sound of my knife and fork clinking on the plate was impressive. After years of eating off plastic trays with a plastic utensil, the look and feel of the silver, china, and crystal seemed wildly luxurious. I'd gone from pauper to prince in one day.

I wiped my hands on the linen napkin much more than I needed to. For me, simply *having* a napkin was a novelty. If I wanted or needed a napkin in the prison chow hall, I had to bring toilet paper from my cell.

But the real kicker was having someone serve me dinner—having another person carefully place my full plate in front of me, smile at me, make sure my glass was filled, and fuss over whether or not I liked the food. For me, this was absolutely mind-boggling. "Prison dining" (insert derisive laughter here) is eating every single meal in the world's worst cafeteria. The cooks don't care, the kitchen workers hate their jobs, and the food is the absolute cheapest and most poorly prepared possible. This experience was like a preview of heaven—the very best meal I'd ever had.

There were speeches and laughter, the reliving of tight moments and maddening delays. Barry told long, hilarious stories that always came back to make a powerful point. The other attorneys at the table made a series of long-winded toasts and then laughed uproariously at their tendency to make long-winded toasts. The Innocence Project had a cameraman tape me promising to never, ever, ever tell another lawyer joke—a vow that's been easy to keep. Lawyers, these lawyers, had saved my life.

Restaurant workers peeked in at us and whispered to one another when they recognized me as the man they'd seen on TV.

My mother was as happy as I had ever seen her—ever. She was talking about all the things she wanted to help me catch up on, and she mentioned casually how eager I was to swim—saying that I'd been an avid scuba diver and couldn't wait to get back in the water.

I had suffered quite a dry spell. The only water I'd dived into for decades was the crowded communal prison shower.

Instantly, one of the Innocence Project angels whipped out her phone and called the hotel where we would be spending the night to make sure they had a pool. They did, in the basement—just waiting for me.

I got the impression that if there hadn't been a pool, we would've stayed somewhere else. I don't know if they were just trying to fulfill an exoneree's wishes or were simply crazy. Either way, I felt honored, unworthy, and deeply touched. After so many years in the company of some of society's worst, these people were a gift from God. They made me feel human again, loved again—alive again.

The Innocence Project had reserved rooms for me—and my parents—at the posh InterContinental hotel in Austin. Some of the attorneys who helped me were staying there, too. That night I learned how to use a key card to open the door to my room—a first for me. When I looked inside, I was stunned. Just the night before I had been in a cell with cracked concrete walls. Now I stood in the entryway to what seemed like the most beautiful room I'd ever seen. There was a marble floor in the bathroom, a king-size bed, a gigantic flat-screen TV, and—best of all—absolute and utter privacy. It made me dizzy.

But what thrilled me most that night was my chance to finally get back in the water. Sadly, I had no bathing suit. Someone whispered to me that I could just wear my boxers—from a distance, they said, no one would notice. Brilliant.

I donned the luxurious white terry-cloth hotel robe and the slippers conveniently waiting in my closet and walked alone to the elevator, not quite sure if it was truly acceptable to march around the hotel dressed like this. I felt terribly out of place in my robe, but

I appeared to be the only one who saw it that way. People smiled at me in the elevator.

When the doors to the pool area opened, a couple entered and called me by name. The man shook my hand and congratulated me. His wife hugged my neck and wished me well. They were complete strangers, but they'd seen me on TV. After so many years of being the bogey man, I had suddenly become everyone's best friend. It was jarring—but good.

At poolside, I found my mom; Nina—still smiling; Rachel Pecker, a kind Innocence Project intern; and Angela Amel, the warmhearted Innocence Project specialist who helped exonerees get resettled. They had been waiting for me. This formidable female phalanx had my back—they gave me maternal love and ferocious protection, understanding and caring friendship, even legal advice. They were there to make sure my first swim was as good as it could be. I don't know that I will ever again feel so sheltered, so lucky, or so loved.

For them, this may have been simply my inaugural swim. For me, it was more like a baptism—a rebirth back into the free world.

I plunged in, and my body instantly remembered what I had always loved about the water—the weightlessness, the way I could glide great distances, the feeling of floating—the utter peace.

I was swimming.

I was flying.

I was free.

John Raley and Barry Scheck soon appeared poolside. John told me his firm had a tradition of celebrating every legal success by sitting in a hot tub and drinking cold beer. An ice bucket with beer bottles sprouting from it like a glass bouquet materialized. John and I got in the hot tub while everyone else gathered around, swapping stories old and new. Barry regaled us with the amazing details of cases past and present—and future. His delivery, even after a few drinks—even after *I* had a few drinks—was mesmerizing.

When hotel management finally came and told us—with regret—that the pool was closed, we wrapped up and headed back upstairs.

To my astonishment, I found in my room an ice bucket—complete with a champagne bottle and elegant glass flutes. Who had ordered it? Who had put it there? It was hard to wrap my head around the obvious fact that someone had done that for me.

Preparing for bed, I walked into the bathroom. The difference between the sumptuous carpet and the bathroom's smooth marble floor registered on my bare feet. Moving from the carpet to the marble thrilled me so much that I performed a little two-step dance, going back and forth, back and forth.

Later, I tried to set the newfangled alarm clock—then gave up and called the front desk, asking for a wake-up call.

Then, with great joy, I sank into the bed—deep into the pile of pillows, between the pressed, cool white sheets, savoring the luxurious cushioned mattress. I turned the light off and just lay there—feeling as though I was reclining on a cloud, savoring the profound comfort and the incredible silence.

For the first time in twenty-five years, I quickly fell fast asleep. Smiling.

Of course, I woke up at 3:30 A.M., rested and ready for breakfast.

My body clock was going to need a reset after so many years of eating, working, and sleeping on a prison schedule that seemed to arbitrarily set the first meal of the day for the middle of the night. And that was just one of the many adjustments I would be making from that moment on.

When we left the hotel, I received another round of applause from the bellhops, the waiters, the people behind the desk, and the guests checking in and out. This stuff was going to be hard to get used to.

We drove off in my brother-in-law Mike's truck, headed for my parents' house. The five-hour drive seemed to speed by, helped along by the celebration going on inside. We rocked the Texas-size pickup with laughter and excitement, questions and plans, the giddiness of finally feeling hope and promise and possibility. It was the drive home I'd dreamed of—for decades.

Walking into my parents' home again was staggering, for a number of reasons. First, at long last, I felt safe—truly safe. At the same time, it was the beginning of my real understanding of how far I had to go in rebuilding my life. For now, the plan was for me to live in my folks' spare bedroom—a sobering reality for a fifty-seven-year-old man.

It would be some time before my state compensation package would be worked out and I would actually have any money in hand. I fretted about being a burden to my parents, after they had done so much. I worried that I would have to ask the people I loved for money after they had already pumped so much money into my case—and put up with so much during my imprisonment. It all triggered small flashbacks to the shame I'd felt for my years of being a drain on everyone—emotionally and financially. I wanted to pick up where I'd left off, but I was a long, long way from being able to do so.

What I didn't anticipate was that so many people, beginning with my family, were going to be so good to me. My sister Vicky and her husband, Mike, put an embarrassing amount of money in my pocket. My younger brother, Matt, repeatedly stuffed bills into my hand. My youngest sister, Patti, and her husband, Riley, were also generous to a fault.

I had been asked to do an interview with *60 Minutes*, and the day I met with a representative of the show, I was also introduced to Caitlin Baker, the daughter of Debra Masters Baker—the other case where DNA evidence showed that Mark Norwood had been involved.

Like Eric, Caitlin had been only three at the time of her mother's murder. The two of us really hit it off. She was so bright and so understanding—we both knew we shared a special, sad bond. But I was stunned when Caitlin gave me her MacBook, saying that, although it was a few years old, I might be able to use it. I was almost unable to control my excitement and gratitude. It was just another example of the sweet, sweet gestures extended to me by so many people in the free world.

Not long after, another person with a link to Caitlin's family called, telling me a friend of his had seen my story on TV—and wanted to give me a fourth-row-center seat at a Willie Nelson concert, and a night at a beautiful condo on Town Lake. I even got to meet Willie himself backstage.

Frankly, this was becoming embarrassing—but every kindness, every act of generosity, even if it was just an open smile or a warm handshake—was reaffirming my belief in the potential for goodness inside each human heart. It can be hard to find—especially so in prison—but the people I met in the free world were redeeming my trust in humanity.

Topping just about everything else, a member of John Raley's church gave me his "old" Chevy Tahoe. Really. After hearing my story, he just gave it to me. When I got the news, I closed the door to my bedroom and wept.

Each day in the free world seemed to erase another day of the darkness I'd endured in prison—and I was so grateful, so profoundly grateful.

A few weeks after my release, my father had a mild stroke. It wasn't bad and he quickly began to recover, but for me, it was sobering. The fact that I was there—I was *finally* there—to help my mom, to do what I could for my dad, to at long last step in and be an active, accountable, participating part of my family gave me unimaginable peace. And it reaffirmed my belief that God's universe runs on its own clock and its own calendar—that my long road to release was not simply a series of coincidences, accidents, setbacks, and eventual victories—that all of this was meant to happen exactly the way it did.

Within a few weeks of my release, I visited John Raley's beautiful home in Houston—but not just to see John and his wife, Kelly. John had kindly set up the first meeting I would have since my release with my son, Eric, and his new wife, Maggie.

I'm not embarrassed to admit that I was nervous—very nervous. I so much wanted everything to go well. I also knew I had a long way to go before Eric could accept me as a real father again. We had to overcome years of lies, decades of misinformation about who I was and what my relationship with Chris had been—and the long, long separation we had experienced. The two of us had a great deal to get past, but I was desperate to begin trying.

I sat with John and Kelly waiting for Eric and Maggie to arrive, feeling something like a teenager with first-date jitters. When the doorbell rang, we all walked to the foyer. John opened the door, welcoming them.

Since my release, I had seen photos of Eric taken by my mother and sister Vicky. I had looked him up online at the Catholic school where he worked as an educator. I'd seen pictures of his graduation and shots of him at work and photos of the day he and Maggie were married. But in my heart, he hadn't grown past the toddler who needed me or his mother to help him with virtually everything—a little blond boy who liked to hold my hand, talk to me while I worked on projects around the house, and sweetly fall asleep in my arms.

The man who walked in the door that evening had changed so much. I had changed, too—not just on the outside but on the inside. Seeing Eric was a bit like attending a high school reunion and vaguely recognizing a face—*knowing* you have a history with that person but being so separated by life experience and years apart that it takes time and work to reconnect.

I had projected so much onto this moment—and Eric had his own fears about meeting with me again. After all, he was still trying to rebuild the truth of *his* life. Now, here he was standing in front of an overly excited guy with gray hair—a villain turned victim, but still very much the man he had learned to hate. We shared a handshake that shakily morphed into a hug.

Sitting down in the living room, we chatted stiffly, and as I looked at Eric, I began to see small signs that I recognized as being part of our lost—but still in there somewhere—connection. We were wearing virtually identical shoes, and our pants looked like carbon copies.

We'd each chosen almost matching shirts for our big day. And when I looked at his face, I saw Chris looking back at me—through all the time and all the pain. It was startling—and comforting. I struggled to keep my emotions in check.

As I talked to Maggie, I saw that my son had chosen a wife with the same stunning blue eyes and long dark hair as his mother. She was warm and kind, encouraging and easy to talk to. I saw Chris in her, too, and I was so profoundly grateful for her presence in his life. Maggie was pregnant, and it wouldn't be long until their first daughter was born.

I didn't know it at the time, but they had already decided to name their little girl Christine Marie, another way in which Eric and his wife kept faith with—and built their family around—his lost, mourned, beloved, beautiful mother.

I could feel myself talking faster and faster, as if sheer speed of speech was a way to make up for lost time. Finally, John had one of his brilliant ideas and ushered us into the backyard, where we sat on a wooden swing under a massive old oak. John must have turned the outdoor lights off when he went inside. Eric and I found ourselves sitting there alone in the dark, finally beginning to share a few of the moments we had been denied for so long.

The swing creaked as we talked on that fall night. We eventually found our rhythm and our common ground—chatting about the peccadillos and personal joys of our shared family. We couldn't see each other's faces, but I could feel him smiling. I smiled, too.

I felt like I had won the lottery. I would discover later that I had projected more onto that night's conversation and first meeting than Eric had. For me, being with him was a homecoming—for him, it was the beginning of a long, dark, difficult chapter in a life that had already suffered more challenges than anyone deserved. Looking back, I recognize with regret that, while I was euphoric, he was struggling. In fact, his understanding of his whole life was falling apart before his eyes.

Eric had not been told much about his mother. Her brutal death and my conviction in the case quickly became such a terribly painful part of family history that no one wanted to—or felt strong enough to—talk about it with him. Even at an early age, children sense that kind of family taboo, and Eric had grown up knowing not to ask—and not to look back—no matter how much he needed and wanted to.

As Eric and I have grown closer, I have been committed to doing what I can to fill in those blanks. I want to tell him as much as I can about Chris and how we had all lived together—so long ago—so happily and so full of hope about the future. That night, when he and Maggie said good-bye, I felt like we had made a beginning—we had scratched the surface of all that lay beneath the bare outlines of each other's lives.

At the doorway, we hugged again. For me, my hug was a thank-you—and a blessed reassurance that, while we had a long, long road ahead, our journey had at last begun.

CHAPTER TWENTY-FOUR

EACH DAY THAT I WOKE UP AT MY PARENTS' HOUSE WAS A FRESH SHOCK to my system.

The sweet silence that's so much part of rural life was jarring to me. Sometimes, it was so quiet I thought I could hear the grass growing. I had spent decades successfully tuning out the chaotic cacophony of Planet Prison—now that I was living in a world so still and so peaceful, I felt overwhelmed.

My ears were no longer battered, but they seemed filled by the *lack* of sound that had been part of my life for so long. There were no slamming cell doors, the loud buzzers were gone, and the years of belligerent shouting had finally been quieted.

The constant, awful roar of anger that permeates every aspect of penitentiary life was gone, and it left a gap in my world that began to fill with extraordinarily beautiful sounds and sensations—simple elements of daily life I had gone without for years.

That first morning in my new bathroom at my parents' house, I realized I could hear water gushing from the sink's faucet as though it were a mighty river. The sound of it gurgling down the drain was almost deafening. I reveled in the muffled noise of my toothbrush scrubbing back and forth on my teeth. I could even hear myself flossing, for crying out loud.

But it was the sound of the razor scraping against my whiskers that really floored me. I hadn't heard that for so long. I remembered hearing it the first time I shaved—or really the first time I actually *needed* to shave. Like so many teenage boys, I began shaving long before I had even a trace of a reason. Back when I was a teenager, when I *finally* heard that crisp scratch of razor on my burgeoning beard, it was a sign that I had arrived—I had become a man. It was the sound of taking care of myself, of caring about how I looked, especially to others. It felt that way to me all over again. I had missed it more than I knew.

Turning on the shower and hearing the gentle spray hit the porcelain tub and tile was a revelation. Behind bars, the showers were so different—they were institutional, crowded and loud, an ugly cattle yard for people accustomed to being treated like livestock—and it always seemed someone you'd rather not see naked was doing something no one should have to witness.

I saw older inmates knocked down on the slick shower floors, would-be musclemen strutting to intimidate or embarrass the female guards required to stand watch, and creeps attacking other inmates when they were at their most vulnerable. I remembered one unforgettable day in the shower in my early years, when I stood next to an older Latino man whose chest sported two giant tattoos of clown faces.

The man's nipples served as the clowns' noses.

The instant I saw this, I burst out laughing. The old guy glared my way. Someone informed me immediately that this was fairly common among men of his age who shared his background and social circles—and it wasn't funny.

Who knew?

You could learn all kinds of things in a prison shower, but there was seldom a chance to embrace the simple joy of getting clean—to appreciate the feel of warm water on skin or smell the sweet scent of a fresh bar of soap. When a person goes without these elements of everyday life long enough, experiencing it all again can be mind-blowing.

I toweled off—with one of my mom's wonderfully soft towels—while I listened to the coffeepot perking away in the kitchen and my mother quietly setting the table for breakfast. Through the bathroom's open window, I recognized the noise of squirrels racing and scrambling about, vaulting through the trees and scavenging in the grass. The ethereal rush of wind through the leaves gave me goose bumps. I privately rejoiced in the persistent buzz of a hardworking bee having its way in my mom's flower bed. When I heard the high-pitched hum of a mosquito sullying the beautiful Texas fall weather—man, even *that* sounded good.

This was music to me—the sound of normal life. I promised myself I would never again take any of it for granted. The intoxicating sounds, scents, and visual gifts of the natural world I'd been banished from—the familiar universe I had missed more than I dreamed possible—gave me boundless joy. I felt like an astronaut who had just come back after a decades-long trip to the barren planet Mars and was celebrating every second of his return to our lush Earth.

Of course, there were profound changes in technology that awaited me—and mastering them was a mixed bag. Because I had been locked up in 1987, I had never used a cell phone—never owned a personal computer, a CD player, a DVD, or any kind of GPS device. TV remotes were a complete puzzlement. What was different for me, though, was that I'd never had to struggle with the progressive nature of technological change. I hadn't had the burden of walking around yelling into a heavy brick-size phone or stumbling through life with a balky PC that would swallow up a person's work without a moment's warning. I came in at the top.

The iPhone my sister gave me was my first brush with new communication technology, and I loved it. My first computer was a MacBook, and it is wonderful. The navigation system in my truck is voice activated, so if I feel lost, I can literally "ask" for help finding my way home.

There were moments when I did feel like I had stepped into the future, but the transition wasn't nearly as difficult as it sounds. I felt like the generation before me had been the guinea pigs. I was the lucky beneficiary of everything everyone else had learned the hard way. I was struck by how digital systems seem to operate so intuitively. Apps were simple to download and understand. Wireless service was everywhere. To my amazement, I had no problem learning from online tutorials. And if I still needed help, there were plenty of people to ask. I could stop practically anyone on the street and get advice and answers.

Other changes in society were more layered and required different sorts of changes in me. For years I had avoided coffee, because what prison serves up as "coffee" tends to be a toxic, blackened, burned-tasting version of what everyone else knows and loves. Newly unleashed in the free world, I was amazed at the number and variety of coffeehouses that now dotted every portion of the landscape. This transformation into Latte Land didn't make any sense until my niece Staci gave me a gift card and a snazzy coffee cup from Starbucks.

My first attempt to order coffee from the Starbucks menu was like being forced to fly a jet, but I have learned. Boy, have I learned. Now, coffee is a daily delight—and it tastes even better than it did before prison. I've discovered something for the first time—again.

I also had to relearn how to walk barefoot, because for twenty-five years my unprotected feet hadn't touched the ground. I didn't dare make contact with the floor in the prison showers or the cells. God only knew what kinds of diseases or debris lay waiting to ravage my unprotected soles. Early on, when I walked through my parents' house without flip-flops, shower shoes, or my old prison pleather boots, I felt like I was marching around naked. The feel of the wood, the warmth of a streak of sun on the floor—it was all confounding and confusing, and somehow it felt wrong to me, even dangerous.

Equally disconcerting was the fact that, for the first time in twenty-five years, I was able to get a good look at myself. In prison there are—of course—very few actual glass mirrors. Inmates had to make do with mirror-shaped pieces of polished metal or plastic commissary "mirrors" that offered fun-house-worthy reflections of their faces. Whenever I was issued a new ID card, I could see a photograph of myself, but that was one of the infrequent ways I got to see what I really looked like or how I had changed through the years.

Now, when I looked in a real mirror, part of me felt I didn't know "that guy." He looked like a very tired version of my old self and sported more gray hair than I'd expected. Mirrors are everywhere in the free world, and it seemed like "that guy" followed me all over the place. I'd see myself in the mirror in a restaurant lobby and, for a moment, feel like "There he is again!"

Slowly, but surely, I adjusted.

Food—all kinds of food, every kind of food—became a playground for me. My mother would ask what I wanted to eat, and I would always say, "Anything, anything at all." I simply could *not* be disappointed, not after eating prison swill for so long.

For me, restaurants weren't just sources of good food, they were locations for life-changing moments of insight. I began to constantly seek out new places that served up dishes or types of food I had never tasted. Sushi? Yes! Indian food? Why not? Italian tonight? Bring it on! A Brazilian steak house? Pull up a chair for me!

The sheer bounty available in the free world was overwhelming.

Not too long after I'd been released, my sister Vicky took me out to a casual place and we decided to have a go at the salad bar. I gleefully loaded my plate with greens, fresh tomatoes, cucumbers, various cheeses, mushrooms, chopped meats, salad dressings, and a big bunch of bread.

When we got to our table, I looked down at my plate—overflowing with so many of the foods I had missed for so long—and I had to fight as hard as I could to keep from breaking down in sobs. I hadn't been prepared to be so emotionally shaken simply by the fixings I'd found on a particularly nice salad bar. For me, however, "losing it" over something small or seemingly insignificant was an everyday reality.

In the first days after my release, my emotions—my despair, gratitude, and relief—were always right there with me, always ready to burst out and remind me of who I was and what had happened, and how much it hurt. Sometimes, darker emotions—the instinctual way I sensed a threat, the anger I had inside me—also came out. As I was leaving that same restaurant with Vicky, I saw another customer—a shady-looking guy—look my beautiful sister up and down, clearly exhibiting what we used to call in church "impure thoughts." It felt like a violation of someone I loved. I quickly acted on prison instinct—glaring at him with murderous rage, like I was going to kill him.

In prison, we had a very crude term for this kind of violent way of staring at a person—but then we had a very crude term for *everything*. Basically, this prison glare boiled down to using your eyes to let someone know that crossing you was going to end up being painful, bloody, disfiguring. This was how we communicated inside—how we protected ourselves, protected each other, and warned off unwanted "special friends." It was a kind of American Sign Language for the very angry and very often violent, and every message said the same thing: "I will hurt you very badly. Don't be a fool."

Oddly, out in the free world, I felt a little bit like a cop on the beat. When I looked around, I saw everybody as a perpetrator, a suspect, or an unindicted coconspirator. Over time I had to work hard to let that lingering suspicion go.

Still, there were moments that caught me by surprise. A few times, when I was in the yard raking leaves and I would hear a siren, that old fight-or-flight response kicked in. The police! My heart raced for a few seconds and I had to talk myself down. It told me that, while I'd made it out, I wasn't fully home yet.

And I had to figure out what came next.

Part of that was answered for me by the direction the legal case took as a result of work John Raley, Nina Morrison, and the Innocence Project had done months before.

Even as they worked to free me through advances in DNA technology, they took steps to make sure I had other options, should the
bandanna not hold the biological evidence I needed to prove my
innocence.

While they were fighting to get the testing done, my team began
to operate on a parallel track to win my release—by arguing that
my right to due process had been violated. Any success they had
there could win me a new trial—and they believed we could have
effectively fought all the weaknesses in the case against me with new
information, new arguments, and new expertise.

Building on that effort, Barry Scheck had told the current district
attorney, John Bradley, that we wanted to depose a number of people in Williamson County law enforcement who had worked on my
case. Bradley, ever the obstructionist, deployed as many procedural
roadblocks as possible.

But when the DNA on the bandanna cleared me, named Mark
Norwood as my wife's murderer, and led to the discovery of another
of Norwood's victims, Bradley's opposition evaporated—not immediately, but when it became clear the tide of public opinion had
angrily turned against him, he came around.

My legal team was now able to push on with the depositions, but
they had to be done in a terrifically compressed time frame. We had
only thirty days to uncover information that had been hidden for
twenty-five years—and it had to be pulled out of people who didn't
want to cooperate and didn't want to admit to their own roles in my
wrongful conviction.

Still, Barry Scheck and John Raley quickly began to take sworn
statements from the people who had been most important in my
conviction. I wasn't involved in the day-to-day planning of their
approach—I was still enjoying adjusting to air-conditioning, hot and
cold water, and a world filled with good and decent people. I didn't
attend most of the depositions. But my lawyers filled me in on what
they were finding.

I learned that Medical Examiner Roberto Bayardo took back

virtually all of his testimony that Chris could have died before I went to work. He admitted that what he'd said during my trial had not been scientifically based—and protested that Ken Anderson had twisted his testimony words in an effort to convince the jury there was a "scientific" reason to believe I was guilty.

Mike Davis, the assistant attorney who helped Anderson convict me, claimed that he simply didn't remember talking to the jury after my verdict or telling them that if they had seen the prosecutor's entire investigative file—instead of just a portion of it—they might have found reason to question my guilt.

That old "I don't recall" tactic would become all too familiar.

We did learn from Sergeant Don Wood, the chief investigator in my case, that he had expected to testify during my trial. He said he was waiting outside the courtroom to be called when Sheriff Boutwell stopped him and announced that *he* would be the law enforcement witness taking the stand. Wood, now savaged by strokes and in precarious health, said that the move had surprised him. He wasn't sure why things had changed.

Doug Arnold, one of the assistant attorneys under Anderson, explained exactly why this had happened. He said that Ken Anderson had an ongoing strategy of not allowing the chief investigator to take the stand. If the investigator didn't testify, Anderson was not required to turn over to defense attorneys all the notes, interviews, and information the investigator had compiled. So Anderson kept his opposing attorneys in the dark, orchestrating a questionable way around legal requirements and, in the process, giving himself an unfair advantage.

Finally, the last deposition was scheduled.

Ken Anderson himself would be sitting at the long, narrow table inside a jury deliberation room deep in the heart of the Williamson County courthouse. Barry Scheck would do his usual expert job of leading the questioning. John Raley would sit beside him, offering alternative ideas and lines of questioning. And they both wanted me to be there.

This would be the first time I had come face-to-face with Anderson since my release. I knew he was now a judge. I knew his friend and cohort John Bradley had done everything in his power as the new DA to delay or derail my release—and to keep Anderson from suffering any consequences for his behavior. I knew Anderson did not want to talk about my conviction or his role in it. But after twenty-five years in prison, as I was still trying so hard to rebuild my shattered relationship with my son and staggering around the real world trying to catch up on everything and everyone I had missed—I felt I deserved to know why this had happened to me.

After hours of questioning—sadly—we got no truth, no insight, and no understanding from Ken Anderson. We heard about how he couldn't remember the details of my case, how he "thought" he would have handed over evidence but couldn't remember actually having done it. We got explanations of how skillfully and fairly he had always run his office. We got speeches on the law and a whole lot of defensive posturing about his approach to trying a case and how he had honed his skills over the years. We got repeated testaments on what a good man he was and what good he had done for the community.

In other words, we got nothing.

I had been sitting patiently the whole time, all dressed up in my sports coat and tie—primed to sympathize with Anderson if he owned up *in the least* to shortcomings in how he'd handled my case. Human beings make mistakes—I understood that. He could have apologized, or said he wished he could go back and do things differently. He could have shown that he understood at least one iota of what I had been through—he could have been honest.

I am not and was not vengeful. I certainly didn't wish him harm. I just wanted to know *why*. Why had he done this to me? What was his motive? Did he have any misgivings at the time? Did he think about his responsibility to *my* life at all?

He didn't give us those answers. Instead, he revealed—sometimes inadvertently—that he still cared more about himself than about the law and that he still wanted to protect his own future more than actually consider what he had done to my life. After so many hours—and so many years—it became too much for me.

I pushed away from the table and headed to the back of the room. I placed my hands on the walls and leaned in—trying hard to keep my anger from boiling over. I heard Anderson squeak to Barry and John, "Your client seems upset."

It was clear he was afraid of me, worried that I would attack him in some "penitentiary" way. I had no plans to do anything like that, but I knew I was probably looking at him in a way that scared this soft man who'd been so hard on so many people—this guy who'd sent so many people to prison and rightly feared he wouldn't last a day behind bars on his own.

Later, during a break in the deposition, John leaned over and told me that the look on my face had frightened Anderson, because it was the kind of look only someone who had been in prison for twenty-five years could master. I told him not to worry. "I'm fine," I said. "He's just a wuss." Actually, I used the kind of word someone who had served twenty-five years in prison would choose.

The transcripts of the depositions and sworn statements were all bundled into an argument to the Texas state supreme court, requesting a special court of inquiry—an examination of whether Ken Anderson had broken the law or the ethics required of a prosecutor in Texas. It was a long-shot case.

But we won.

The Texas Supreme Court appointed Rusty Hardin—a Houston legal legend—as the special prosecutor. He would essentially be trying Anderson in front of a judge who would decide whether the case would go forward to a criminal court. Judge Louis Sturns, of Fort Worth, would be presiding. He was known for his even temperament and fair decisions

At the same time, the State Bar of Texas announced it would be launching its own investigation, to see if Anderson's handling of my case warranted disbarment. That meant he could lose his position as a judge, his financial security, and his status. There was even a possibility he would face jail time.

I began to realize that this investigation was about much more than just me—or what had happened to me inside our flawed legal system. This was about fairness, about making certain that Texas prosecutors understood that their first priority should be the proverbial search for the truth—not a personal quest to rack up convictions, garner power, and move up the political ladder.

I did not want what had happened to me to happen to anyone else. The Innocence Project and attorneys like Barry Scheck, John Raley, and Nina Morrison were making a crucial difference in our system of justice. I wanted to do the same.

Even though I would have liked nothing better than to simply go home and begin rebuilding what was left of my life, I couldn't walk away from my case or the glaring problems it exposed. If making a difference meant spending more time in courtrooms, if it meant speaking to state lawmakers—if it meant becoming more of a public person than I had ever intended to be—I had an obligation to do it. I had to show at least some measure of the commitment so many people had offered me back when I was stuck behind bars, without any legal hope. There were people just like me still in prison. If the system didn't change, there would be more in the future.

With this court of inquiry, Ken Anderson would now learn what it was like to be on trial for his life—to have every statement, every action, and every decision pulled apart, examined for proof of his flaws, his failings, and his guilt.

But he would have something I did not—he would face a fair and honest prosecution, an unbiased judge, and a public interested in hearing both sides of the case.

Ken Anderson would get justice. That could be what he feared most of all.

CHAPTER TWENTY-FIVE

IN THE TWENTY-SIX YEARS SINCE I'D FIRST COME TO THE WILLIAMSON County Courthouse seeking justice, the small-town Texas charm hadn't changed—at least not on the surface. There were still tiny cafes in which to grab a cup of coffee or a piece of pie—or both. There were vintage shops around the town square that did a brisk business with tourists looking to take home a piece of the sweet long ago.

The historic buildings and the way neighbors still waved at each other from pickup to pickup lent the place a timelessness—a sense that here, things were the way they had always been.

Luckily, that was no longer true. Things here had changed profoundly—and what was about to happen in the county's courthouse would ultimately spread that change throughout the state.

In February 2013, when I came back to Williamson County, I was seen not as the villain in a terrible murder but as the victim in a chilling case of wrongful prosecution.

Believe me, the view this time was better.

The court of inquiry about to be called to order was a one-of-a-kind event in Texas. This form of hearing was an obscure process designed to investigate wrongdoing, usually some kind of illegal or improper act committed by someone who had been serving in an official capacity. Throughout our country, and certainly in my home state, there were very few legal avenues for seeking accountability from the powers that be. Prosecutors, judges, investigators, police—the people who very much had the authority and influence to send you away for life—could not be sued, or brought up on criminal charges, or be made to pay personally or professionally for their "mistakes." A court of inquiry was one of the few ways to demand accountability, but it had never been used against a prosecutor for his choices, methods, and actions in pursuing a murder case.

This was a test.

But it wasn't *only* a test. It was a warning to the powerful that they should play fair with people's lives, an example of how accountability had finally come to the courtroom—not just for the defendant but for the system itself. The fact that Ken Anderson was now a sitting judge made the event all the more shocking.

In an ironic twist, Anderson's fate would be determined in a courtroom just down the hall from his own legal kingdom—the grand setting where he had served as a state district judge for years, ensconced behind his own high bench, draped in his own dark robe. It was terrifying to me that the man who had treated me so unfairly now sat every day in judgment of others.

As I approached the new Williamson County Courthouse on the morning the inquiry began, I felt no apprehension—no flashbacks, no fear. This time, no one was after me. I would not be found guilty. I would not end up in jail. And none of what happened in this hearing would gut my bank account or strip my parents of their savings.

On this day Ken Anderson would be the one weighing those kinds of worries. He would be just another nervous man sitting at a defense table, keeping his head down, hoping for mercy or luck, or what he probably believed he deserved—special treatment.

Rusty Hardin and his superlative staff were more than ready to press the case against Anderson. Hardin and I had met a couple of times in the days leading up to the hearing, and I felt confident in his mastery of the evidence and keen understanding of the case.

Judge Louis Sturns would be functioning essentially as a one-man grand jury. He'd been brought in to hear testimony and arguments and then decide whether there was probable cause to believe that my former prosecutor had broken the law. If Judge Sturns could be convinced of that, Anderson's case would be headed for criminal court, and a warrant would be issued for the former prosecutor's arrest. Anderson would be booked. He would have to make bail.

I knew I was going to be called as the first witness that morning, and the last time I'd testified in a Williamson County courtroom things had not gone well, to say the least. Intellectually, I knew everything was going to be different this time, but still I appreciated John Raley's ardent coaching before we got to court. "Michael, do not be flippant on cross-examination. Don't volunteer information. Simply tell your story, answer the questions, and always speak from your heart."

I was certainly ready to do that.

We got to the courthouse before the doors were unlocked and stood outside, shivering and clutching our coats and shooting the breeze with some of the reporters who had been so important in illuminating my situation for the public.

Brandi Grissom, from *The Texas Tribune*, had beaten all of us to the courthouse that chilly day—something that was entirely typical of her. I'd come to believe she had the kind of investigative chops, determination, and tenacity that might have led her to solve this whole thing if she had been on the story back in 1986.

Pam Colloff, a gifted writer and editor from *Texas Monthly*, was waiting with us, too. She had spent months working on my story. Then she wrote it with eloquence and heartrending detail in two expansive articles. It seemed the whole country had come to know, understand, and care about what had happened.

When we were finally allowed in, we slowly made our way through the airport-worthy security shakedown and headed toward the courtroom. My mother, who felt she had waited far too long for this day, basically bolted ahead of the rest of us to grab herself a premium seat.

She saved one for me as well. Thanks, Mom.

By the time we sat down, Rusty Hardin and his team were taking control of the room. They carried audiovisual equipment, boxes of notes, depositions, evidence, and God knew what else. It would soon become clear that this team's greatest asset was hidden inside Rusty Hardin's head. His brain is a legal computer with a unique understanding of the workings of the human heart. Hardin knows how to speak to real people. He is able to explain great pain or unfairness in a way that can easily be understood. He knew how to characterize honestly—and colorfully—the shenanigans that had gone on during my trial. He knew how to communicate the consequences of those actions for me and far too many others.

The Williamson County bailiffs at the front of the court—who had never before worked with Judge Sturns—nervously told everyone entering the room that the judge *hated* cell phones. They said that if the hearing were punctuated by bings, clicks, ring tones, rock songs, or any other digital distractions, there would be hell to pay. I checked my phone and my mother's about ten times.

The courtroom was packed with familiar faces. Barry Scheck, Nina Morrison, John Raley, and all the other attorneys who'd pitched in on my case were there to greet me—and each other—with bear hugs. They huddled in small pin-striped clumps all over the courtroom to talk about the incredible turnaround this day represented.

There were representatives from the State Bar of Texas, waiting eagerly for evidence that would help them decide whether Ken Anderson should lose his law license.

A few Texas state lawmakers were on hand to witness the goings-on. State Senator Rodney Ellis, who was helping push through legislation designed to keep my nightmare from being repeated, sat a few rows to the rear of me. I knew he was there before I even saw him. His distinctive raspy laugh and buoyant voice let me know that here in the courthouse—just like in the state capitol—Senator Ellis had my back.

Directly behind me sat Caitlin Baker, whose mother had also been killed by the man who killed Chris. Debra Baker's husband, Phillip, and her sister, Lisa, were also there. I noticed Caitlin had recently had the name Debra tattooed on her upper arm to mark the twenty-fifth year since she'd lost her mom.

All of us carried Kleenex. All of us would need it.

Beverly Reeves, an attorney friend who was putting all of us up at her Austin home for the duration of the court of inquiry, sat behind me, on the same packed courthouse bench as the Baker family.

There were two video cameras inside and a phalanx of TV cameras waiting in the hall.

The room was stacked with local defense lawyers who'd previously faced off against Ken Anderson or argued cases before him, or just wanted to see legal history in the making. The place had become a magnet for attorneys who wanted a rare peek at a prosecutor being forced to explain and defend his actions. The legal community knew that too many prosecutors did what Anderson had done in my case.

On one of the benches near the back of the room, Anderson's son sat quietly—looking angry. I didn't approach him, but I felt bad for him and the entire family. Still, I knew that this hearing had to go forward. It wasn't about me and it wasn't about his dad. It was about justice.

Judge Sturns, a tall, elegant man who looked like he'd been born to wear a black robe, swept in through a door behind his bench. A hush swept over the room as he began the hearing.

Rusty Hardin stood up. "We call our first witness, Michael Morton, to the stand." I was sworn in and took a seat in the witness chair next to the judge.

Rusty asked me to recount the day of Chris's killing, to share details about how Sheriff Boutwell had treated me, to remind the courtroom of the way three-year-old Eric had reacted to the tragedy.

I should have seen my emotions coming, but I didn't. Suddenly, it was terribly difficult to speak. Talking about that day—about what Eric had seen—always seemed to summon up such raw feelings. I plunged on, but on occasion, I had to stop midsentence, regain control, and then begin again.

Hardin asked me what my twenty-five years in prison had been like. "Brutal," I told him, trying to be upbeat. "But after a couple of decades I got used to it."

He wanted to know more about what I'd had to adapt to. "I got used to the lack of privacy, the restriction of movement, the forced associations, the lack of seeing my son. The million and one little things that you take for granted that you can't even imagine—clothes that are comfortable, people who are honest, food that tastes good, a comfortable bed to sleep in."

I didn't mention the more brutal aspects of prison life: the bloody fights, the crude behavior, the sense of shame that accompanies every sunrise and is reinforced again and again all day long—the negative assumptions every world-weary guard or warden, prison bus driver, or parole board member made about me for so long.

He asked about my reaction when I first read the transcript of that long-ago phone call between my mother-in-law and Sergeant Wood, where Chris's mother told the investigator that Eric had given her a graphic description of Chris's death.

I told Rusty I had been stunned, simply stunned.

He asked me how I kept bitterness at bay.

"The grace of God," I said—and I meant it. I couldn't have done it on my own.

I went on to tell him, "I don't want revenge. I don't want anything ill for Judge Anderson. But I also realize that there are consequences for our actions and there needs to be accountability. Without that everything falls apart."

I looked at Ken Anderson and saw that he wasn't looking at me. He had his head bent down and was staring—into the table, into his notes, into the abyss. He certainly appeared less sure of himself than he had twenty-six years earlier. Back then he had dominated the courtroom—pacing about, pounding on tables, shedding theatrical tears in front of the jury, and making up wild, disgusting stories about what I had done sexually with my wife's dead body.

In 1987 Anderson had been a young man with his whole future ahead of him—but then so had I. He'd been thinner—and had more hair and more energy. Just like me. Now, sitting beside his high-priced team of attorneys, Anderson looked much older, puffier and paler. He was clearly tired and stressed. He felt unfairly pursued. He felt he didn't deserve this treatment. And he looked like he couldn't quite understand how all of this had happened to him.

I knew what that felt like, too.

Hardin asked me what I hoped the court of inquiry could accomplish.

I felt my face redden and my eyes fill with tears. I couldn't control it. This meant a great deal to me. I very much wanted this process to be fair. I didn't want any more pain for anyone—I simply wanted our lopsided practice of criminal justice to reach a better balance. I didn't want anyone else to go through what I had—and I knew firsthand that there were other people behind bars who, like me, didn't belong there.

I looked straight at Judge Sturns and spoke directly to him. "I ask that you do what needs to be done, but at the same time—to be gentle with Judge Anderson."

Ken Anderson didn't even look up.

Back when I had been released, I'd seen him hold a press conference, telling reporters how sorry he was that "the system" had screwed up. It was astonishing that he still wouldn't admit what had happened to me—or his role in it. His beliefs and his attitude were going to make everything much harder for him.

Everyone in court had to sit through hours of Anderson's video-taped deposition, long bouts of questioning that produced no real answers. It was like a replay of Nixon's version of Watergate. Anderson described how he didn't remember in about seventeen different ways.

He said he *knew* he turned over any exculpatory evidence to my attorneys—then said he didn't actually recall doing so, again and again.

Much of the back-and-forth in the video deposition focused on what came to be known as the "monster transcript"—the recorded phone call between my mother-in-law and Sergeant Don Wood.

Chris's mother said she had been home alone with Eric when he suddenly began talking about what he had seen. She said he had started by telling her that "Mommy was asleep under the flowers," the explanation I had given him at the cemetery when he asked where his mother was.

She told Sergeant Wood that Eric had spread a blanket on the floor of her bedroom and begun kicking it, saying, "Mommy, get up." Chris's mother said she had started to take notes and ask Eric questions. Over the phone, she read her notes to the investigator. The first time I'd seen this conversation, found in the police file and pried out through legal action, I had been incredulous. Eric, though he was only three years old at the time, had given investigators a detailed description of what had happened inside our home—and who had killed Chris.

Eric: Mommy's crying. She's— Stop it. Go away.
Grandmother: Why is she crying?
Eric: Cause the monster's there.
Grandmother: What's he doing?
Eric: He hit Mommy. He broke the bed.
Grandmother: Is Mommy still crying?
Eric: No, Mommy stopped.
Grandmother: Then what happened?
Eric: The monster threw a blue suitcase on the bed, he's mad . . .
Grandmother: Was he big?
Eric: Yeah.
Grandmother: Did he have gloves?
Eric: Yeah, red.
Grandmother: What did he carry in his red gloves?

Eric: Basket.
Grandmother: What was in the basket?
Eric: Wood.

Eric's story contained details that only the police knew, including the blue suitcase the killer had piled on Chris's body. He said that the "monster" had carried wood, which was what had been used to bludgeon Chris. Eric's grandmother told Sergeant Wood she then asked the question she was most afraid to hear answered.

Grandmother: Where was Daddy, Eric? . . . Was Daddy there?
Eric: No, Mommy and Eric was there.

Rita Kirkpatrick then told Sergeant Wood to "get off the . . . domestic thing now and look for the monster and I have no more suspicions in my mind that Mike did it." Rita referred to the killer as "the big monster with the big mustache," apparently repeating a description Eric had given her.

Sergeant Wood asked no further questions and did not appear interested in speaking with Eric himself. Instead, he pushed back, trying to convince her that the "big monster" was simply me in disguise. He said I was probably wearing my scuba suit.

This combination of ignorance and incompetence was no surprise to me. What shocked me was what Ken Anderson had done with this information—he had hidden it, from me and from my attorneys. He'd buried it deep in a file and kept it there for a quarter century. He had not taken it into consideration when deciding whether to file charges against me. It had not tweaked his conscience when he stood before the jury and tearfully pleaded with them to find me guilty and send me to prison.

The question that I wanted an answer to was Why? For what purpose had he kept this information from becoming public during my trial—or my appeals—or my requests for DNA testing?

There were no answers forthcoming from Ken Anderson.

In the video deposition, he said memorably, "There's no way on God's green earth, if that was in my file, I wouldn't have told them that Eric said that a monster had killed his mother."

If Anderson thought he was going to get backup from the assistant attorneys working in his office at the time, he was wrong.

Former Prosecutor Kimberly Dufour Gardner testified she had been stricken when she learned in 2011 that I was innocent. She said she'd truly believed I had killed my wife based on what Anderson had shared with the other attorneys. She said she had heard Anderson discussing my mother-in-law's phone call about the "monster" with Mike Davis, the assistant prosecutor who had helped Anderson try my case. She said she recalled listening to Anderson lay out the details of the phone call. "I remember him leaning up against a door-jamb with his arms crossed, saying 'The kid thinks a monster killed his mother.'"

Later, she told the court that Anderson had gone on to say he—like Sergeant Wood—believed that the "monster" was me wearing my scuba suit. They had apparently touted that theory internally as a way to explain why there weren't any bloody clothes found at our home. Gardner said much of the discussion had focused on Eric being too young to testify and Anderson's belief that Rita's comments could be classified as "hearsay."

Gardner described Anderson as a "mentor" and told the court, "I don't want to be here, but I know what I heard."

Even more damning was the testimony of Doug Arnold, another former assistant prosecutor who was now a Williamson County judge. Judge Arnold had contacted my attorneys after my release, telling them what he knew about Ken Anderson's trial practices—and what he knew about my case. He said, "I felt horrible for Mr. Morton and I felt I owed it to him."

He went on to testify that he "felt terrible about what was going on here at the time, with people trying to quash subpoenas." He recalled for the court a conversation he had had years ago in which Anderson told him that he would simply decide not to call the lead investigator to the witness stand, thereby avoiding his obligation to turn over the investigator's full file and notes.

That was exactly what had happened during my trial. Only Sheriff Boutwell had taken the stand. The only notes my team got to see were those assembled on the first day of the investigation. Everything else—the phone call transcript, the neighbors' reports of a mysterious green van, the man who left that van and walked into the wooded area behind our home, and more—remained hidden from the defense. We didn't know what police had learned, we didn't see evidence that raised doubts about my guilt, we didn't know what to investigate because we didn't know what existed.

It was unfair.

It was morally wrong.

And it was illegal.

And at least one other woman died because police and prosecutors went after the wrong man. I felt sick for the family of Debra Baker as they pressed close to each other, hearing exactly how Williamson County police and prosecutors' mind-boggling ineptitude and arrogance had set the stage for the murder of someone they loved.

My original defense team—"the two Bills"—testified as well, making it clear that they had received nothing of consequence from Ken Anderson's office.

"Did you ever know anything about . . . a conversation between Rita Kirkpatrick and Don Wood about her grandson witnessing the murder?" Rusty Hardin asked Bill Allison.

"No," he responded.

"How certain are you of that?" Hardin pushed.

"One hundred percent," he said, nodding for emphasis.

It was sadly ironic to see how the evidence Anderson had hidden meshed so completely with the argument my attorneys had made at my trial—that an intruder was responsible for Chris's murder. Bill Allison and Bill White had figured out what happened the day Chris died but could not put their hands on the evidence to prove it.

I could see, too, that my case and its outcome had taken an emotional toll on Bill Allison. Anyone who believes lawyers always maintain a "healthy" emotional separation from their clients didn't see his face that day in court. When Rusty Hardin asked him what he had believed about my case for the past twenty-six years, he answered honestly and with great pain. He said he felt "that an innocent man had been convicted and [had] his son taken away from him by the state." He paused and added that it was "hard to explain how I feel. I have felt for a long time that I had really let Michael down somehow."

The truth is, of course, that Bill Allison was the reason my case was investigated by the Innocence Project. He never stopped advocating for me.

It was easy to see which witnesses were most controversial—they drew the biggest crowds. That was certainly the case for John Bradley, the man who had taken over as Williamson County district attorney when Ken Anderson was elevated to the bench. Bradley was known for doing whatever he could to win, an attribute he shared with his mentor.

It was Bradley who'd fought hardest—and longest—against DNA testing that could shed light on Chris's killer's identity. There had already been testimony about how they'd met privately to discuss strategy for delaying my requests for testing. Bradley and Anderson appeared to have worked together to brainstorm legal arguments that would slow-walk my case through the courts. They'd both spoken dismissively about my case to the media.

Bradley, who seemed to be perpetually tanned—believe me, that's the kind of thing someone who's spent twenty-five years in prison notices—was up next on the stand. He'd lost his seat in a bitter primary fight to another Republican, a woman who came in vowing to clean house, not knowing exactly what kind of mess was waiting there. One of my lawyers had heard that, when she moved into her new office, she opened one of the drawers of the desk John Bradley had used. Lying inside was a dead snake someone had placed there for her to find. Welcome to the Williamson County Courthouse.

John Bradley was called to the stand by Anderson's defense team in an effort to aid his besieged friend. He took the oath while seemingly oozing contempt for the whole process. He obviously didn't believe he or Ken Anderson should be questioned about their behavior as district attorneys. He acknowledged that he was "not the most neutral person in this case."

No kidding.

He was defensive throughout his testimony, saying Anderson had provided every bit of evidence he had been asked to produce. He painted Anderson as a victim of overzealous second-guessing. He claimed that he had delayed DNA testing because there simply was no protocol for handling requests like mine.

I couldn't help remembering one of Bradley's other efforts regarding DNA testing. He had participated in an online discussion among Texas district attorneys, advocating for simply destroying DNA evidence after trials. He'd lamented that "innocence . . . has proven to trump most anything." He thought a better approach "might be to get a written agreement that all the evidence can be destroyed after the conviction and sentence. Then, there is nothing to test or retest."

I shudder to think how that kind of agreement would have affected my life.

Finally, after four days of testimony and questioning, and countless increasingly nasty arguments between Rusty Hardin and Ken Anderson's team of legal eagles, the man on the hot seat was called to testify.

This was it. Ken Anderson was finally going to answer questions about my case—in front of God and everybody. The courtroom fell silent as he approached the stand, took the oath, and sat in the chair where he had put so many other people on the spot.

Like most of the other spectators, I had imagined we would see a smooth, experienced prosecutor-turned-judge, a witness who would be difficult to pin down—a man who knew very well the ins and outs of making a good impression on the stand. I was worried it wasn't going to be possible, even for a pro like Rusty Hardin, to get him to reveal anything of who he was or how he had made decisions in my case.

Instead, we saw the complete collapse of the façade that Ken Anderson had carefully maintained for so many years. He was not accustomed to answering hard questions, only asking them. He did not come off as a fair-minded or focused public servant, nor did he seem to comprehend how his actions had affected innocent people. He revealed that he still did not understand the agony his actions had caused in my life or the lives of others—like the Baker family.

He was indignant, frustrated, angry, and he made it clear from the beginning that he believed he shouldn't have to be there, saying he was the victim of an all-out "media frenzy." He described himself as a paragon of public service, recounted his years as a Boy Scout leader and Sunday School teacher. He bragged about his office's tough stance against child molesters in the 1980s, when not many prosecutors focused on trying these awful criminals.

When he said his office had "a lot to be proud of and we still do," his voice cracked with emotion. He also got teary as he laid out how hard the past eighteen months had been on him and his family. "I had to spend money to hire lawyers. And I worked my entire life and now they have it," he told the judge.

One of his attorneys, recognizing the danger of Anderson's self-pitying description of what he had gone through—versus my decades in prison—asked him to speak directly to me about how he felt after having been hit with "false accusations" about his actions.

He turned toward me, his mouth twisted with emotion, and said, "I know what me and my family have been through in the last eighteen months, and it's hell. And it doesn't even register in the same ballpark with what you went through, Mr. Morton. So I don't know that I can say I feel your pain, but I have a pretty darned good idea how horrible what we've gone through for eighteen months has been, with false accusations and everything else, and what happened to you is so much worse than that. I can't imagine what you're feeling."

I had been sitting there, ready to accept an apology, but that's not what he offered. It was as if his situation and mine were not connected, as if he had nothing to do with my charges, my trial, or my imprisonment—he was just another man who felt bad that it had happened. He went on to say—again—that the system had "screwed up," adding that "I've beaten myself up on what could have been done different and I frankly don't know."

He just didn't get it—still.

Anderson insulted virtually everyone participating in the court of inquiry by saying it would be a "blessed day" if a court of inquiry were never again used in Texas. He snorted and called the charges against him "so bogus it's unreal." He admitted that he hadn't even troubled himself to go over the details of the murder case that had upended my life. Even at the urging of his legal team, he had not deigned to sit down, read the trial transcript, and see for himself what evidence had and had not been presented. He left the impression that it was all somehow beneath him.

For the next several hours, Anderson offered defiant, meandering answers to every question about why he had not turned over the transcript recounting what Eric said he had seen in our home when Chris was killed. He shrugged off questions about why my attorneys never saw the neighbors' reports of a strange van behind our house.

He was a terrible witness—belligerent, haughty, put-upon, and self-pitying. His appearance that day was a kind of professional and personal self-immolation. At several points his attorneys tried to indicate to him that he should stop making things worse—but he didn't listen. His attorneys pleaded with Judge Sturns to let Anderson take a bathroom break—a transparent attempt to get him off the stand so they could talk some sense into him. The judge's decision projected the first real clue of how he felt about the case. He did not let the former prosecutor leave the stand to get what would have been the most basic legal advice possible—for God's sake, when you are this deep in a hole, stop digging.

Anderson's attitude on the witness stand was destroying his reputation more effectively than anything I had said or claimed in court. He was burying his long career with his own braying self-regard.

And Hardin, a master at getting witnesses to reveal themselves, was working his lethal, legal magic on Ken Anderson.

Hardin zeroed in, using my former prosecutor's own words to challenge his choices in my case. "How could a prosecutor who cares so deeply about children not remember *anything* about a child seeing his mother killed in a case that he prosecuted? How could that be? How could you forget it?"

Anderson answered flatly, "I have no recollection of a particular piece of evidence of that nature or in that detail." He explained that he would not have put trust in Eric's assertion that I had not been there when Chris was killed. He said that Eric was a "traumatized three-year-old child. You can't attach any significance to anything he said at that point."

Hardin countered, "He was right, wasn't he? He was right!" He pointed out that Eric had independently come up with details about the crime scene that no one else knew. "Why in the world wouldn't you want to investigate based on what that little boy said?"

Anderson responded, "You'd have to ask Boutwell that." Of course, the sheriff had been dead for almost two decades.

Anderson went on to complain that his *real* problem was that he had simply been "too good" as a prosecutor. He said he wasn't sure he could even prosecute cases successfully with all these new laws requiring full disclosure to the defense.

He insisted he *had* shared all of the exculpatory evidence with my attorneys and claimed they had just not followed up on the information.

At one point Anderson became so angry at Rusty Hardin, that he began shouting. Hardin was quoting from a vanity book Anderson had written in 1997, called *Crime in Texas*, which apparently touched briefly on my case. Hardin had been holding the book up and reading aloud what Anderson had written about me. In the process, he mistakenly said that the book contained an entire chapter on my case.

Ken Anderson snatched the book out of Hardin's grasp and proceeded to read for the court the title of each chapter. He was incensed at Hardin's error. Seething, he announced to the courtroom that my name had been mentioned only in a short introductory section. Apparently I didn't merit more than that.

It was a moment that encapsulated everything that had gone wrong in my case, everything that was wrong with the criminal justice system's failure to hold prosecutors like Anderson accountable. Anderson focused on details—insignificant bits of information that revealed nothing. He missed the big picture entirely.

AFTERWARD, I TOLD REPORTERS THAT WHILE I HAD HOPED FOR MORE from Anderson's testimony, he was a man who had been in a position of power for almost three decades, and for the first time, he had to answer for his actions—clearly, he was very uncomfortable with that.

I recognized that Ken Anderson was terribly bitter and struggling with denial and anger. Long ago, I had fought those same demons. I prayed that someday—like me—he would find peace.

It would be weeks before we knew how Judge Sturns would rule. I had to prepare for another courtroom drama—the murder trial of the man who had killed my wife.

CHAPTER TWENTY-SIX

WINDSWEPT SAN ANGELO, TEXAS, MAY BE IN THE MIDDLE OF NOWHERE, but for one week in March 2013, the arid high-country college town was the center of my universe. It was where the man who killed Chris finally faced justice—long delayed, but no longer denied.

The trial was held there after Mark Norwood's attorneys won a change of venue because of the overwhelming publicity in the Austin area surrounding my release and his arrest. The decision had the effect of turning the entire connected community of family members, attorneys, witnesses, and reporters following the case into something of a gypsy caravan. Our hearty troupe arrived in West Texas dragging boxes of legal files, suitcases, cameras—and a kind of tired hope.

It was not a short trek to San Angelo. The city is more than two hundred miles from Austin and almost four hundred from Houston, entailing long drives past small towns and Texas-size expanses of empty, open space.

Maybe this would mark an end. Maybe this trial would finally set some of us free—emotionally and psychologically, not just physically. I wasn't the only one who had been a prisoner of Norwood's terrible deeds.

By the opening morning of the trial, the gang was all in place. Eric and his wife, Maggie, came. My mother and my sister Vicky were there, too. Supporters, lawyers, and friends of mine came in for a day or two at various points in the week—and then left from the city's tiny airport, a place plagued by a scary combination of high winds, wild temperature changes, and small planes.

I just hoped we'd all survive the week.

Chris's sister Mary Lee, the woman who had raised and eventually adopted Eric, also came. It was almost unfathomable that we would once again be together in a courtroom reliving the details of Chris's last days, the description of how she died, the horror of what had happened to our interlocked families. It swept us up and forced us back to the moment we each heard what had happened, back to the days when our tears were fresh.

Mary Lee—like Eric—was still adjusting to the new reality about me and about Chris's murder. We were cordial but no longer close. Still, I was grateful to her for keeping Eric safe. And Mary Lee had also played an important role in preserving the truth about her sister's murder. Long ago, when three-year-old Eric started talking to his grandmother about what he'd seen, it had been Mary Lee who insisted that she take notes and keep a detailed transcript of the conversation. That long-hidden account had helped set me free.

Unlike in my trial, this time Mary Lee and I were hoping for the same outcome—a guilty verdict. Finally, I knew we were on the same side.

I had been warned that this would be a tough case to argue and a difficult conviction to win. I wasn't sure what to believe. The DNA evidence seemed to lend such certainty to the state's case against Norwood. On the other hand, the unpredictable and sometimes inexplicable decisions of a jury were not unfamiliar to me.

While there was much more hard evidence against Mark Norwood than there had ever been against me, twenty-six years had come and gone since he'd entered our home and set in motion a cataclysmic nightmare that engulfed two families. The strongest evidence we had of the chronic criminal's involvement in Chris's murder was his DNA—found intermingled with her blood on the bandanna discovered behind our home.

That evidence was powerful—strong enough to get me released from prison. The DNA profile was complete enough to link Norwood to another tragically similar murder. But would it convince a jury to send him to prison for life? We wouldn't know until we tried.

My trust fell upon Adrienne MacFarland and Lisa Tanner from the Texas Attorney General's Office, named as special prosecutors in the case. We met a few times to go over my testimony.

MacFarland was senior at the AG's office. Tanner was quite accomplished in prosecuting cold cases and had the gift of being able to sound both folksy and completely comfortable explaining the complex forensics of DNA evidence—something that would be very important in San Angelo. Tanner would handle most of the courtroom argument, but both of these women were good lawyers and good people. Along with their excellent staff, the whole team inspired confidence.

The judge had appointed two qualified lawyers to represent Norwood. Both of them were very capable of connecting with a jury and quite experienced in defending people who had done the indefensible. I knew that their job would be to plant seeds of doubt—about the evidence, about the testimony, about how much time had passed and how faulty people's memories were.

As we walked to the courthouse that first morning, San Angelo's bright sun was battling a chilling breeze for control of the thermostat—creating a climate that felt oddly hot and cold at the same time. It was like having chills and a fever—an apt metaphor for how I felt. I was relieved and worried, pleased that this was happening but brokenhearted that it meant we would all have to revisit Chris's murder again.

I was most worried about Eric. Everyone else in our family had been through this before. We knew what had happened to Chris, and we'd had decades to absorb it and try to make our peace with how she died. Eric would be learning the truth, in all its dreadful detail, for the first time. I ached for him, but I knew that he needed to understand how he'd lost his mother. And he needed to hear what his life was like before her death.

We arrived at court early, greeted by our ever-present contingent of reporters and photographers—people I now knew by name. I even knew the names of some of their kids. My mother welcomed many of them with hugs and loud expressions of her glee that this day had finally arrived.

The large pillared courthouse was impressive—all carved concrete, massive steps, and legal majesty. It looked like an important place where important decisions were reached. Inside, it was a bit different than I'd expected. It had been built in the late 1920s, and whoever designed it had captured unique elements of the era's architectural exuberance.

The original painting style inside appeared to have been restored. It was colorful, to say the least. Most courthouses are pretty dull. Built with an eye for utility first and foremost, they tend to boast a great deal of open, easily cleaned space. Here, columns with carved and painted trees and branches, flourishes and flowers marked the entry. Perhaps the rainbow of color was a reaction to the starkness and austerity of life in West Texas. Maybe it was an attempt to distract the often-bereft people who entered its doors. It was a beautiful place in which we would speak of ugly events.

Judge Burt Carnes, a tall, white-haired Texan whose family had a lengthy law enforcement background, had come in from Williamson County. He wore blue jeans under his black robe. I knew this because he stayed at my hotel and I saw him leave for court every morning, dressed like an elegant cowboy on a weekend getaway. In court, we all got to see his getup again because he whipped his robe off the instant we took a break—he had to. The old courtroom's heating system seemed to work without regard for the weather outside. The combination of the constant heat, the bright sun streaming in through the large windows, and his heavy, dark robe must have been unbearable.

That sense that all of the trial participants—officers, witnesses, and reporters—were spending our days and evenings jostling up against each other extended to the old, narrow hallways and tiny restrooms, where we were in constant contact. It was possible to stand in line outside the restrooms for long minutes surrounded by witnesses, jurors, a television reporter, and the judge.

Hardest of all may have been the close proximity of the Norwood family. The accused murderer's mother, brother, and sister were there—all of them physically similar to him. The differences, though, were on the inside. His sister and brother seemed nervous and unsure of how my family and I would react to them. I didn't blame them. They seemed like good people who were in terrible pain about their brother's situation.

Mark Norwood's mother believed with all her heart that her son was innocent. She mourned the trial as the first step in yet another wrongful conviction. She compared her son's situation to mine—to my face—again and again. I heard her telling reporters, even bystanders, that her son was being railroaded. I understood. I could see my mother's pain reflected in her eyes. I knew how much my conviction had hurt my mom. Mark Norwood's mother was wrong, but I knew her heartache was real.

We sat next to each other in the hall, chatted during breaks, and did not talk about our very different feelings toward her son. What we thought didn't matter. It would be the job of the legal system to locate the truth that lay buried in decades of lies.

At the old courthouse, everyone had to surrender cell phones upon entry. You would have thought that the reporters, attorneys, and spectators were being asked to give up limbs. Because I had spent so many years without an electronic leash, it didn't bother me, but I was the exception. There were long protests, requests for special treatment, attempts to talk the lobby guards out of enforcing the rules—all to no avail.

San Angelo was very "old school," and for me, that was just fine. This was a long-ago case, a crime that took place in a world that no longer existed. For me and for the other people who loved Chris, this was an old, old ache. It made sense that the last chapter of this long-unfinished story would be written in a setting that seemed not to have changed much in the years she'd been gone.

I knew the key to this trial was going to be what the jury would hear about Norwood—and there were strict limits on that. I would not be introduced as someone who had wrongly served decades in prison for Chris's murder. Prosecutors believed that knowing I had spent so much time in prison could be a factor in how the jurors viewed me—rightly or wrongly. It was decided that I would simply be a grieving husband who finally—after all this time—was hoping for closure.

Further, there was no guarantee the jury would hear that Norwood's DNA matched evidence found at the Debra Baker murder scene. The admissibility of that fact would be decided as the case was tried. The legal team prosecuting Norwood wanted the jury to know that he had a long criminal record and was linked by DNA to another shockingly similar murder. So did I, and I prayed the judge would rule in our favor.

That first day, the old courtroom benches were nearly full, most of them with prospective jurors. Somewhere in that crowd of San Angelo faces—farmers, teachers, police officers' in-laws, and salespeople—were the twelve men and women who would decide whether Mark Norwood was guilty of killing Chris.

My family and I took seats near the front. Eric sat down beside us, with his wife on one side and Mary Lee on the other. We were all braced to hear things we didn't want to hear, to see images so awful that those of us who'd viewed them before hadn't forgotten the horror—even after more than a quarter century.

The back door opened, and Mark Norwood walked in, his hands cuffed in front of him, a deputy at his side.

The room fell silent.

I had seen photos and video of the man. I knew what he looked like. But we had never been in the same room—we had never breathed the same air. I saw that Eric was staring hard at him as the gangly, tall wreck of a man moved toward his seat at the defense table. He seemed to walk with a defiant swagger—a wordless way of saying that no one and nothing in that courtroom mattered to him.

I was actually surprised to see him walking. That morning he had arrived at the courthouse in a police car and been transferred to a wheelchair for the short trip to the courtroom. Reporters said that Norwood claimed to be too weak to walk because of the ongoing hunger strike he was on to protest the jailhouse food. He seemed to have difficulty discerning between the inconvenience of his own unhappy taste buds and the heartbreaking death of an innocent woman.

At the Nuremberg trials, the political philosopher Hannah Arendt described the actions and the architects of the Holocaust with a simple, memorable phrase—saying that the whole lot represented "the banality of evil." Her long-ago words applied well to the man before us.

Mark Norwood was dull and ordinary, ignorant and ugly—a man who possessed no exceptional qualities except that he had been cruel enough to take the life of a sleeping innocent, at least twice. In the process, he had delivered decades of pain to so many good people.

He wore his ragged gray hair pulled back into a thin ponytail. His sideburns were haphazard, scraggly muttonchops, just as they'd looked in various mug shots over the years. He did not appear healthy. His clothes hung off of him. The skin on his arms was loose and saggy. His massive hands were knobby, scarred, and wrinkled.

Norwood mindlessly walked in front of the large, brightly lit screen prosecutors were still adjusting so they could display pictures and documents during the trial. He cast a fleeting dark profile across the spotless white background as he moved toward the defense table.

Mark Norwood may have been a shadow of the man he'd been twenty-six years earlier—but he was still the man who had broken into our home and broken our hearts. He was the "big monster with the big mustache" Eric had seen, and I could tell that this man's presence in the courtroom was profoundly shaking to my son. It shook me, too, but not in the way I had expected.

I knew he had murdered Chris. I knew he was the man who had launched my life in an unimaginable direction. If I had been this close to him shortly after Chris's death, I would have killed him—without a doubt, without hesitation, without an iota of remorse.

Since then, I had learned the hard way that there are worse things than dying—and that was what I wanted for Mark Norwood. I wanted him to go to the netherworld I'd been banished to—for the rest of his life. I wanted him to lose all of his freedoms, large and small. I wanted him to be miserable—for a very long time—and then die behind the cold, uncaring walls of prison, alone.

But it was hard, after all this time, to finally see him sitting there smugly, so close to the people I loved. His dull eyes scanned the room—looking at the crowd, looking my way, looking at Eric—but not really seeing anything. He may not have known who I was. I wondered if he could fathom that the dark-haired man sitting near me was the three-year-old boy he had terrorized so many years earlier.

I wondered if he was even capable of understanding how much pain he had caused.

Jury selection began with an acknowledgment that many of those in the courtroom were younger than this case—they hadn't been born when Chris died. After intense questioning from both sides revealing that some potential jurors had relatives who'd been victims of violence and others feared wrongfully convicting a person, while a handful simply did not want the responsibility of deciding someone's fate—a panel was chosen.

The State of Texas versus Mark Alan Norwood was under way.

Norwood took out the listening device he'd held against his ear throughout jury selection, stood up, and said in a loud voice, "Your Honor, I plead not guilty."

Lisa Tanner began her opening argument. "Twenty-six years, seven months, and five days ago, Ronald Reagan was president of the United States . . . and Christine Morton was living the American dream." Tanner told the story of how we met and married, how we went out the night before Chris died to celebrate my birthday with our newly healthy son. She described how I had left for work early the next morning and how our neighbor had seen Eric sitting on our front porch whimpering, all alone, around noon. She told the court what the neighbor had found inside and how I had rushed home.

Significantly, Tanner did not say anything about my being a suspect or my arrest, about my trial or my time in prison. She talked about the official investigation and described how Chris's brother, frustrated by the lackadaisical work of the police, had set out to see if he could find any evidence on his own. She explained how he had found the bandanna behind our home and carefully saved it and handed it over to police. She explained that testing at the time revealed there was blood on it, but technology hadn't yet evolved enough to reveal whose blood it was.

Tanner then jumped ahead to 2011, when the bandanna was tested again and the blood was finally identified as being Chris's. She explained that someone else's DNA was found intermingled with Chris's blood—and how a computer database search identified that DNA as belonging to Mark Norwood. She described how investigators had determined that, in 1986, Norwood had lived close to our house, working as a carpet layer for the construction company that built the homes in our development—how he might even have worked on our home before we moved in.

Then Tanner went deeper into the case, explaining how investigators had found a long-ago friend of Mark Norwood's who now lived in Nashville—a man by the name of Sonny Wann. Upon hearing Sonny's name mentioned, Mark Norwood's mother let out a long, loud moan—an acknowledgment that Sonny's entry into the story line was going to be bad news for her boy.

She was right.

After my release, when investigators from the Austin police cold case unit went to visit Sonny, they began chatting with him about his gun collection. Tanner said the police asked him if he had a .45. He said he had only one. When he brought it out to show the officers, they were stunned. It was my old pistol. The serial numbers matched. It had been stolen from our closet on the day Chris was killed.

Tanner told the rapt jury that the investigators visiting Sonny never brought up Norwood's name or told Sonny why they were there. They were just chatting with him. She said Sonny told investigators that he'd gotten the gun when the small construction company he owned was working on a remodeling project at a house in Austin. Sonny said he bought it for fifty dollars from one of the men he'd hired to help out on that renovation. He casually told police the man's name—Mark Norwood.

Sonny Wann knew Norwood well. They had worked together off and on—not only on various building projects but also at a diner owned by Sonny's former mother-in-law. In fact, Sonny had dated Norwood's ex-wife and had moved with her out of state. His was not a fleeting recollection of someone he had known only briefly.

Lisa Tanner said they had tracked down the owner of the home Sonny and Norwood had worked on and gotten a receipt showing when the project began—August 1986, the same month as Chris's murder.

She told the jury the evidence to convict Norwood had been there all along, and she asked them to finally—at long last—find him guilty.

The defense opened their case by telling the jury that it was their job to force the state to do its job—to prove the case. They said they were asking the same of the twelve people sitting in judgment. They said it all boiled down to "can you trust the evidence?" They told the jury about the presumption of innocence. They finished by exhorting jurors to keep in mind the possibility of evidence contaminated by sloppy storage techniques or careless collection. They told them to look out for lies by some of the witnesses—a clear reference to Sonny.

Once again, I was called to the stand as the first witness. As Lisa Tanner led me through questions about my life with Chris and her last days, I realized this was the first time I was telling this story in front of Eric. When prosecutors put pictures of our old home up on the big screen, I knew this was the first time Eric had seen images of the house he'd lived in as a little boy.

They showed pictures of the house surrounded by crime scene tape, with Chris's car still sitting in the driveway. It took me back to what I had seen when I pulled up at home the day she died—police everywhere, neighbors gawking—normalcy forever gone. With each photo they displayed, I could almost hear the shutter of the camera the way I'd heard it in our home that day—and the flashes of light in our hallway as the police photographer took picture after picture of Chris's battered body still lying in our bed.

Tanner handed me my old pistol, the one Norwood had stolen the day he killed Chris. I hadn't seen it or touched it in twenty-six years. It was like a ghost to me—a remnant of a long-ago life that seemed familiar, but faded. I recognized it and ruefully acknowledged it was mine. Was this gun the reason Norwood had killed Chris—for the paltry fifty dollars he got for it? Was that all her life had been worth to him?

Prosecutors put up a picture of Chris and Eric, their heads leaned in toward each other, both of them beaming. Eric looked so healthy and Chris looked so happy. I remembered taking the picture—never imagining it would be shown at a trial for the man who murdered my wife.

I saw Eric tear up and run his hands through his hair. I could see he was struggling to stay composed. Maggie took his hand and held him close.

Elizabeth Gee, the next-door neighbor who had delivered such damning testimony at my trial in 1987, took the stand. Lisa Tanner had told me that Elizabeth had continued to believe I was guilty—even after my exoneration and release, after Norwood's arrest, after all the coverage of this case. Lisa said people from the attorney general's office had to finally sit her down and let her know, in no uncertain terms, that I was truly innocent. They told her that everything she had believed about Chris's murder and about our marriage was profoundly wrong—and that the testimony she gave in my trial had done great damage.

Apparently, she had come around. This time on the stand, she did not accuse me of ripping out the marigolds Chris had planted, and she did not testify—wrongly—that I referred to my wife as "bitch." She actually said some kind things about Chris and me as parents, telling the jury we never let Eric out of our sight—that we were with him, everywhere and always. She said that was how she knew something was very wrong at our home on the day Chris died. Our little boy was outside alone, something we would *never* have let happen.

Her testimony was followed by that of investigators who had worked on the original case.

Then a man from the Austin Police Department Crime Lab took the stand. His testimony would explain the investigation at the crime scene while the prosecution team put up photos showing what police and sheriff's deputies had found.

Eric pushed close to my mother and Mary Lee. Maggie curled up against him. He was literally surrounded by women who loved him, as if they were forming a force field to protect him. The victims' advocate from the attorney general's office also moved closer to Eric as the testimony from the crime scene was introduced.

Anthony Arnold, a longtime crime lab specialist, led the courtroom through photos one by one as Lisa Tanner asked for explanations or additional information about what was being shown. It was a stark lesson in the incredible indignity of death, a reminder that a murder victim is so often reduced to little more than a piece of evidence, her body turned into just another crime scene exhibit. The delicate pink nightgown Chris wore to bed that night was photographed in harsh light, her bare form underneath visible through the thin fabric. I hurt knowing that Eric was seeing his mother like this.

Arnold described how police had step by step exposed Chris's body, taking pictures at each point. Many of the photos were benign, showing the reading material we had stacked in our bookshelf headboard. There was a picture of the recipe folder that Chris kept there, packed with ideas for dishes she planned to serve at family dinners or neighborhood get-togethers. There was a snapshot of the book I had been reading in bed on the nights before the murder.

Eric was holding his head down as the prosecution's assistant called up each photo when Lisa Tanner asked for them by exhibit number. He would look up when he was reassured that it was okay, something half of the courtroom was doing as well. Everyone there knew there was a possibility of seeing something too terrible to ever forget.

Arnold was testifying about how the crime lab team had finally uncovered Chris's head, looking ever closer to see exactly what had happened.

Tanner called for the assistant to put up another photo.

Their system for shuffling through the exhibits and displaying them on the big screen was clumsy and vulnerable to human error—such as mistakenly putting up a photo out of order. Tragically, that is exactly what happened. The assistant accidentally put on screen a close-up picture of Chris's head taken during the autopsy. All the blood had been washed off and her brain, her crushed face, the damage to one of her eyes, and her shattered teeth were visible to the entire courtroom.

Her face no longer looked like her.

Her face no longer looked human.

Everyone gasped, and a shock wave of truth about how violently and horribly Chris had been killed swept through the jury, the judge, and the spectators.

At first the assistant did not realize that this terrible photograph was up on the big screen. Lisa Tanner, clearly horrified, rushed to the assistant, pleading with her to get that shot off the screen—now. The damage, however, was done. Everyone had seen it.

Eric had seen it.

He dropped his head into his hands as his wife and both families enveloped him. Now he knew the pain of what we all had been living with for so long. He understood why one side of the family hated me, believing I had done this to someone they loved so much. He got a glimpse of the pain I felt, having lost my beloved wife in such a horrific way.

Now, he knew why her death had been so rarely discussed, why it had damaged so many people he loved. He knew how bad it had been. Knowledge may be power, but it can come with a high price.

Arnold continued his testimony, leading the courtroom through what police found in our bedroom that day. Some of the photos were hard to look at—showing blood spray that reached the ceiling, Chris's blood splashed onto framed family photos, chunks of tissue and bone that had been catapulted across the room by the blows inflicted on her beautiful face. There were close-ups of Chris's delicate hands, one of them clutching a long dark hair, the other with her little finger broken after she had instinctively raised her hand to protect herself.

When Roberto Bayardo, the medical examiner who'd performed the autopsy, was called to the stand, Eric, his wife, and Chris's sister left the courtroom. They had seen more than enough.

Bayardo testified that Chris had suffered at least eight blows to her head. He said he believed that she had probably not lived past the second strike—that she would have been unconscious almost instantly and died very quickly. Her lack of suffering was hard to believe when prosecutors put up additional autopsy photos. They were the stuff of nightmares. Bayardo explained how he'd found long, jagged splinters of dark wood embedded in Chris's head. He believed they were shards of whatever had been used to bludgeon her as she slept.

For much of this testimony, I was outside the courtroom. I learned what had happened and what had been said afterward, through others in court—my family, friends, reporters, even spectators sitting in on the trial. Everyone knew how hard it was for me not to be sitting in there. But the defense had told the judge they planned on recalling me and didn't want me tainted by what other witnesses were saying. I spent most of my time waiting in the small office the prosecution team had set up across the narrow hall from the courtroom.

It was where witnesses about to go on the stand gathered. Waiting there gave me the chance to speak with people I hadn't seen in years—to see some of them for the first time in over two decades. They were people who'd made a huge difference in my life—both good and bad.

I spoke with John Kirkpatrick, Chris's brother—the man who'd found the bandanna that set me free and led to Norwood's arrest. John had always been a quiet, exacting person. I'd never known him to emote much. But on this day, he told me that Chris's murder had been so painful for him that he hadn't spoken of it at all in the years since she died—even to his wife. He said that his two children were not aware that Chris had been murdered until he was forced to tell them when I was released in 2011.

As we talked, it became clear that speaking about her death and his discovery of the bandanna was incredibly difficult for John after so many years of repressing what had happened. I knew Chris and John had been especially close, and I ached at the pain he had struggled with all these years. He and his family lived in the Pacific Northwest—as far as they could get from the heartache they'd left behind in Texas.

I could see that he wanted to do a good job of testifying. He still cared so much about Chris. I hoped doing this would help him find peace within himself.

Inside the courtroom that day, when John was on the stand, the blue bandanna was carefully removed from its evidence envelope. It was held up like it was the Shroud of Turin—a piece of material that had the power to change everything.

Lisa Tanner held it up for John and asked him to identify it, which he did without hesitation. He recounted the story of trying to "channel" the thoughts of the killer because he was impatient with the lack of police involvement in the case. He recounted finding it lying in the street, saying, "It was just there by itself, waiting for me to find it."

He told the jury about the moment he had learned of Chris's death in a phone call from his father. He said he answered his home phone that day and heard his late father say, "I'm going to tell you the worst news you're ever going to hear in your life."

I was told later that John had choked up on the stand and that portions of his testimony were terribly hard for him to get through. But his recall of events and his recounting of his role in finally solving her murder had been riveting. The details had all stayed with him—buried deep inside, waiting for him to finally share them with the world.

While John was testifying, I talked with his wife, Dianne. Much of what she shared could have passed for banter at a cocktail party—information about their lives and their jobs, their kids and their faraway home. As we talked, I couldn't help thinking about all the time that had passed, all the experiences we would have shared if Chris had lived. She was our link, and when she was gone—so were they. It was good to see them again.

Also waiting in the witness room were the two forensic specialists from the Orchid Cellmark lab who had extracted Norwood's DNA from the bandanna—and eliminated me as a suspect. They seemed thrilled to meet me. To them, I was a DNA celebrity.

They told me this was the first time they'd shaken the hand of someone they had helped exonerate. Their daily work was anonymous, clinical—sterile in every sense. My standing there in the flesh turned their impersonal work into something tangible; it put a face on what their scientific skills meant for real people. They asked if I would pose for a picture with them that they could take back to the lab. I told them the pleasure was all mine—and I meant it.

They took their turns in court, in addition to a slew of former Williamson County sheriff's investigators. The cops who had botched my case all took the same basic tack—they had done the best they could with the technology they had at the time. Seeing some of them was a reminder of how ill prepared and poorly trained they were, particularly considering the power they had once had over my life and the lives of all the trusting residents of Williamson County.

The shadow of Sheriff Jim Boutwell hung over the proceedings. He had set the tone, he had led the team, he had determined me to be guilty on the day he walked in our front door. It was the job of the deputies and investigators, the jail guards hoping for a promotion, and the truck drivers dubbed detectives simply to bring in the evidence they needed to prove my guilt in the eyes of a jury.

They did that and absolutely nothing more. If they had looked harder, they might have found Sonny Wann.

In videotaped testimony—he was too ill to travel to San Angelo and terrified of flying—Wann told how he had purchased my old gun from Mark Norwood. He described Norwood as a "big ole boy" and said he was a hard worker. Still, the distrust with which he viewed Norwood, the hardscrabble world in which they both had lived, and the animosity between the two men overshadowed his words. Wann claimed he'd had a sexual relationship with Norwood's first wife once they moved out of state. He said Norwood was always broke and asking for money. He mentioned that he had never seen him act violently, but Wann's words hung in the air—leaving the sense that Norwood may well have been violent *outside* of Wann's company.

The next steps were crucial. Mark Norwood's ex-wife was going to take the stand.

Judy Norwood was a petite brunette who seemed terrified at the prospect of even being in the same room as her former husband. Her story was sad. She and Norwood had met in Tennessee when she had been fourteen. He had insisted that she sue her parents to win the right to marry him, even though she was underage. They had married in 1983, when she was only sixteen—then had a son together and moved to Austin the following year. They lived about twelve miles from our house.

She described a sad life, marked by financial failure and a fast-deteriorating relationship with her then husband. She said Norwood stayed out late at night, telling her he was working but warning her not to ask him any questions. She described how she had taken multiple jobs to keep the family going financially but quit after she came home one night from work to find that Norwood had left their very young son alone.

The most jarring element of her testimony was her mere presence. Judy Norwood looked too much like Chris and Debra Baker for it to be a coincidence. Like Norwood's victims, she had long dark hair and was tiny in comparison to her tall, once powerful ex-husband. Judy Norwood had been raising a young child at the time, just as Chris and Debra had been.

Her nervousness at being near Norwood, her fear at testifying in front of him, told the jury everything they needed to know about his capacity for violence and his long pattern of bullying and cruelty to women. She visibly trembled and cried when prosecutors put up on the screen a large picture of Mark Norwood and their son, Thomas. The little boy boasted a broad, innocent smile. His glowering father stood behind him—with a bandanna dangling loosely from his right front pocket.

Reporters covering the trial told me she broke down when she left the courthouse and was followed by cameras to her car. She clearly wanted to drive as fast and as far as she could from this case—and this killer.

Later that day jurors were kept out of the courtroom while prosecutors tried to convince Judge Carnes that he should allow testimony on the murder of Debra Baker. Their reasoning was that the Baker murder—a nearly identical brutal bludgeoning that took place a year and a half after Chris's death—constituted a "signature crime."

Lisa Tanner was persuasive as she ticked off the similarities. Both women were beaten to death as they lay sleeping. In both cases, the blows were focused on their heads. They had both been beaten with an unidentified blunt object, and both victims' purses had been rifled through. In each case, something of value had been stolen from the house—at our house, my .45 pistol was taken, and at the Baker home, the killer had stolen a VCR. Particularly telling was the way the women's bodies had been left—bloodied and covered with pillows and other items.

Eerily, Chris and Debra Baker were close in age, similar in appearance, and raising young children. The killer had not raped either of the women. But in each case, Mark Norwood had left behind damning evidence—his DNA. Both killings had also taken place early on a Wednesday morning, on the thirteenth of the month. At the time Debra Baker died, Judy Norwood and her husband and son had lived only two-tenths of a mile from her home.

The judge ruled that the Baker case could be shared with the jury, a decision that left the prosecutors—and my family—exultant.

The first witness to share Debra Baker's story with the jury was her eighty-nine-year-old mother. She was pushed to the front of the courtroom in a wheelchair and recounted how she had come looking for her daughter after concerned co-workers called to say Debra had not shown up for work that day. She described entering her daughter's home calling to her, only to find Debra bloody and lifeless in her bed, her crushed face covered with pillows.

She didn't have to tell the jury how heartbreaking the past decades had been for her—not knowing who had killed her daughter, not knowing if he was out there, free to kill again. Years of agony underscored her every word.

Debra Baker's bright and fiery daughter, Caitlin, was front and center to see her long-lost mother remembered—and to watch as the man who'd savaged her family's lives when she was just a toddler was forced to sit silently and listen to the pain of the innocent people he'd hurt so profoundly. Her brother Jesse sat beside her, finally receiving a small measure of justice for her death.

Phillip Baker, Debra's husband, was there, too—supporting his daughter, his son, and his murdered wife's sister, Lisa. Together, the Bakers' presence and the facts of their case, along with ours, painted a damning and disturbing portrait of the accused murderer who sat before us. The difference between this trial and my own twenty-six years earlier? Actual, physical, undeniable evidence of guilt.

There was little for Mark Norwood's attorneys to offer in his defense. His elderly mother, Dorothy, long suffering and drenched in denial about her son's violent life, told the jury that her son had grown up in a tight-knit Air Force family. She said they had moved around the world, often having only each other as close and permanent companions.

Norwood's brother Dale watched with his daughter at his side. His sister Connie listened to it all in silence and despair. They had done nothing to deserve this.

The defense relied on building doubt rather than laying out an alternate series of events. "Maybe" the bandanna had been contaminated, "maybe" one of us had tracked Chris's blood onto it, "maybe" Sonny Wann had lied about buying the gun from Norwood— "maybe" Wann had the gun because *he* was the killer.

They put Wann's ex-wife on the stand to testify that her former husband was a liar. Their daughter, estranged from her father for years, took the stand to agree with her.

His attorneys also brought up the fact that, in one of the crime scene photos, a bandanna was visible on the floor of our bedroom— having been tossed there when our dresser drawers were dumped. It looked different from the one found behind our home containing Chris's blood and Norwood's DNA. I was recalled to the stand to tell jurors I remembered it as a long-abandoned style artifact of the 1980s. Way back then, Chris's sister Mary Lee had worn that bandanna as a belt. Everyone in the courtroom who'd lived through the fashion-challenged eighties nodded in recognition—they remembered the look, too.

The jury got the case before lunch. I had a feeling deliberations would not be lengthy. I'd seen the judge leaving the hotel for court that morning, carrying his packed bags.

Within a few hours, we were told there was a verdict.

As the courtroom filled with spectators, attorneys, reporters, and family members still hurting from Mark Norwood's brief and brutal appearance in their lives, I couldn't help thinking about the day when I had been convicted. I was profoundly grateful that the death penalty was not asked for in my case. And that was part of the reason that Chris's family and I had not asked for it in Norwood's trial.

There had been enough death. There had been too many tortured families. If Mark Norwood were found guilty, he would automatically be given a life sentence. His mother and his family would not have to suffer further by being dragged to the execution of someone who long ago began breaking their hearts. They, too, were due some decent treatment.

The disheveled shell of a man who sat at the front—scratching his head, fidgeting with his listening device, swallowing, smirking, and staring into space—was not the man who killed Chris. He was all that was left of that man. He was a person whose ugliness of character and guilt had already exacted their toll.

He had already been convicted—in his own heart and his own head—long ago. He *knew* he was guilty. He had known all along.

When the jury foreman read the verdict, I did not feel joy or revenge or power or closure. I felt relief for all the people who still loved Chris so much and the strong family who still loved Debra Baker. I felt we could finally exhale.

I hoped that, in the days ahead, there would be a trial for Norwood in the murder of Debra Baker. I hoped that for her family and for her memory.

I hoped that trial would someday lead former prosecutor Ken Anderson to accept in his heart that his actions—whatever drove them—had unintentionally led to the murder of yet another innocent, much-loved woman.

The two families hugged. There were tears, but no triumph.

I hugged Norwood's brother as well. Outside the courthouse, he tried to apologize. But the words wouldn't come. He struggled, then collapsed into my arms and sobbed. He cried for what his brother had done. He cried for what I'd been through. And he cried for himself and his family. Their new pain and their prison sentence was just beginning.

The Norwood verdict had come after I'd been out of prison for almost eighteen months. But it was on that day that I felt I was finally free.

EPILOGUE

IT WAS STILL DARK.

Stepping outside into the cool shadows of the early morning, I held my cup of hot coffee close. I could smell the pine trees and see birds beginning to flutter out of the black branches looking for breakfast. Far out on the lake, I could hear the splash of an occasional fish leaping high and then plunging back down into the quiet, deep water.

I've been living in this house on a lake in East Texas for only a few months, but it already feels like home.

It's taken a long time, and the help of one person in particular, to get here.

We met the old-fashioned way—in church. Cynthia was part of the same small-town congregation as my parents. In fact, my family had known her well for years. They liked her. She was about my age, and her three children had grown and gone on to their own successes. She was fun and smart and pretty and—lucky for me—single.

I knew none of this when I was asked to speak at the church, not long after my release. The salt-of-the-earth folks who make up the membership had meant the world to my mother, in particular. They'd helped her tremendously during my imprisonment—letting her vent, supporting her for standing by me. They even remembered me on my birthday and holidays.

My mother's Sunday School class at this church had bought me the plastic "penitentiary typewriter" for one of my first Christmases behind bars. That typewriter changed my life.

Now, this same church was about to change my life again.

I had only been out of prison for a few months, and my freedom was fresh enough that I still felt lost. I didn't know how to fit into this new world or whether I would ever really be able to feel at home.

I was still casting about, trying to figure out how I should look. Before I was locked up, I'd had a mustache. Then, I was forced to be clean shaven for twenty-five years. Now I had the liberty to grow a mustache or long sideburns—or heck, even a gigantic lumberjack beard! For me, at least at this point, any facial hair that would have been off-limits in prison was suddenly on the menu.

Which explains why I showed up for my speaking engagement at church wearing what looked like a mustache, both above—and, oddly enough, *below* my mouth. I thought it was a goatee. In retrospect, it actually looked more "goaty." In other words, I was not sartorially ready to meet the woman who would eventually agree to spend the rest of her life with me. Meeting someone was the furthest thing from my mind. I was simply worried about speaking publicly for the first time.

I was also painfully aware that I had not entirely shaken my "penitentiary personality." I knew I didn't see life the way other people did. I didn't react to daily ups and downs the way others did. I was very much a work in progress. As the old saying goes, God wasn't finished with me yet. I had a lot of rough edges that needed smoothing, a lot of pain that needed to be processed, a lot of life I needed to catch up on.

But I owed these people so much, for helping me and for helping my family. I wanted to show them how much it meant to me. I wanted to let them know how their faith in me—and my faith in God—had helped pull me out of prison alive.

I got up to the front and began with a casual comment—that ultimately changed everything in my life. I told them that one of the first things I'd learned after coming out of prison was that people wanted to know what life was like on the inside.

I'd determined that I wasn't going to talk about it that night. So I offhandedly told the audience that if they wanted to learn about my life in prison, they would have to buy me a cup of coffee. I went on and finished my speech without embarrassing myself—except for the poorly considered facial hair.

That night, I chatted briefly with Cynthia. She was gentle and kind—and had a real spark of intelligence in her eyes.

I filed our meeting away under "maybe someday." I certainly knew that I wasn't ready to jump into the dating pool.

A few days later, my parents' phone rang. It was Cynthia—calling for me. She said she wanted to buy me that cup of coffee.

I was stricken.

Needless to say, a woman had never asked me out. I wasn't even sure if this counted as being asked out. Where did meeting for coffee fall on the scale that ran from dinner and drinks (clearly a date) to trying to assist some hapless soul who needed help reentering the real world (not a date)?

I realized anew how out of social practice I was. I don't think Cynthia had a clue that the desperate man on the other end of the line felt like he'd just been handed a lit social firecracker.

But I swallowed hard—and said yes.

That cup of coffee was our beginning. We met and talked for four hours—but not about prison. The next day we did it again—same coffee place, same good conversation, same powerful connection.

Cynthia and I shared a worldview, a system of beliefs, and a set of dreams. It felt as though I'd known her for a long time. I knew instantly I could trust her. I felt safe with her. We laughed easily and liked the same books and movies and music. We began going out to dinner, going to plays, going to church, and going forward—together.

She had a job, but whenever she could, she joined me at public appearances as I worked to bring change to our criminal justice system. She was with me at the state capitol to lobby for a new law that would help keep my nightmare from being visited on someone else. The bill that lawmakers worked hard to push through was somewhat embarrassingly called the Michael Morton Act. It codified exactly how and when prosecutors would share information with citizens who stand accused of a crime.

The proposal passed the Texas House and Senate unanimously, and on May 16, 2013, it was signed into law. Cynthia was there to keep my head from getting too big when the governor and other prominent politicians shook my hand and patted me on the back. She was there to lovingly remind me that, while this might be a life achievement, it was not a lifestyle.

I loved her for that—and so much more.

She was with me at Ken Anderson's court of inquiry and there beside me a few weeks later, when Judge Louis Sturns ruled that my former prosecutor should, indeed, face a criminal proceeding for his actions in my case.

Soon after the ruling was announced, Ken Anderson was taken to jail, booked, and released on bond. He later resigned his position on the bench and negotiated a guilty plea that forced him to surrender his law license but minimized his time in jail to just a few days. Still, his sentence sends a powerful message to other prosecutors.

Most important to me is the fact that all of Ken Anderson's cases will be reexamined by Williamson County's new prosecutor, with the help and guidance of the Innocence Project. They will start by looking at the convictions of people who are still serving time. There may be someone else like me behind bars right now—waiting for truth to set him free.

Cynthia and I were married shortly before Mark Norwood was tried for Chris's murder. We'd been dating for more than a year. I very much wanted her at the trial with me. I remembered my own trial in 1987 and how alone I'd felt, even though I was surrounded by dedicated lawyers and loving family. I knew the upcoming trial was going to tear open old wounds. I was going to have to relive the very worst time in my life.

I needed help. I needed to have someone there who was closer to me than my attorney or my family. I needed a shoulder to cry on, a calm voice to talk me through. I needed a hand to hold. I needed Cynthia—someone who understood me and where I had been, someone who was willing to help me find my way back home. When I got down on one knee, she said yes.

Today, we live on a beautiful lake with a big deck and a blue heron as a regular visitor.

Life is good.

Eric and I get together as often as we can. I remember being his age and the trouble Chris and I had juggling a new home, our friends, our young kid, and our careers. We had to schedule parental visits weeks in advance. We felt we were so busy.

Now, it's my turn to push for more time—and I count my blessings that I am here and free and able to see Eric and his precious family as much as I do.

Part of the wisdom that has washed over me in my past two years of freedom is the realization that Eric has had to make a more difficult journey than I have—because, through all the years, I knew some things that he did not.

I knew all along that I was innocent.

I knew all along that I loved him.

And I believed all along that—someday—this would all be set right.

Eric has had to adjust again and again—and again—to different realities. I am grateful for the way he has welcomed me back into his life. He and Maggie have just become parents again—this time to Patrick, a handsome and healthy little boy. Their beautiful little Chrissy is two.

I am hoping in the years ahead I can relive at least a piece of Eric's childhood by watching their children grow up. I want to be a good grandpa.

For now, I am practicing my parenting skills on the set of baby kittens Cynthia's formerly feral cat just delivered. The four little fur balls, in an assortment of colors—and probably an equal number of fathers—are still mewling loudly in their warm bed in our home workshop.

Their eyes have just opened, and they are squinting at their blurry and bewildering new world, wondering where they are—and trying to figure out where they fit in. They are shakily beginning their new lives.

I know something about how that feels.

And I know what it is to finally find your way.

On this glorious dawn, Cynthia walks up behind me, reaches out, and takes my hand. I am free. I am home. And I am in love.

Finally, the long night has ended.

The sun is rising.

Author's Note

THIS MEMOIR IS MY RECOLLECTION OF WHAT HAPPENED AND ITS IM-
pact on me. Memories can be slippery, subjective things. Therefore,
whenever possible, I have relied on court records, journal entries,
and eyewitnesses to re-create conversations and verbal statements. If
I've erred anywhere, please forgive me. I did my best to be accurate,
but I'm only human.

Acknowledgments

NO BOOK IS WRITTEN IN A VACUUM. FIRST AND FOREMOST, I MUST thank my new wife, CYNTHIA. She is my present. She is my future. And without her this would have been the height of folly.

I can thank no one if I do not thank JOHN RALEY. Had he not spent year after year fighting for me—without pay, without recognition, and with no guarantee of the outcome—I would have a very, very different life. He is my brother.

I am also indebted to the angels, the advocates, and the consummate professionals at the Innocence Project. I cannot measure the magnitude or adequately express my gratitude for all BARRY SCHECK has done. How does one repay such an unfathomable debt?

Mentioning the Innocence Project is pointless without metaphorically kissing the hand of NINA MORRISON. Her penetrating intellect, dazzling smile, and unending, infectious enthusiasm kept me from the abyss more than once.

I am also compelled to thank the Innocence Project's ANGELA AMEL for smoothing my transition into the free world. No one was sweeter, more compassionate, or as thoughtful. The same is true of RACHEL PECKER, the IP intern when everything came to fruition. There are too many lawyers, staffers, interns, and patrons to list. But I bow before each of you.

An army of attorneys won my release. BILL WHITE and BILL ALLISON, my attorneys at trial, preserved the record—and without that, I'd still be in the pit. JACKIE COOPER and DIANA

FAUST did much of the heavy lifting in those dark early years. JERRY GOLDSTEIN and RUSTY HARDIN—as they always do—wowed everyone with their finesse, poise, and stellar lawyering. KAY KANABY and CYNTHIA HEPNER, from John Raley's office, made the Norwood/Baker connection, long before anyone in law enforcement. KELLY RALEY, John's wife and fellow lawyer, inspired, assisted, and kept her husband on track. Then, she found Eric. John's law partner BOBBY BOWICK exhibited patience, tolerance, and grace, while John labored in the vineyard for years. PATRICIA CUMMINGS saw more, did more, and knows more of what happened behind the scenes in Williamson County than anyone. BEVERLY REEVES facilitated more connections than I will ever appreciate. ADRIENNE McFARLAND and LISA TANNER, with the Texas AG's office, secured the Norwood conviction. And LAURA POPPS made sure Anderson never practices law again.

After all my initial negative experiences, some journalists have made me reassess the profession. PAM COLLOFF did such a thorough job researching my story, I suspect she actually works for the CIA, not *Texas Monthly*. BRANDI GRISSOM's integrity and professionalism are unmatched. CHUCK LINDELL showed the Austin hometown folks how print journalism should be done. SHANNON WOLFSON demonstrated that her local TV news reporting was topped only by the size of her heart. And LARA LOGAN, with *60 Minutes*, gave me the best interview advice imaginable. Thank you, one and all.

I was dubious when Austin lobbyist THOMAS RATLIFF approached me. But he delivered, walking me through the sausage-making legislative process. Then, SENATOR ELLIS and SENATOR WHITMIRE made it happen. It pays to work with pros.

I am thankful that NELLIE GONZALEZ introduced me to AL REINERT. The documentary was a success. Al made it look easy. The good ones always do.

All personal trials have a spiritual element. On the inside, ANDY BRINK and RANDY SKILES were just two of the gentle souls who shepherded me through the dark years. On the outside, BRUCE

WELLS provided the environment, the support, and the love I needed. He does that for everyone.

I cannot forget TOMMY PHILLIPS, my friend on the inside.

MARIO GARCIA stood beside me, before Chris was killed, as a character witness at my trial, every day I was in prison, and as a friend today. Semper Fi, mi amigo.

From the goodness of his heart, TOM OWEN gave me a vehicle. He'd never met me, until he handed me the keys. His gesture made me weep.

Unbeknownst to almost everyone, JACK ANDERSON kept my ever-growing prison journal for over twenty years. Without that selfless, herculean effort, most of what's in this memoir would be lost to the vagaries of human memory. Thanks, buddy.

This book never would have happened without editor SARAH KNIGHT or agent PAUL FEDORKO. And then there was MARY MAPES, confidante, guide, aggravator, soother of ruffled feathers, pragmatist, sage, PC filter, counselor, accomplice, and friend.

And saving the best for last . . . my family got me through. Prison can be a soul-killing place. My parents, BILL and PAT MORTON, kept me afloat, literally and figuratively. My sister VICKY WARLICK and her husband MIKE WARLICK did, too. My brother, MATT MORTON, and baby sister, PATTI HODGES, were always there, thank God.

I cannot finish without thanking my son, ERIC, for the strength and the bravery to tackle and accept the complete inversion of everything he thought he knew. I don't know if I would have done as well. Without the gentle prodding of his wife, MAGGIE, and his angelic mother-in-law, BARBARA MAHONEY, we might still be estranged.

Again, thank you, God.

"You have turned for me my mourning into dancing; You have put off my sackcloth and clothed me with gladness."
—PSALM 30:11 (NKJV)

About the Innocence Project

UNABLE TO PERSUADE THE TEXAS COURTS THAT THE SYSTEM HAD CON-
victed an innocent man, Michael Morton turned to the Innocence
Project to help clear his name. Founded in 1992, the Innocence
Project is a national litigation and public policy organization that is
dedicated to exonerating the wrongly convicted through DNA evidence and reforming the system to prevent further injustice.

To date, more than three hundred people in the United States
have been exonerated by DNA testing. The Innocence Project has
helped in more than 170 of those cases. To learn more about the
groundbreaking work of the Innocence Project and what you can
do to help prevent wrongful convictions, please visit www.innocence
project.org.

About the Author

Michael Morton was born in Texas, grew up in California, and moved back to Texas in high school. While living in Austin, Michael was convicted of murdering his wife—a crime he did not commit. He spent almost twenty-five years in prison before being exonerated through the efforts of the Innocence Project, pro bono lawyer John Raley, and advances in DNA technology. Michael Morton is now remarried and lives on a lake in rural East Texas, relishing and appreciating what others may take for granted.

NOW SEE THE AWARD-WINNING DOCUMENTARY

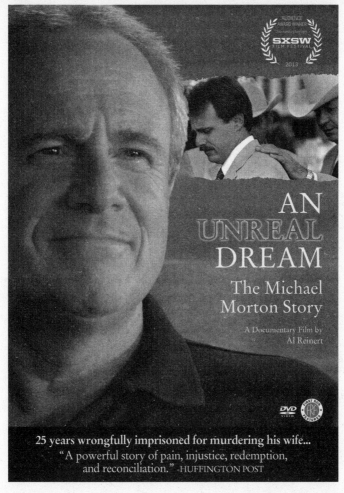

From two-time Academy Award-nominee Al Reinert comes the powerful, inside look at the story of Michael Morton. Featuring exclusive interviews with nearly everyone involved in Morton's case, the film ultimately reveals that the price of a wrongful conviction goes well beyond one man's loss of freedom.

Available for purchase on DVD.
Order your copy today at firstrunfeatures.com/unrealdreamdvd.html

 FirstRunFeatures.com

Mount Laurel Library
100 Walt Whitman Avenue
Mount Laurel, NJ 08054-9539
856-234-7319
www.mtlaurel.lib.nj.us